AF608201

COMMUNITY-BASED LANGUAGE LEARNING

Community-Based Language Learning

A Framework for Educators

Joan Clifford
Deborah S. Reisinger

Georgetown University Press / *Washington, DC*

© 2019 Georgetown University Press. All rights reserved. No part of this book may be reproduced or utilized in any form or by any means, electronic or mechanical, including photocopying and recording, or by any information storage and retrieval system, without permission in writing from the publisher.

The publisher is not responsible for third-party websites or their content. URL links were active at time of publication.

Library of Congress Cataloging-in-Publication Data

Names: Clifford, Joan, author. | Reisinger, Deborah Streifford, 1969– author.
Title: Community-based language learning / Joan Clifford and Deborah S Reisinger.
Description: Washington, DC : Georgetown University Press, 2019. | bibliographical references and index.
Identifiers: LCCN 2018004911 | ISBN 9781626166363 (pbk. : alk. paper) | ISBN 9781626166356 (hardcover : alk. paper) | ISBN 9781626166370 (ebook)
Subjects: LCSH: Language acquisition—Social aspects. | Community education | Experiential learning. | Languages, Modern—Study and teaching.
Classification: LCC P118 .C58 2019 | DDC 401/.93—dc23
LC record available at https://lccn.loc.gov/2018004911

♾ This book is printed on acid-free paper meeting the requirements of the American National Standard for Permanence in Paper for Printed Library Materials.

20 19 9 8 7 6 5 4 3 2 First printing

Printed in the United States of America

Cover design by Naylor Design, Inc.

Contents

Acknowledgments

This work would not have been possible without the support of the Duke Service-Learning Community-Based Language Initiative, the Department of Romance Studies, and the Cultures and Languages Across the Curriculum Initiative at Duke University. We are especially grateful for the encouragement of our colleagues Gregson Davis, David Malone, Eric Mlyn, Liliana Paredes, Richard Rosa, and Inge Walther, who actively helped us advance the goals of this book.

We are grateful to our colleagues who formed our global community of learning, and especially to those who shared their experiences of teaching community-based language classes. A heartfelt thank you to the Duke Faculty Write Program for its support of public scholarship.

Thank you to Annie Abbott and Darcy Lear for leading the way. We are especially indebted to Adam Hollowell and Melissa Simmermeyer for their valuable feedback on multiple iterations of this work. Their friendship and professional commitment to writing supported us in innumerable ways. To the organizations and community members that partner with our students and with which we have built lasting relationships, we wish to express our sincere appreciation. To our amazing students, thank you for all you continue to teach us.

Finally, we would like to extend our deepest gratitude to our families for their love and support. To Udo, Max, and Lena, who have been patient, encouraging, and inspiring. To our parents, who modeled how to advocate for social change. And to all the immigrants who make this country their home: Welcome.

Introduction

World language educators have an important role to play in how higher education prepares students for global citizenship. Language teachers have long implemented community-based learning (CBL) strategies in their classrooms, asking students to connect with language communities around the world. Although some teachers have focused on building relationships with native speakers through study abroad experiences, others have turned to local communities. We, the authors of this book, have worked in both arenas for the past two decades. We teach world language courses (in Spanish and in French, respectively), lead global education programs, and support service-learning curricular and co-curricular programming. As we began to develop CBL programs at our institution, however, it became clear to us that we had not been adequately prepared to address the complexities of community partnerships: What kinds of second language (L2) activities push students to think critically about social inequities? How should we create strong and sustainable community partnerships? What strategies support students who experience dissonance? As questions multiplied, and others resurfaced, we decided to research the broader field of CBL. As we did, we learned that local CBL in the L2 presents unique opportunities—and challenges—not present in CBL courses that are taught and administered in English. This book is the result of our investigation into those distinctions, and it will, we hope, contribute to the training of current and future researchers and practitioners.

Our recognition of the differences between CBL-English and CBL in the L2 motivated us to consolidate different resources and promising practices. We do not claim that local community-based learning with L2 learners (CBLL) is a new phenomenon, but we have not found a robust or cohesive literature of the field. We believe that distinguishing CBLL from CBL-English better prepares world language educators to design more successful and sustainable community-based experiences with local L2 speakers. Ultimately, CBLL leads to a more complete understanding of how language proficiency and social justice consciousness are complementary learning outcomes. In linking these two outcomes, we integrate conversations from the fields of world languages (second-language acquisition), service learning, community engagement, and critical theory to argue that languages are a tool for social change.

Let us more closely detail the principal observations and challenges that spurred our interest in developing practices specific to CBLL.

First, in the largest sense, models of CBL that posit theories based on English language exchanges do not adequately reflect the specific needs of student language learners. Although these models sometimes place students in contact with multilingual speakers—and indeed, some of these students are nonnative speakers of English themselves—CBL-English differs greatly from CBL in an L2 because the majority of students are language *learners* who are put into communication with native or heritage speakers of that same language. Quite simply, students who take courses in English and who do community work in English (with partners who may or may not master English) do not share all the same concerns of students who are learning an L2 and who are completing coursework and partnership activities in the L2. In our experience, L2 learners are often tentative in their community partnerships, in great part due to (1) a lack of confidence in their ability to express themselves in the L2, (2) difficulty understanding the linguistic production of their native speaker partners, (3) the need to adapt to a new environment and learn specialized vocabulary, and (4) the need to learn cultural norms and acquire political and historical knowledge of the L2 country and/or culture. Feelings of inadequacy and confusion, or challenges to identity, not only slow the pace of projects but also necessitate tailored activities to address them. Considerable time both inside and outside the classroom is necessary to support the unique needs of L2 learners, and to build ethical, generative, and productive relationships with the community members.

Second, CBL-English models do not address the specificity of working with populations with limited or emerging English proficiency who do not fully access the dominant culture. As a result, students can find themselves in positions of power for which they are underprepared or even unprepared. In some cases, they serve as ad hoc language interpreters or cultural brokers, with little to no training. It is important to consider how a student, without the first-hand knowledge gained from head-of-household or parental responsibilities, must become conversant with a different perspective in order to navigate the school system or the health care system. There are multiple types of literacy needed to become a cultural ambassador that go far beyond the linguistic skill set. For example, one of our students, Danielle, was tutoring a school-age child when a car drove into the apartment building where the child's French-speaking family resides, collapsing part of the building. For the next two hours, Danielle found herself serving as an interpreter for the police and the paramedics, and eventually the Red Cross. As she calmed local residents and helped the family decide whether to shelter in place with friends or accept $300 toward a hotel room, she reported being terrified of saying or doing "the wrong thing." Danielle, herself, had never encountered this type of situation before, and yet she had suddenly become the linguistic and cultural interpreter in a complex intervention. Undeniably, this situation would be a crisis even for renters who speak English well and comfortably navigate the dominant culture, but a lack of linguistic and cultural access further exacerbates the situation. We must consider how to equip students to recognize and negotiate these linguistic and cultural challenges.

Third and finally, local landscapes in the United States make CBL partnerships unique. During international experiences, students engage in CBL in a foreign geographic location, in another dominant culture, and often in another language; they cannot escape their immersion experience easily, which offers many challenges, including culture shock and feelings of isolation. Students working in the United States, however, are surrounded by a culture that they often know and that they can navigate with some ease, guided by learned norms and personal experiences. CBL work in local language communities or with local L2 speakers thus offers a temporary immersive context, somewhere between a "new place" and a "known place." After students engage with native or heritage speakers locally, they return to places of comfort: to familiar surroundings, to their friends, and to their common language. (Here, we are generalizing the definition of college to reflect its more traditional structure in the United States—as a four-year residential campus with undergraduate students living in residence halls, as part of a contained community that may be walled off from the town or in a downtown setting but is nonetheless separate; we understand that this distinction is not true of all college settings, especially those of community colleges. Likewise, when we reference the "local community," we assume geographical distinctions between campus and community such that students interact with both the town community and the campus community [primarily made up of peers] in different ways.) In working with local communities in the United States, then, our students may experience CBLL as a limited interaction outside the bubble of the college environment. They may make "others" of the L2 speakers living in local communities, and because of the sometimes-limited interactions of their CBL experiences, they can be challenged to build authentic relationships based on connections, belonging, and inclusion.

This book seeks to provide foundational knowledge for establishing successful community-based learning partnerships in the L2, or CBLL. The first three chapters aim to provide a theoretical framework for approaching CBLL. In chapter 1 we develop a detailed model of CBLL that distinguishes it from CBL-English and presents it in the context of several pedagogical and political frameworks. Chapter 2 outlines the learning outcomes for language students engaged in CBL, aligning the model with L2 acquisition theories and national standards for world language education. There, we develop an approach that includes both pedagogy and practice. In chapter 3 we examine how to assess students, faculty members, community partners, and programs. We discuss the role of critical reflection within the assessment continuum and offer ways to align assessments with student learning outcomes that span the modes of communication.

The second half of this book centers on challenges and solutions in practice. Our examples refer to our experiences with students working within local language communities and with local L2 speakers who include native and heritage speakers of Arabic, Hindi, French, Mandarin, Spanish, and Swahili. Numerous activities provide opportunities for critical reflection and active participation. Chapter 4 explores the complex interplay of identity and language in CBLL partnerships. In chapter 5 we examine how dissonance and resistance manifest in students, teachers, and community partners, and how they contribute to transformative learning. Chapter 6 concludes by exploring the principles and realities of authentic and ethical relationships in CBLL. It is our hope that this book will be useful as a guiding framework, as a tool for reflection, and as a manual for working with students and communities.

CHAPTER 1

A Theoretical Framework for CBLL

By the end of this chapter, readers will be able to:

- Define a variety of community-based learning (CBL) models, including service learning, international service learning, and global service learning
- Distinguish CBL within language learning contexts (CBLL) from other models
- Elaborate distinguishing features of CBLL that lead to successful programming
- Explain how Bloom's, Kolb's, Dewey's, and Freire's theories and models inform CBLL
- Identify the role of critical pedagogy in CBLL

DEFINING COMMUNITY-BASED LEARNING

There is a vast literature that explores definitions and practices of community engagement (Carnegie Classifications 2018; Kellogg Commission 1999). According to Mooney and Edwards (2001, 182), "Community-based learning refers to any pedagogical tool in which the community becomes a partner in the learning process." Broadly speaking, community-based learning (CBL) serves as an umbrella term for activities that engage students within their communities and is often equated with service learning. With increased interest in civic engagement on college campuses (Ward and Wolf-Wendel 2000), however, a number of new terms are emerging, whereas others have been redefined to turn the focus from working *with* rather than *for* communities. As a result, even the words "community," "civic," and "service" have become mobile signifiers that take on different meanings in different contexts. How do we define "community-based learning"? Is sending a student to observe a flea market CBL? Is CBL only equated with service? Who are the members of the "community"? Who is doing the learning? The selection of a word or the choice of a term by each institution, as well as this publication, are part of an ongoing and important conversation in the field of community engagement.

Generally speaking, colleges and universities define and adapt CBL to their own institutional cultures. Some universities have undergraduate programs in service learning (Duke, Missouri, Oregon), whereas others use the terms *community-engaged learning* (Stanford), *community-based learning* (Georgetown), and *civic engagement* (Northwestern, Richmond). The lacks of clear definitions and a shared language are significant, for several reasons. CBL researchers and practitioners must use precise language in order to develop a clear understanding of what kind of engagement we wish to reference (O'Connor et al. 2011, 5). In order to support, research, and evaluate community engagement, a common and shared definition is crucial. Rather than seeing this as reductive, however, we believe that a naming system can help all parties share understanding and learning. For the purposes of this book, then, we use "CBL" as an umbrella term that provides models of how to engage in curricular and co-curricular experiences with local communities. As pedagogy, CBL encompasses service-oriented interactions with the community, such as service learning, as well as other solidarity-building practices that transform worldviews, highlight social issues, co-create knowledge, and foster authentic relationships based on connection. Generally speaking, CBL can interest and motivate students by providing a foundation for exploring intellectual and social issues through rigorous engagement, discussion, and reflection.

To distinguish our discussions from the broader model of CBL, and to accurately home in on the specificity of engaging in community interactions in an L2, we use the term *community-based language learning*, or CBLL, throughout this book. CBLL refers specifically to interactions that take place between L2 students and heritage/native speakers of the target language residing in the United States. This dyad includes students who speak English and who reside in the US (including international students who are not native English speakers) who are learning an additional language, and community members who are native or heritage speakers of those languages and who also reside in the US (e.g., Chinese immigrants, Congolese refugees, heritage Spanish speakers). By naming CBLL, we intentionally foreground important elements of language, communication, and culture that differentiate CBL with heritage and native speakers in the L2 from CBL that takes place entirely in English.

We wish to be clear that we do not assume that students on US college campuses are all native speakers of English born in the United States, because we know that international and heritage students make up an increasingly significant percentage of US college students. Although these students must have proficiency in the English language to attend a university, they are not necessarily fluent in the dominant culture; as such, their backgrounds can upset binary structures that posit the student as a knower of culture and the community member as an uninformed recipient of culture. Furthermore, when we examine these binary models and their related assumptions, we notice that they sometimes fail precisely because US students, usually young adults, are not always fluent in all aspects of their own "culture"—for example, they cannot reliably help heads of household decode electricity bills, fill out applications for permanent residency, or prepare for parent–teacher conferences. These cultural "deficits" reflect not only a limited knowledge of the "real world" but also, of particular importance, socioeconomic and class differences among students and between some students and the L2 speakers with whom they interact. So, though students reside in the United States, and may speak fluent English, their expertise is often limited to their knowledge of the English language and to a finite set of personal experiences of the culture determined by their age, their socioeconomic status, and, sometimes, their citizenship. Good examples of CBLL, then, include and prioritize interactions in which the community partner and community members serve as coeducators, because neither the students nor the educators are the ultimate authority or knower of culture. Students and educators must be open to expertise from beyond traditional classroom sources.

Just as we do not assume that all students are native speakers of English, we must not assume the homogeneity of language communities. For the purposes of this book, we sometimes refer to clusters of heritage speakers or native speakers of languages other than English as "language communities." These clusters could be based on shared spaces (e.g., apartment complexes, schools, businesses, and neighborhoods) or ideologies (e.g., religious affiliation, politics). We acknowledge that this naming is problematic. Such a classification may inadvertently make "others" of individuals and groups that are already experiencing social and economic marginalization. It may also erase the experiences of L2 speakers who are dispersed or who do not belong to a particular community. There are differences in socioeconomic status, ethnicity, race, language, nationality, religion, cultural norms, and so on both within and between local immigrant populations that are not explicitly included in the designation "language communities." In chapter 4 we explore this issue in some depth and offer activities that can help students explore how language shapes identity and relationships of power.

CBLL AND GLOBAL LEARNING MODELS

Other CBL frameworks that promote intercultural synergies among individuals who speak different languages include international service learning (ISL) and global service learning (GSL). We want to take a moment to draw important distinctions that inform our understanding of these models, before turning to define service learning later in the chapter. According to Bringle and Hatcher (2011, 19), ISL is "a structured academic experience in another country in which students (a) participate in an organized service activity that addresses identified community needs; (b) learn from direct interaction and cross-cultural dialogue with others; [and] (c) reflect on the experiences in such a way as to gain further understanding of course content, a deep understanding of global and intercultural issues, a broader appreciation of the host country and the discipline, and an enhanced sense of their own responsibilities as citizens locally and globally." CBLL shares all these components with ISL, except that ISL is limited to a service activity that takes place abroad; CBLL, conversely, occurs in the local community where the student's university is located—in this case, the United States. In an effort to expand the ISL model, some practitioners have suggested that "service learning with global frameworks can take place at home *or* abroad" (Whitehead 2015). As Whitehead (2015, "Global Learning" section, para. 2) writes, "*global service learning* is an emerging, holistic practice that encompasses service experiences both in the local community and abroad." She explains: "In fact, global learning can occur in a wide range of activities, including international interactive video conferences; engagement with international students and scholars; projects that are inclusive of global perspectives and approaches; and globally focused integrative courses, capstones, and internships." Her broader definition thus opens the focus of ISL to include the multitude of global experiences that students now access via their home academic institutions. This reframing to include both the global and local dimensions may be compelled in part by the movements for internationalization and community engagement at US colleges and universities.

Another noteworthy change is that study abroad offices at many universities now include programs based in the United States, giving way to terms such as "global education," "study away," and "domestic programs." By advocating for a change in nomenclature, Whitehead (2015, "From International to Global Service Learning" section, para. 3) explains that "such a reframing involves shifting the focus from the *location of the service* to the *content of the service*." Although we agree that a renewed focus on content is an important shift that introduces more rigor to community-based work, we do not wish to neglect the important role of *place* in CBLL; nor do we wish to speak of service only. In fact, we see the distinction between local and global programming as significant and even crucial for further developing our students' critical thinking. And though learning about the world can occur in both local and international environments, some learning objectives, outcomes, and challenges inherent in place specificity are distinct. The place of the student in the community and the role of language in community interactions are the distinguishing characteristics of CBLL pedagogy. Together, these factors determine how students question identity based on power and privilege, providing unique opportunities for developing intercultural communicative competence, awareness of social and political issues, authentic relationships, and ultimately transformative learning.

Students who participate in service learning abroad (a form of ISL) often wrestle with culture shock, reverse culture shock, and identity construction—to a degree that training in the five stages of culture shock is an integral part of most ISL programs. CBLL students may experience some degree of *place-based culture shock*, but it is seldom at the level that occurs in an immersive environment abroad, where students are rarely part of the dominant culture. Once CBLL students leave their community encounter, for instance, they return to "normal/native" surroundings; most are likely to resume eating the foods they enjoy, finding comfort in familiar sights and sounds, and speaking the languages of their campus communities. In contrast, students living abroad often remain outsiders vis-à-vis the dominant culture, encountering cultural and linguistic barriers throughout their day. A US student working on a service project in Ecuador, for instance, returns to her host family, where she continues to be surrounded by an unfamiliar, stimulating environment. CBLL students, conversely, may spend only 1 hour per week in their service environment. Each experience offers a different orientation of the "window into another world"; study abroad orients the window to view the new host country, though CBLL presents students with a window onto their own culture, which functions as a mirror. The culture "shock" experienced by CBLL students is not insignificant and can even be more acute, because the student rarely anticipates encountering culture shock in his or her own country. In contrast to the GSL student's glib judgments on the host culture abroad ("That is so weird") or cultural relativism ("It's just different here"), CBLL students can be shocked by their own culture's practices ("Do we really do this?"). Students placed with a local resettlement office, for instance, are often surprised by the public policy restrictions that shape the organization's mission, whereas those working in school settings are usually upset to discover the lack of resources and poor funding mechanisms; this may be a CBLL student's first encounter with structural racism. Here, culture shock takes place in relation to the student's own culture and raises a different set of challenges, as students begin to explore and question US systems.

CBLL students also confront their own senses of privilege and worldviews in unique ways. Some assume they know best, and embody a save-the-world mentality that reflects cultural relativism and perpetuates a charity model of service. Often, students will assume that their known practices are superior and that immigrants should adapt to the dominant culture of the United States and/or follow practices familiar to the student in order to be successful. Students need support to develop a critical eye to enable them to discern how their understanding of success might not be valid for all persons. Cultural norms also influence how parents raise their children, set expectations for education, or conceptualize independence. Students should thus be prepared to grapple with the contrasting worldviews that may arise in CBLL encounters, and learn strategies to identify the power and privilege embedded in many of their perceptions and practices; we explore the transformative power of these moments of dissonance in chapters 5 and 6. As educators within a CBLL model, then, we must impart to our students the responsibility of both learning about other cultures and critically assessing one's own assumptions. This awareness will enable students to continually work on recognizing the dynamics created by differences in power and privilege. These unique components of local L2 immersion demonstrate why it is useful to concretize a distinctive CBLL model.

Another important distinction that frames CBLL pedagogy is its *unique linguistic landscape*. In theory, both ISL and GSL include work in communities where the L2 is spoken, whether here or abroad. Still, the role of language and language learning is couched within the learning of culture, and rarely named outright. In her description of GSL, for instance, Whitehead (2015, "International to Global Service Learning" section, para. 4) writes, "Wherever it takes place, global service learning requires deep, grounded knowledge of community cultures along with respect for the knowledge and experiences of community members. Attention to cultural, economic, historical, political, and social issues affecting the community, as well as to those issues' local and international contexts, is essential." The missing reference to language or linguistic issues here is worth noting. It is this absence that we wish to address, for though GSL supports objectives shared with CBLL—including "such learning outcomes as civic knowledge and intercultural knowledge and competence" (Whitehead 2015)—CBLL specifically brings to the forefront the unique role of language in navigating this work. The dynamic of US-based students interacting with local L2 speakers deserves close examination, because language educators face very specific challenges in designing and implementing CBL in this context. As we explain in subsequent chapters, educators must consider the role that language plays in communication and interpretation, from making space for what is not said (because it cannot be communicated) to leaving time in class for processing the role of language in relationship building, and for planning for additional activities that support language learning relevant to local L2 speakers. In sum, CBLL fits into the larger category of CBL but merits additional and separate treatment due to the nature of working in another language that students are actively in the process of acquiring. The merit of CBLL is in its articulation of the context that exists because of the presence of languages and language learning for students and community members.

Reflections for Instructors

1a. *ISL versus GSL.* How is CBLL distinct from ISL and GSL?

1b. How might the distinctions between these two terms affect:

- how a student interacts with a community organization or a community member?
- the themes included in a lesson?
- the differences in power and privilege based on place?
- the ways a student experiences differences in worldviews?

2. *Different volunteer experiences.* Mariel is spending a semester in France, where she lives with a host family. Once a week, she visits a local elementary school, where she tutors a group of French children in English. José lives in the United States, and is enrolled in a Spanish service-learning course. Once a week, for 1 hour, he tutors English in a class on English as a second language (ESL) at a local elementary school. His friend, Fiona, also tutors at the elementary school through a student club; she works 5 hours per week. Fiona does not speak Spanish.

How might the experiences of Mariel, José, and Fiona differ? How might they be similar? Reflect on the dynamics between tutors and tutees (power and privilege), opportunities for structured reflection and personal growth, knowledge of cultural norms and the school system, and the like. Next, map each of these situations onto one of the models discussed (ISL, GSL, or CBLL).

SERVICE-LEARNING MODELS AND CBLL

CBLL overlaps significantly with the aims, sensitivities, and methods of service learning (SL), even though they are not identical approaches. In this section we define SL, as well as identify some of the methods within SL that inform CBLL.

Bringle and Clayton (2012, 105) define SL as "the integration of academic material, relevant community-based service activities, and critical reflection in a reciprocal partnership that engages students, faculty/staff, and community members to achieve academic, civic, and personal learning objectives as well as to advance public purposes." Within SL models, most community interactions can be divided into either *direct* or *indirect* service. In a direct service model, students tutor English language learners, staff a table at a health fair, or assist in the distribution of clothing or food at a homeless shelter. In an indirect service activity, students prepare a report for a nonprofit organization, paint a classroom in a church, or glean sweet potatoes that are then donated to the food bank. Whether these experiences are curricular or co-curricular, direct or indirect, they can all contribute to significant learning outcomes for students, as long as they include critical reflection, an essential component of CBL that we explore in depth in chapter 3.

Butin's conceptualizations of SL models offer another way to examine CBLL structures. Butin (2003) outlines four perspectives on SL that reflect distinct approaches to its teaching and practice: (1) a *technical* perspective, which links SL to cognitive outcomes; (2) a *cultural* perspective, which expands students' understanding of self in the local and global community; (3) a *political* perspective, which examines foundations of power; and (4) a *poststructuralist* (or antifoundational) perspective, which analyzes how SL might construct or disrupt particular social norms of being and thinking. Instructors often combine these approaches (especially 1 and 2), and though the first three align the act of service with a particular theme, the poststructuralist model challenges most how a student thinks about the world.

These SL models also apply to CBLL and are helpful for better understanding how students build and sustain relationships. They challenge educators to study carefully and to negotiate our goals and learning outcomes with our community partners. SL is one valuable way to build partnerships, but we wish to acknowledge that working in solidarity with the community does not always mandate a service activity. There are other important components to building authentic relationships, some solely based on social time, that we explore in this book.

Reflections for Instructors

1. *Characteristics of CBLL.* Considering Butin's theory, how would you categorize the activities given in table 1.1? Which perspective best aligns with your conceptual goals of CBLL? Would you change the activities from direct to indirect service models to better meet your goals?

2. *Service-learning models.* What SL models are currently in place at your institution? Are there specific models that your institution might adapt—or not—depending on its campus culture? Is there a model that you feel aligns best with your institution's or department's goals?

3. *Which type of service?* Does one kind of service better meet your anticipated learning outcomes than another? Direct or indirect? Cultural or poststructuralist? What types of events or interactions help build solidarity with the community?

(continued)

TABLE 1.1

	Technical	Cultural	Political	Poststructuralist
English language tutoring				
Translating a school flyer				
Door-to-door surveys on health concerns in neighborhood				
Citizenship application workshop				
Presentation in L2 at a heritage language school				
Playing games with senior citizens in L2				

CBLL, RECIPROCITY, AND SOLIDARITY

To examine the role of relationships in our work with language communities and L2 speakers, we look more closely at the notion of the "reciprocal partnership." Most definitions of SL identify the practice as grounded in ethical, collaborative, and reciprocal relationships (Bringle and Clayton 2012). In CBLL, we also strive to build mutually beneficial relationships that serve not just the student but also the community. CBLL overlaps with SL in many ways, so we can learn a great deal about CBLL by examining the fundamental tenets of SL. To better understand how to build healthy reciprocal relationships in CBLL, we can implement many of the central traits of SL.

In their article "Reciprocity: Saying What We Mean and Meaning What We Say," Dostilio and others (2012, 22–25) identify three types of reciprocal relationships that characterize SL. The first, *exchange-oriented reciprocity*, is defined as the "interchange of benefits, resources or actions," a process that maximizes individual gain while also promoting collective action. An exchange orientation can produce a benefit to the community but is criticized for not advancing thinking about structural changes. University students getting teaching experience in an after-school program would fall into this category. The second type, *influence-oriented reciprocity*, is defined by the condition of interrelatedness. In other words, "personal, social, and environmental factors iteratively influence the way in which something is done," although not necessarily in a bidirectional way. An influence orientation can get bogged down in interrelatedness and not actually work to the benefit of the relationship; there is a fine balance in tending to both personal and interpersonal work, and not just accepting diversity. Dostilio and others share an example from a collaborative research study about health disparities. During the course of the study, academics and community members share their distinct perspectives about the reasons for the disparities, which in turn influences the direction of the study questions; the process and outcomes of the research are adjusted accordingly. The third type, *generativity-oriented reciprocity*, describes the transformation or production of something new. In this model, reciprocity "refers to interrelatedness of beings and the broader world around them as well as the potential synergies that emerge from their relationships." Unlike the first two relationships, the third orientation sees SL partnerships as a way to effect change, actively considering the roles of power, privilege, and oppression. In this form of reciprocity, partnerships develop over time and include multiple participants who work for long-term change, organizing new structures to push big ideas forward. This generative reciprocity is also known as transformative reciprocity (Stanlick and Sell 2016). Katz Jameson, Clayton, and Jaeger (2011, 264) discuss this transformational aspect through the lens of establishing a relationship of "co-educators, co-learners, and co-generators of knowledge." CBLL can map onto these SL models of reciprocity in ways that are especially important for language education. For pedagogical reasons, then, CBLL instructors should be both deliberate and transparent in choosing and monitoring the type of relationship they help students establish in the community, acknowledging the complexity of building these generative reciprocal relationships. A discussion of how this orientation fits into the building of authentic, transformative relationships will be further developed in chapter 6.

Although often overlooked by practitioners in the United States, international perspectives on CBL also help elucidate how to develop relationships with local communities. As language educators who have expertise in other cultural frameworks, we are in a unique position to provide first-hand cultural knowledge that other community engagement practitioners may not have. For example, the above-mentioned types of reciprocity are an important value to consider in the formation of CBLL partnerships, but they also reflect a US-based framework that does not always take into account other, international conceptualizations of CBL. Though we do not explore this issue in great detail here, we wish to draw attention to the importance of expanding our understanding to include wider global perspectives. Looking closely at how service is connected to the concept of solidarity in Latin America, for example, can help inform practices for successful community interactions within our local Latino/a communities. Tapia (2012, 193, 197) states that within the conceptualization of SL in Latin America, solidarity is defined by "actions [that] are developed *in conjunction with* the community and not *for* it," and that solidarity is "social engagement linked in with transforming a situation and the quest for a fair and equitable society." The fact that many schools in Latin America also serve as home bases for grassroots service networks could have an impact on how immigrants from these countries perceive US-based service projects. Knowing more about international service practices could improve local relationships because it would allow us to understand expectations, actions, and perceptions from many points of view—not only the US point of view. Another important aspect of connecting solidarity to CBLL is that by working in solidarity with the community, students will develop a relationship directly with community members. Through this direct interaction, they will observe economic, health, and educational disparities, and, with coaching, they will learn how to advocate for eradicating them. Solidarity emphasizes being present in the community, actively listening, and collaborating together to enact change. Although reciprocal relationships in US CBL models may share these characteristics, we cannot assume that all reciprocal relationships will be as comprehensive and change-oriented in their outcomes as relationships built in solidarity.

Strategies that expand the understanding of partnered relationships include imagining how service is performed or enacted in other places in the world. In the context of school-based CBLL, for instance, we should explore relationships between the school and the local community in the relevant country: What are appropriate or common practices between parents and teachers in the country of origin? Do they communicate regularly, and if so, who initiates the communication? How do students manage homework within their family dynamic? Do parents step in and manage, or are students expected to take charge of their own studies? Before working with a Chinese family that recently arrived in the United States, it would be helpful to understand the expectations the family may have for interactions with university students. Similarly, when working with Congolese refugees, we should determine what are appropriate behaviors between volunteers and community members in the Democratic Republic of the Congo. Is it common practice for volunteers to be present in schools or for students to volunteer? If so, what are common expectations, both culturally and socially? Knowing more of the history and practices of community engagement in the home country of the community with whom students will interact helps to build intercultural understanding, improve communication, and develop a nonjudgmental awareness of cultural practices. It is imperative to learn about how different cultures perceive community partnerships. To this end, the educator or the students in the CBLL course might survey local L2 speakers to understand their notions of service and of learning, based on their prior experiences

Reflections for Instructors

1. *What is your local linguistic landscape?* Using the MLA map (https://apps.mla.org/map_main), list the languages that are spoken in your area. Next, using table 1.2, identify contacts that you have at community organizations that might interact with L2 speakers and language communities—including schools, libraries, churches, housing agencies, police, courts, law firms, social services, immigration advocacy groups, financial institutions, museums, community centers, parks and recreation, health clinics, hospitals, retirement facilities, and support groups. In what ways might your students be able to work in solidarity with these individuals and groups?

TABLE 1.2

Local language	Community organizations that interact/support L2 speakers	Ways to work together

2a. *Generative reciprocity.* Using table 1.3, describe the activities performed in the list of common CBLL experiences, and then identify how they represent or could be transformed into a relationship based on generativity-oriented reciprocity.

TABLE 1.3

Common CBLL experiences	Description of activities	Generative reciprocity
Tutoring ESL	*—Students meet with ESL students weekly* *—School trains and monitors student work* *—CBLL and ESL students learn together and socialize*	*Tutors and school personnel write a grant to hire a full-time ESL instructor at the school*
Volunteering at a health clinic		
Assisting with naturalization applications or at a citizenship workshop		
Visiting an assisted living facility		
Working in a community garden		

2b. Would you define any of these activities as working in solidarity with the community? Explain.

3. *New lenses.* Can you imagine how your students would perceive their community interactions differently through the lenses of reciprocity and solidarity? How can you prepare students to notice structural disparity and discern the perspectives of the various stakeholders in this system? How do students perceive their role in maintaining and/or changing existing power structures?

in their country of origin. Ultimately, this will lead to improved intercultural understanding. If students, community partners, and community members become aware of different conceptualizations and beliefs related to engagement, relationships will be more open and transparent.

CBLL AND TRANSFORMATION

Before addressing other pertinent topics, we wish to situate CBLL within current educational thought. When considering experiential learning and critical reflection, it is crucial to evoke Bloom and others' *Taxonomy of Educational Objectives* (1956, revised in 2001) and Kolb's (1984) Experiential Learning Theory. Bloom's model defines learning "as a hierarchical sequence moving from the lower-order thinking skills (identify, describe, apply) to the higher-order thinking skills (analyze, synthesize, evaluate)," and it is key to the creation of the DEAL model for critical reflection outlined in chapter 3 (Ash and Clayton 2004; Ash, Clayton, and Atkinson 2005). Kolb's Experiential Learning Theory is a foundational model because it promotes "structured reflection to connect experience with concepts, ideas, and theories and generate new and applicable knowledge in concrete 'real-life' situations" (Kiely 2005, 6). Together, Bloom's taxonomy and Kolb's learning cycle help articulate the impact on students of community interactions in CBLL.

Another important way to think about the relationship of experiential learning and reflection stems from the work of John Dewey, an educational reformer and pioneer for social change in the early twentieth century. Dewey defines education as "experiential learning . . . reflective activity, citizenship, community and democracy" (Deans 1999, 16). When the experiential component of CBLL is accompanied by observation, reflection, and critical thinking, it promotes enhanced learning. Dewey explains that "learning and knowing emerge from the situation, from 'the forked road of doubt,' and are realized through action" (Deans 1999, 17). This decision-making in the "forked road" represents an important trigger for learning. Students need plenty of opportunities to reflect on how community interactions correspond to their own formation and beliefs, because each student enters the relationship at a different level of readiness. From pre-visit orientations to post-encounter "unpacking," we recommend a variety of reflection activities throughout the CBLL experience. Depending on the objectives set by the instructor, reflections can target distinct audiences (self, group of students, student(s) and community, student and educator) or specific domains of learning (cognitive, interpersonal, or intrapersonal). Content may expand on a specific topic that is related to class (immigration, health disparities, social inequities, communication, etc.) or may challenge the student's personal growth (leadership, intercultural competence, belief system, etc.). Reflection should include not only the consumption of knowledge but also the very sources that produce it. Such activities could entail a study of the diversity of voices represented in teaching materials, or they might target discourses related to "foreignness" or the "other." Reflections should be continuous, challenging, connected, and contextualized (Eyler, Giles, and Schmiede 1996). Formats for reflection will vary according to the skills and content of the particular learning objective; these include written, oral, presentational, and multimedia formats. For the language learner, reflection activities may provide especially useful ways to practice and reinforce L2 skills, but there may also be a role for reflections carried out in English. In chapter 3 we explore how reflection fits into the assessment continuum and explain how to align reflection activities with the American Council on the Teaching of Foreign Languages' (ACTFL's) three modes of communication: interpretive, interpersonal, and presentational.

Critical reflection is a tool for engaging in perspective transformation. We see how perspectives are transformed in Mezirow's (2000, 19) writing on learning, when he states that learning happens in four ways: "by elaborating frames of reference, by learning new frames of reference, by transforming points of view, or by transforming habits of mind." Understanding this process of learning is central to comprehending the possibilities of perspective transformation. Although many disciplines explore student learning, from gender studies to neurohumanities, our interest here lies in understanding transformative learning. Mezirow (2000, 17) defines learning as "habits of mind," or "a set of assumptions—broad, generalized, orienting predispositions that act as a filter for interpreting the meaning of experience." To distinguish learning and transformative learning, Kasl and Yorks (2012, 507) define learning as "a change in cognitive habit of mind" and transformative learning as "a change in *habit of being*—a holistic relationship to one's world experienced through coherence among one's multiple ways of knowing." The transition from thinking about change to making change happen is a useful metaphor for understanding CBLL's role in transformative learning, which we develop in greater detail in chapter 5. Osborn (2000, 66) underscores the role of critical reflection in transformation, stating that it "involves challenging the boundaries of our educational thought and practice and rearranging or dissecting the constructs that we employ in an effort to understand the relations of power that underlie them." Through critical reflection, we deconstruct the mechanisms that support power relations and engage students in a critical pedagogy that shapes habits of mind and being.

Paolo Freire, arguably the most influential theoretician of and advocate for critical pedagogy, shows that action and reflection can help "reveal reality." In *The Pedagogy of the Oppressed* (1970, 244), Freire writes that "knowledge emerges only through invention and re-invention, through the restless, impatient, continuing, hopeful inquiry human beings pursue in the world, with the world, and with each other." Freire characterizes this "educational meaning-making process as dialogic (i.e., created through dialogue) as opposed to banking (i.e., depositing meaning into students' heads)" (Schapiro, Wasserman, and Gallegos 2012, 367). It is through these dialogic transformations that learning is initiated, and it is through action and reflection that reality is revealed. Freire (1970, 39) claims that

> the more radical the person is, the more fully he or she enters into reality so that, knowing it better, he or she can transform it. This individual is not afraid to confront, to listen, to see the world unveiled. This person is not afraid to meet the people or to enter into a dialogue with them. This person does not consider himself or herself the proprietor of history or of all people, or the liberator of the oppressed; but he or she does commit himself or herself, within history, to fight at their side.

Personal and political transformations are achieved through dialogue and the development of "critical consciousness," or the unveiling of reality (Deans 1999, 15). We see CBLL's roots in this foundational belief that it is through critical reflection that "learners develop an awareness of power and greater agency (political consciousness) to transform society and their own reality" (Taylor 2009, 5). Some scholars have explored how SL intersects with the transformative or social justice paradigm when it "embraces a service ethic emphasizing a scholarship of engagement and collaboration with communities to address both the symptoms as well as the root causes of inequities" (Verjee 2010, 9). This intersection recalls Freire's commitment to privileging the voices and the influence of the oppressed in addressing the root causes of socioeconomic inequities.

Reflections for Instructors

Triggers for Growth. What transformations in values and actions have you seen (or do you anticipate seeing) in your CBLL students? What do you think triggered (or might trigger) this personal growth? How have (or might) critical reflection and dialogue supported the process? What barriers impede perspective transformation?

CRITICAL PEDAGOGIES AND CBLL

As students encounter challenging situations in the community, they may encounter new perspectives that place their assumptions in full view, causing them to become uncomfortable and even defensive. Such reactions are common, and though sometimes painful, they can be crucial steps to fostering personal growth and change. In order to support students through this phase, we advocate using a critical pedagogy framework (as advocated by Freire, Giroux, and Osborn) that provides a road map for building students' consciousness about social inequities. As educators interested in political agency and activism, we embrace this approach because it helps us anticipate the types of support that students need as they are pushed to (re)consider their worldviews. Arries (1999, 41) provides a compelling summary of how incorporating an SL experience transformed his introductory writing course in Spanish into a critical cultural studies course. He suggests that "service can empower students, enabling them to demystify complex aspects of language and society." In addition to proposing ways to support students as agents of change, throughout this book we encourage readers to consider how to make explicit the "hidden curriculum" and systems that perpetuate the binaries of the dominant versus the foreign culture. Osborn (2000, 51) defines the "hidden curriculum" as "that program of socialization in the schools that runs parallel to the explicit curriculum and inherently serves to benefit those whose cultural capital resembles that of the dominant culture, thus marginalizing others." In chapters 4 and 5, we bring attention to these structures and share strategies for shifting learning in the classroom. By engaging in critical pedagogy, there are many ways for educators to reconceptualize the curriculum and the classroom experience.

Critical pedagogy takes a variety of forms, many of them stemming from Freire's emphasis on disrupting power to create social change. Principles of critical pedagogy include "facilitating the development of students' critical consciousness by enabling them to identify, question, and challenge oppression, hierarchies of power, and the beliefs and practices that support domination" (Kajner et al. 2013, 37). Such an approach aims to develop students' capacities for critical judgment and social commitment to the world. Students learn to become critical agents who actively question and negotiate the relationship between theory and practice, critical analysis and "common sense," and learning and social change. Critical pedagogy studies "knowledge claims" in order to reveal the systems of belief that support these claims, with the final goal of exposing oppressive practices. According to Kajner and others (2013, 37), "such pedagogy facilitates healthy skepticism about power, opens space for students to question and comprehend their own privilege, and provides conditions for students to understand their positionality." By disrupting power, co-constructing knowledge, encouraging experiential learning, and participating in critical reflection about society, this pedagogy exposes repression, poverty, and injustice. The discomfort, the dissonance, and the resistance that often result from CBLL are all critical to cognitive, interpersonal, and intrapersonal growth. CBLL provides a way for students to concretely see that "the sheer complexities of social reality—when carefully and systematically examined and reflected upon—yield opportunities for the realization that justice (or the lack thereof) is contingent upon our engagement with the world" (Butin 2007, 181). In such a framework, students learn to see themselves as agents of change who can act to transform society.

Social justice education focuses on oppression by modeling social justice in the classroom. As Adams (2016, 28) writes, this practice "challenges traditional education through applying principles of social justice to both the explicit and hidden curriculum to expose unequal power relations that privilege some while disadvantaging others at individual, institutional, and societal levels." CBLL educators can implement socially just learning environments by examining power dynamics in the classroom—such as who is speaking, and to whom—and by modeling equitable relations and social structures. Still, socially just classroom environments do not guarantee positive outcomes, and interactions between students and communities may actually perpetuate stereotypes or reinforce assumptions (Butin 2008; Himley 2004). Butin (2008, 80) stresses that "justice-learning allows us to focus as much on the process of undercutting dualistic ways of thinking as on the product of deliberative and sustainable transformational change." In order to engage students in ways that can enact change in communities and in society as a whole, we must consider how to position CBLL as a model for both transformative learning and social change.

According to Mitchell (2008), "traditional service learning" emphasizes service to an individual, and thus perpetuates a charity model that has lost its connection to social justice. This exchange-oriented model potentially damages relationships and community partnerships, perpetuating power differentials. Mitchell (2015, 21) defines *critical service learning* as an approach "that is attentive to social change, works to redistribute power, and strives to develop authentic relationships." She stresses that educators who apply this pedagogy must support students in their discovery that service can both alleviate *and* perpetuate systems of inequity (Mitchell 2008, 53). A student who regularly visits a neighborhood school to tutor students in ESL might help the students better decipher their homework assignments; but ultimately, this exchange may result in reinforcing power dynamics and preconceived notions of server and served. Critical SL, conversely, focuses on service as a vehicle for change, connecting to the generative or transformative reciprocity model. As Davis, Kliewer, and Nicolaides (2017, 50) write, "Mutual sharing of power that produces generative reciprocity enables all stakeholders to join together synergistically to build capacities and produce outcomes that none could otherwise produce separately." If we consider the example of teaching ESL, for instance, students engaged in a critical SL model might work within the educational system to advocate for hiring more qualified ESL teachers to support the population of English-language learners. Although this more generative model contemplates social change, it can be challenging to achieve real change in the context of a one-semester course. It is therefore imperative to consider carefully the messaging about the types of relationships that are proposed and the impact of the goals that are associated with our community interactions.

When we look specifically at language and critical pedagogy, we recall that the very act of learning a new language is "a largely humanistic endeavor rather than an elite or strictly methodological task" (Giroux 2011, 179). This statement reflects the ACTFL's World Language Readiness Standards, which declare that "language and communication are at the heart of the human experience" (ACTFL 2016). These language learning guidelines embed communication in a larger context of communities, connections, comparisons, and cultures, underscoring that language cannot and should not be studied in a vacuum but rather in the context of interconnectivity. As Giroux (2011, 179) explains further, "the force of [language's] importance has to be tied to its relevance as an empowering, emancipatory and democratic function." In other words, the very task of studying another language is political. He explains that

> as it becomes clear that you cannot decouple issues concerning language usage from issues of dialogue, communication, culture and power, matters of politics and pedagogy become crucial to how one understands pedagogy as a political issue and the politics of language as a deeply pedagogical consideration. I have argued for a number of years that language as both an object and subject of mastery, understanding, and engagement is the site in which people negotiate the most fundamental elements of their identities, the relationship between themselves and others, and their relationship to the larger world. (Giroux 2011, 174)

Giroux reminds us that we can no longer treat language learning as simply a "technical issue"—studying linguistic patterns and memorizing vocabulary—instead, we must envision it as a site of struggle and resistance where our identities are at stake. As we consider language as "a mode of learning and dissent," we see that it is "crucial to configuring and translating the boundaries between the public and the private, and attending to questions of politics, power, public consciousness and civic courage" (Giroux 2011, 174–75). Language is central to the work of democracy and social justice. By focusing our attention on the powerful role of language in society, and by practicing communication in a language that is not necessarily our own, we negotiate our identities and access alternative ways of understanding the world.

FINAL THOUGHTS ON THE POLITICS OF CBLL

In the United States, many beliefs and behaviors are increasingly guided by a neoliberal framework. This economic paradigm, which champions a laissez-faire approach to policy and education, defines citizens as consumers who compete for finite resources. Under neoliberalism, market forces determine winners and losers, and any effort to reduce inequality is deemed a counterproductive, unnecessary interference. Neoliberalism warrants discussion here because of its impact on education, and on the understanding of what it means to be a citizen. As Raddon and Harrison (2015, 138) write, "To be a neo-liberal citizen is to valorize individualism; to self-identify as a consumer; to naturalize and accept the discipline of competitive markets and their sorting of 'winners' and 'losers'; to shift away from an earlier generation's conception of the citizen as a rights bearer." This notion of neoliberal citizenship conflicts with earlier definitions of citizenry that valorize social equity. The resulting tension is compounded by an increasing emphasis on community engagement in K–16 education—one that is motivated by research documenting high-impact learning and improved student retention.

Although CBL has taken root in the past two decades, its expansion under a neoliberal model changes relationship models and desired outcomes. As Monbiot (2016, 3) writes, "Another paradox of neoliberalism is that universal competition relies upon universal quantification and comparison. The result is that workers, job seekers, and public services of every kind are subject to a pettifogging, stifling regime of assessment and monitoring, designed to identify the winners and punish the losers." This overemphasis on assessment and monitoring often gets in the way of creative lesson plans and innovative curricula. In addition, the commodification of CBL accentuates the monetary translation of hours served, rather than the learning outcomes connected to societal and civic issues. Community engagement has become a graduation requirement for some high schools, and a way to improve some students' chances of getting into a "good" college; in college, CBL becomes a building block for a résumé that will lead to a "good" job, or a better chance to get into a medical school of choice. As its motivations are increasingly divorced from relationship building, learning, working in solidarity, and social change, CBL is reduced to a portfolio builder or a feel-good moment that lacks connection to student learning outcomes.

As US society reorganizes and reallocates social services according to market pressures, significant economic shifts will likely affect community organizations and members. Sometimes, budgetary cuts by federal or state governments force nonprofits to revisit their mission and reallocate funding sources; other organizations are forced to close their doors. In some cases, religious organizations step in to fill needs created by shuttered governmental programs. Even large, for-profit corporations have responded to this shifting paradigm, with corporate responsibility statements that express social awareness or adherence to a certain belief system; many more donate a share of their profits to charities and nonprofits, thereby increasing their marketability.

Increasingly, "social entrepreneurship" is tied to community engagement as a proposed way of sidestepping neoliberal instrumentalism. Social entrepreneurs function "as change agents in the social sector," constantly adapting their mission to create and sustain social change (Dees 2001). As university programs have blurred the lines between CBL, innovation, and entrepreneurship, social entrepreneurship initiatives have flourished. Neoliberal models feed the growing presence of social entrepreneurship education in higher education. As Raddon and Harrison (2015, 5) write, "Neo-liberal subjects are driven to emulate business entities by becoming more personally innovative, entrepreneurial, and efficient even in areas of life where markets do not operate." Large foundations host global competitions for the best social innovation, for instance, with students creating smartphone apps that help refugees find jobs, or that improve delivery mechanisms for medicines in rural Africa. Are these efforts antistructural, bypassing traditional business models and bureaucracy? Are they profit-making tools disguised as social ventures? Where is the reciprocity, the solidarity? Does it matter? With the rise in socially responsible enterprises in the United States, it is important to reflect on how market-driven behaviors may differ from those in other societies. The emphasis in the US on individual action does not always align with what motivates community engagement in some other cultures. Does the country of origin hew more closely to a socialist ideology? Do community members expect schools to provide a social support network for the community? Thinking about these issues can help us prepare our students for cultural misunderstandings that arise when these ideologies conflict with one another.

Neoliberal models of higher education purport to be politically neutral, strategically avoiding the moral judgment and social responsibility that characterize critical pedagogy. As Giroux (2010, 191) concludes about the current state of education, "there is little interest in higher education for understanding pedagogy as a deeply civic, political, and moral practice." In fact, under this new model, social justice is no longer nonpartisan but is increasingly politicized, as belonging to the left (McGivern 2010). This framework is in direct conflict with critical SL, which is "marked by an intentional commitment to a more just and equitable society" (Mitchell 2008, 62). Kubota (2014) explores how using critical pedagogies in language teaching allows him to address controversial issues without an indoctrination of ideas. He suggests that the focus on attitudes or knowledge might promote deeper understanding of controversial issues and uncomfortable moments that arise. In this book we attempt to bring attention to these issues and provide resources that can guide students, teachers, and community partners to deeper learning. For example, we discuss inclusive terminology that raises consciousness about how service may perpetuate marginalization and othering. The naming of languages as "foreign," "second," or "heritage", for instance, can sustain an "us/American" versus "them/foreign" binary (Osborn 2000, 61). Likewise, the use of the term "language communities" often evokes imaginary communities that are artificially created by the dominant discourse, when in fact such groups are diverse and varied. In chapter 4 we address the challenges of naming in greater detail.

As educators, we believe strongly that CBLL can and should play a vital role in world language education. CBLL provides students ways to improve language proficiency and intercultural competence but also models how communication is a vehicle through which we expose social inequities and promote systemic change. Education is a political act, but it does not need to be partisan. By modifying how we name and identify "language communities," for instance, we can transform the study of language into a critical study of the world, providing a transformative platform on which our students may explore how language, power, society, politics, and identity are all interconnected.

Reflections for Instructors

1. *Institutional dialogue.* How might you transform existing models of CBLL at your institution to include themes related to social change? How does your institution talk about communities within and beyond the campus borders? What are current narratives about immigrants, refugees, heritage speakers in your city?

2. *Faculty journal.* During the CBLL course or program, write down observations and reactions to help track your own challenges and breakthroughs. Although you are probably well prepared to seize on a "teachable moment" from the disorienting dilemmas (Mezirow) that arise for students, track your own disorienting dilemmas. It can be useful to use quotations to reflect on CBLL as well; we include a number of these in chapter 3.

3. *Instructor consultations to build knowledge about social justice.* Consider consulting with different members of your community and educational institution in order to gain more knowledge about issues that you want to explore further. Visit the LGBTQ center on campus or in the community. Review the toolkits and resources on the Southern Poverty Law Center's website. Meet with a librarian at the local library to find out what kinds of community resources they offer. More resources are listed in appendix E for your consideration.

Activities for Students

1. *What is CBLL to you?* Distribute an envelope to each student that contains the following words, each one on a small piece of paper. Invite students to spend 10 minutes organizing the words in a way that reflects their personal view of service. Students should use only the words they wish; few will use all. Offer glue and tape, and suggest creativity. This activity can be used at the beginning of the semester, and again at the end, to see how attitudes, values, and practices may have changed or evolved. These words are

> charity, self, community, democracy, citizenship, compassion, leadership, problem-solving, change, collaboration, solidarity, reciprocity, learning, empathy, knowledge, culture, hero, discrimination, power, voice, transformation, politics, dialogue, crisis, conflict, communication, compassion, barriers, stereotypes, . . .

CHAPTER 2

Student Learning Outcomes

By the end of this chapter, readers will be able to:

- List potential learning outcomes of CBL and CBLL
- Identify common student learning outcomes in CBLL
- Apply the intentional design model to CBLL
- Explain how CBLL develops intercultural communicative competencies
- Articulate how CBLL advances language proficiency

LEARNING OUTCOMES IN CBL AND CBLL

Community engagement is considered a high-impact educational practice (according to the Association of American Colleges and Universities) that "increase[s] the odds that students will invest time and effort; participate in active challenging learning experiences; experience diversity; interact with faculty and peers about substantive matters; receive more frequent feedback; and discover the relevance of their learning through real-world experiences" (Jacoby 2015, 11). CBL offers a unique platform that develops opportunities for a multitude of learning outcomes. Eyler and Giles (1999, 6) trace the different learning outcomes that community-engaged pedagogy achieves, stating that "students link personal and social development with academic and cognitive development; . . . experience enhances understanding; understanding leads to more effective action." CBLL students attain and, in certain cases, surpass the learning outcomes established for CBL-English students.

Although there is increasing interest in exploring the benefits of combining world language study and CBL, it has been in the civic engagement research agenda for many years. Hale (1999, 13–14) clearly identified the growth potential of CBLL nearly two decades ago:

> In academic service-learning placements, students usually work with people of different cultures, genders, races, ages, national origins, faiths, languages, sexual preferences, economic, and educational levels. However, they are rarely required to speak or even learn the language of the community into which they are placed or to gain in-depth understanding of the culture in which they are working. Sometimes, this knowledge is absorbed at a subconscious level, but when language and culture are intentionally integrated into the curriculum, the transformative potential . . . grows exponentially.

As Hale concludes, it is the *intentional* integration of language and culture into the curriculum that distinctly amplifies transformation. This chapter looks first at the broader student development outcomes of CBL and then focuses on the additional opportunities presented by CBLL that emphasize learning outcomes related to intercultural communicative competence and language acquisition.

To set the stage for this discussion, we introduce the case study of Ben, a student enrolled in an advanced Spanish service-learning course that places him in a legal aid office for the semester. There, he provides support for lawyers who are representing Spanish-speaking clients in legal cases. Ben's work ranges from clerical tasks, calling and setting up appointments with Spanish-speaking clients, to accompanying Spanish-speaking clients in the courtroom to provide informal support. In his class blog, he reports being troubled that one of the Spanish-speaking clients "does not seem to have any agency": She is not proficient in English, and though she has access to an interpreter in court, he notices that she is overwhelmed by the situation. He is able to help explain some of the legal proceedings and notices that his assistance seems to have a positive impact on the client's comfort level. He begins to feel more confident in his ability to communicate effectively with a native speaker.

Reflections for Instructors

1. What does Ben gain from this experience in the community?
2. How does the knowledge of a language enhance Ben's CBLL experience?
3. What advantages and disadvantages exist for students, organizations, and clients when language students are placed in community organizations?

Community-based learning provides opportunities to expand interpersonal, intrapersonal, and cognitive domains in student development. Students learn more tolerance for ambiguity, dismantle stereotypes, build compassion, and establish reciprocal and authentic relationships. Researchers also note personal growth in areas of leadership, efficacy, and lifelong commitment to service. In this way, community engagement helps higher education produce "critically, civically, and globally minded graduates who possess problem-solving and leadership abilities" (Cress et al. 2010, 3). As students develop critical thinking and problem-solving skills, they better understand the complexities of social issues. Through this heightened civic consciousness, they deepen their commitment to social change and social justice, and become more engaged as global citizens. These students experience moral development and spiritual growth, as well as increased motivation. Students also obtain skills that are useful in their professional lives and are valued by employers. Looking more closely at demographic difference, researchers have also found that first-generation students experience a greater sense of validation, belonging, and connection with the institution. In this chapter, we focus primarily on outcomes specific to CBLL. For more resources on student learning outcomes related to CBL-English, we suggest in particular Giles and others' (2001) *At A Glance: What We Know about The Effects of Service-Learning on College Students, Faculty, Institutions and Communities, 1993–2000* and Jacoby's (2015) *Service-Learning Essentials: Questions, Answers, and Lessons Learned.*

L2 research indicates that when CBL is incorporated into world language study, students experience the same benefits that they do in CBL-English, such as building professional skills (Berreneche 2011; Rosengrant 1997; Thompson 2015). In CBLL students develop a greater awareness of social and political issues (Nelson and Scott 2008; Petrov 2013). Finally, similar to CBL-English, CBLL promotes problem-solving skills (Carney 2004). Pascual y Cabo, Prada, and Lowther Pereira (2017) specifically researched heritage language learners (HLLs) in CBLL courses. HLLs are students who have proficiency in or a cultural connection to the language through family, community, or country of origin; their linguistic abilities are different enough from L2 learners to merit distinct teaching approaches (Potowski 2002). According to the authors, "By engaging in meaningful work that challenged their habits of language use and their intermediate-level proficiency in Spanish, students came to realize what they could do with their language" (Pascual y Cabo, Prada, and Lowther Pereira 2017, 81). Because of CBLL, HLLs perceived their linguistic and cultural competence as a positive attribute within the professional context (Pascual y Cabo, Prada, and Lowther Pereira 2017; Thompson 2015). Guillén (2010) shows that HLLs experience increased self-esteem when engaged in positive CBL experiences in the L2 and that previous insecurities related to linguistic competence are replaced with growing pride in their community work. Likewise, DuBord and Kimball (2016) show that HLLs have better outcomes than L2 learners in the areas of problem solving and dialogic communication (flexible and creative communication).

Research from more than two decades clearly and consistently shows that L2 students who engage in CBL show increased motivation and more positive attitudes toward language learning (Boyle and Overfield 1999; Caldwell 2007; Carney 2004; Grim 2010; Hale 1999; Morris 2001; Nelson and Scott 2008; O'Connor 2012; Pak 2007). These gains hold true for HLLs as well (Pascual y Cabo, Prada, and Lowther Pereira 2017; Petrov 2013). Morris (2001, 252), for instance, finds that "attitudes towards language learning and the speakers of the target language can improve by allowing learners to negotiate meaning with target-language speakers and by understanding the communicative and cultural contexts in which language is used. In conclusion, attitudinal change occurs through social contact and social practice. Motivation and attitudes can be enhanced by fostering access to the target-language community." In a similar vein, Pellettieri (2011) reports that increased contact with native speakers in CBLL improves students' willingness to communicate in the L2. Studies also show a greater confidence in using the L2 (Hellebrandt and Varona 1999; Hellebrandt, Arries, and Varona 2003; Plann 2002; Wehling 2011; Wurr and Hellebrand 2007). It must be stated, however, that it is very difficult to separate the influence of the community component from that of the academic classroom experience because there are so many variables at play in the learning environment (Barreneche and Ramos-Flores 2013).

According to some experts, CBLL students experience gains that are uniquely linked to the language component, including higher levels of language proficiency (Abbott and Lear 2010; Lear and Abbott 2009; Malkin 2010) and expanded vocabulary (Elorriaga 2007; Plann 2002). There has been relatively little research in this area, and we believe that this would be a useful area to develop. Still, DuBord and Kimball (2016, 301) question the importance placed on L2 advances, noting that they should not be the primary outcomes for CBLL. They warn that "the community setting teaches skills that are not generally measured in academic settings. For both HLLs and L2 learners, research suggests that cultural competence and making community connections are of greater value than narrowly defined language gains in CBL." We agree that learning outcomes related to intercultural competence and social justice are more measurable in CBLL. Still, while L2 gains may be secondary, they are nonetheless important outcomes to attain and assess.

In addition to linguistic gains, research shows that L2 learners engaged in CBL demonstrate improved cultural understanding, including a reduction of stereotypes (Nguyen and Kellogg 2010; Pak 2013), an increase in cultural awareness (Beebe and DeCosta 1993; Caldwell 2007; Hale 1999; Morris 2001; Varona 1999), and an expanded understanding of the community (Wu and Dahlgren 2011). Pascual y Cabo, Prada, and Lowther Pereira (2017) and Carracelas-Juncal (2013) report a positive impact on HLLs' own cultural identities. CBLL develops a sense of solidarity, empathy, or belonging (Long 2003; Pascual y Cabo, Prada, and Lowther Pereira 2017) and presents opportunities to explore diversity (Gascoigne Lally 2001). Reflecting on her study of low and high intermediate L2 students, Zapata (2011, 100) confirms that CBL in the L2 can promote a deeper cultural understanding, and yet she also suggests another learning outcome; she states that "the participants' CSL [community service learning] work helped them become more aware of aspects of the target culture (such as diversity, problems that immigrants and workers face in Canada, etc.) and positively affected their view of their L2 as a tool for change (e.g., to help less fortunate people)." In our experience as well, CBLL students often become "language activists," promoting language learning among their peers. In a similar manner, Leeman and Román-Mendoza (2011, 492) report that HLLs who engage in CBLL demonstrate increased social agency and "a new sense of themselves as activists for social change." Understanding that the L2 is a tool for social change (Caldwell 2007; Zapata 2011) is a powerful learning outcome for CBLL that is further explored within the discussion of outcomes related to social justice at the end of this chapter.

Before we delve more deeply into the considerations of designing student learning outcomes, the interplay of CBLL and intercultural communicative competence, as well as the relationship between CBLL and language acquisition, let us return to Ben, the student in the legal aid office from the beginning of the chapter. The way students negotiate meaning determines the level of communication and the depth of relationship that is possible with the community. In this example, Ben witnessed how systemic inequities manifest in the legal realm. He also gained cultural knowledge about the local Latino/a community and learned about marginalized voices in his town. As he honed his critical thinking skills, he also heightened his civic consciousness, demonstrating greater compassion and a broader understanding of social issues. These outcomes are possible for all students, whether they are interacting with the community in English or in the L2. But because Ben spoke Spanish, he was able to use the L2 to interact in the community and engage in perspective taking, thereby creating a deeper connection with community members. Through critical reflection, he gained confidence in his language skills, learned specialized vocabulary, and called on skills of tolerance, compassion, and flexibility. If he had enrolled in an English-only class about law and immigration, or taken a non-CBLL Spanish class about the same subject, it is unlikely that he would have attained these goals to the same degree, if at all.

Reflections for Instructors

Outcomes. What are possible learning outcomes when working with local L2 speakers? How can you target language-acquisition learning outcomes through CBLL?

CONSIDERATIONS FOR DESIGNING STUDENT LEARNING OUTCOMES

In the previous section, we outlined the ways in which students benefit from CBLL opportunities. Here we want to be more explicit about how educators can create syllabi and set up experiences that will help facilitate those outcomes.

When teachers design new courses, they can be easily drawn into a linear model of curricular planning. As Wiggins and McTighe (1998) note, "Many teachers *begin* with textbooks, favored lessons, and time-honored activities rather than deriving those tools from targeted goals or standards." A department might require a certain textbook, for instance, thus prioritizing course materials. For example, a Spanish instructor teaching a 300-level content-based course in Spanish on immigration might begin preparation by compiling a list of books and films to share with students. Based on these materials, the educator will develop a course syllabus, plugging in dates for reading assignments, papers, and tests. The educator will then begin to prepare lesson plans with related content and activities; if it is the first iteration of the course, the instructor will often do so just before each class, as a function of what happened in the previous one. Assessments, too, are often created just before the date indicated on the syllabus. If this instructor wishes to incorporate a CBLL component into the course, the instructor might reach out to a local immigration office that works with the Latino/a community. On the syllabus, the educator will indicate the total amount of service hours that must be completed, noting that students will complete weekly blogs to reflect on their experiences. This instructor-centered approach to course design fails to take into consideration student learning outcomes, or the needs of the community.

A "backward design" approach (Wiggins and McTighe 2007) grounds the curriculum in student learning outcomes (SLOs). In this model, which is endorsed in the American Council on the Teaching of Foreign Languages' (ACTFL's) twenty-first-century skills map, teachers begin planning a course (or a unit) by identifying their desired results, which are framed as student learning

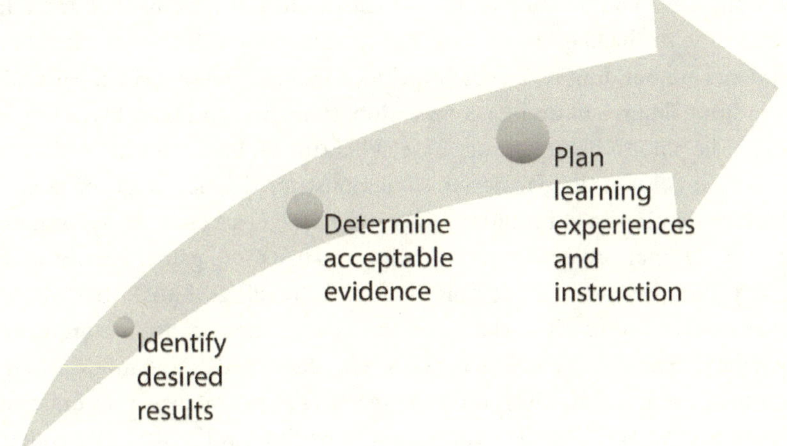

FIGURE 2.1
Source: Authors, based on Wiggins and McTighe.

objectives or SLOs: "What do I want my students to know, understand, and be able to do?" (See appendix A for a complete list of key stages, considerations, criteria, and accomplishments.) Teachers then identify three to five outcomes for student learning, before designing both formative and summative assessments that demonstrate if students have achieved these results and to what degree. From there, teachers plan learning experiences, which include lectures, reflection activities, and homework assignments. Such intentional design emphasizes having community conversations early in the planning stages, ensuring a more collaborative, ethical, and student-centered approach to CBLL course design. SLOs can also remind us to include students in the planning stages, from establishing learning contracts to offering opportunities for self-authored work. SLOs are the key drivers of course development and assessment and should not be overlooked (see figure 2.1).

Knowing that CBLL will deepen student knowledge of immigration, the Spanish educator in the previous example wants to explore the possibility of placing students in a CBLL partnership with an immigration law office that serves a number of Spanish speakers. Using a backward design model, the instructor considers how a CBLL component would enrich or alter existing student learning outcomes. One of the *desired results*, for instance, is to develop students' knowledge of the complexity of immigration practices in the United States. Another student learning outcome is L2 advancement in the three modes of communication. A third SLO, tied to the CBLL component, is intercultural communicative competence (ICC), which would not have likely been a target outcome in the classroom setting alone. But how will the educator know if students are building ICC, which includes skills not necessarily measured in the traditional curriculum like compassion, tolerance, and humility? How will students be able to demonstrate these skills (to the instructor, to each other, and to their community partners)? To demonstrate this new learning goal, the instructor develops a continuum of *acceptable evidence* (writing assignments, role-plays, a final project) that will help measure these gains. Finally, and at the very end, the educator identifies *materials* (readings, films), that will help students develop these ICC skills and then creates and scaffolds complementary reflection activities and lesson plans. This backward design model disrupts traditional curricular models and offers teachers a systematic way to undertake the pedagogical and logistical challenges of working with CBLL. By enacting intentional design in CBLL, student learning outcomes can be enhanced, multiplied, and diversified, offering students the opportunity to be more engaged in their learning and ultimately perform at a higher level.

Reflections for Instructors

1. *Brainstorming SLOs.* Imagine a CBLL course you would like to design and implement. What would you like your students to be able to know, understand, and do as a result of their work in your course? What changes would you like to see in your students? Wiggins and McTighe (1998) suggest brainstorming curricular priorities by first listing ideas worth being familiar with, followed by listing items that are important to know and to do, and finally by identifying elements of "enduring understanding." Use figure 2.2 to brainstorm SLOs.

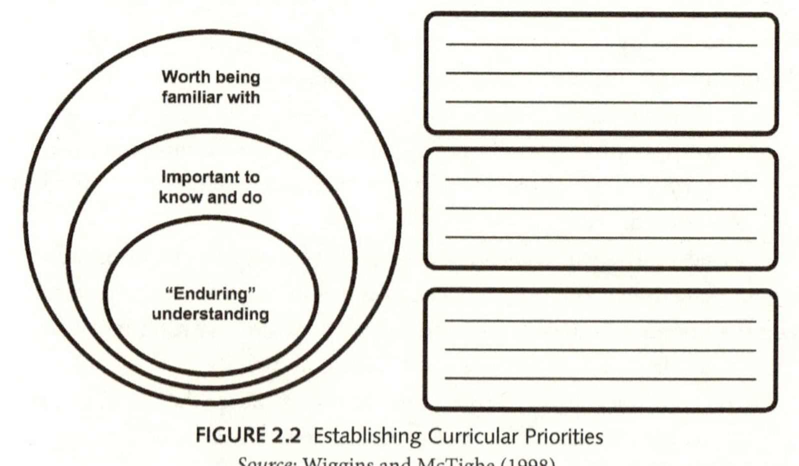

FIGURE 2.2 Establishing Curricular Priorities
Source: Wiggins and McTighe (1998).

(*continued*)

2a. *Measurable outcomes.* When educators write SLOs, they should focus on what students will know and will be able to do. SLOs describe observable and measurable outcomes; verbs like *learn*, *know*, *understand*, and *appreciate* should thus be avoided because they generally describe internal and unobservable behavior. By using more precise language, we articulate our own expectations, and make the learning process more clear for students. Verbs such as *identify*, *explain*, *interpret*, *modify*, *predict*, and *design* represent observable and measurable actions. Bloom's Taxonomy may be useful here, although some researchers have suggested that it offers a purely intellectual and disembodied approach to learning that does not reflect many of our SLOs (Bertucio 2017). In table 2.1, rewrite each SLO to reflect measurable outcomes.

TABLE 2.1

Students will learn how to engage with L2 speakers in culturally competent ways.	
Students will understand social inequities.	
Students will appreciate cultural differences.	

2b. *Establishing SLOs.* Now, use the following chart to write five SLOs. What should students know and understand? Be sure to write clear statements that reflect *S*pecific, *M*easurable, *A*chievable, *R*elevant, and *T*ime-bound goals—SMART goals—for your students. As you do this, consider the wide range of your goals; these may include course content, communication, critical thinking, awareness of community, commitment to service, career development, self-awareness, sensitivity to diversity, life skills, and so on. Here are a number of examples (and see table 2.2):

- Construct an argument defending opposing points of view on immigration reform.
- Articulate and support an argument for refugee resettlement in the L2.
- Produce written documents in the L2 that explain health care laws.
- Evaluate personal or family ethics and traditions in relation to those of other people.
- Formulate or clarify personal values, attitudes, ethics, and beliefs.
- Explain changes in thinking about the community, its challenges, and their solutions as a result of the service-learning experience.
- Summarize your knowledge of community issues, needs, strengths, problems, and resources.
- Articulate the value of community for socially constructive purposes.

TABLE 2.2

As a result of your participation in this course, you will be able to:

SLO 1 ____________________

SLO 2 ____________________

SLO 3 ____________________

SLO 4 ____________________

SLO 5 ____________________

THE ROLE OF COMMUNITY PARTNERS

When developing student learning outcomes, it is paramount to solicit and include community partner input. Intentional conversations with community partners are crucial for setting outcomes that benefit both student and community, and the educator must invest the time to listen deeply to the needs of community partners when establishing a CBLL relationship. It is the educator's responsibility to make sure that outcomes are clearly stated and are consistently being met by all parties. To build a successful CBLL curriculum, the desired learning outcomes for the students *and* the desires and needs of the community must be at the center of the design. Educators should thus start the curricular design process by considering how appropriate and effective the CBLL interactions will be for all stakeholders and then work backward to build an appropriate scaffolding to ensure that impact mirrors intentions.

From the beginning of their working relationship, then, educators should invite community partners to create shared outcomes. Lists of joint goals, memoranda of understanding, sets of best practices for communication, and predetermined evaluation systems can help parties negotiate compromises early in the process. The establishment of *standards of practice* can further help sidestep conflicts. Practices should be based on principles of fairness, equity, and inclusion; they should reflect a shared commitment to a clear purpose, and a clear plan for reaching those outcomes. Practices can be included in a course syllabus, shared at an initial meeting between students and partners, or even co-created at an orientation that takes place early in the semester. Educators should also plan for an orientation that includes students and the community partner, in which they learn about an organization's history, its needs, and its goals. Equally important is deciding the format of the orientation. What are the goals of the orientation, and who decides them? Who will deliver the content, the teacher or the community partner, or both? Where will the orientation take place, in a classroom or in the community? These questions also remind us to be mindful of the limited resources and targeted missions of nonprofit organizations and schools; though some nonprofits committed to training future leaders will take on a coeducational role enthusiastically, other organizations are not equipped to train and monitor volunteers due to capacity issues. When students are unaware of an organization's need to follow regulations or of issues related to liability and sustainability, student volunteers may critique or show impatience about practices, wanting to push original initiatives when organizations do not have sufficient infrastructure to support such endeavors. Students should thus be made aware that volunteers can be both an asset and a burden to community organizations. Not understanding the mission, infrastructure, and particularities of the partner organization can lead to misunderstandings and problematic relationships.

Let us return to our Spanish teacher to consider how to implement these ideas in a concrete way. Before the semester's start, in addition to considering the learning objectives for students, the instructor should sit down with the immigration law office's volunteer coordinator to discuss their goals: Which of the organization's needs will drive the partnership? Do they need office support such as translation, grant writing, or Web design services? Or do they need interpersonal work, such as tutoring, conversational practice, or citizenship training? What do students need to know and understand about the organization and its clients in order to create a meaningful and reciprocal partnership? Finally, how can we move the CBLL experience from a charity model that services the organization to a more engaged partnership that trains students to work for social change? What would it mean for the organization to educate students to be change makers instead of office workers? Or, how can students learn to see office work as an essential part of organizational need and a place of unique, if unexpected, learning? These big picture questions must characterize early discussions and shape SLOs so that instructors can create appropriate assignments that help students reach these goals.

Expectations for language use should also be part of early conversations with the community partner, particularly when notions of target language use may be different for the instructor and for the organization. Although many community organizations relish CBLL partnerships because they do not have bilingual staff members, there are also community projects in which English needs override L2 concerns, and English must be the common language. For many educators, however, interactions with community members are considered a vehicle for activating students' L2 production, and they may push for L2 usage in partnerships. Ethically minded educators must be cautious of using the community as a laboratory, however. If the Spanish teacher's goals are to increase students' L2 proficiency, but the immigration law office prefers to conduct business with its clients in English, there is misalignment. The teacher might instead see the value in placing students at the organization in order to provide opportunities to develop intercultural competence and deepen knowledge about the community, rather than target language acquisition. Being knowledgeable about the mission of the organization will help determine the type of linguistic exchanges that can occur, and whether it is possible to meet the goals of all stakeholders. In order to avoid placing students in situations where they cannot be successful and where the community partners' needs are not being met, educators must work with community partners before the course's iteration, to identify needs and to set intentional outcomes together.

Reflections for Instructors

1a. *Connecting with refugees.* A Swahili teacher learns that there is a refugee resettlement organization in the local community and proposes connecting students with Swahili-speaking refugees from Eastern Africa. What learning outcomes might be possible through this agency? What key questions might they wish to explore? As you prepare a list of three SLOs and two key questions, be careful not only to consider the students' needs but also to make an effort to consider the perspectives of all parties.

1b. Imagine now that the refugee resettlement organization invites students to do in-home visits and assist the adult members of the families in learning English. Design a role-play or dialogue for your students in which one student assumes the role of the instructor and another student takes on the role of the community partner. The goal of the conversation is for both parties to share their objectives and concerns. How will the instructor communicate curricular goals to the organization? Are there ways to clarify the role of language (English and L2)? How will the community partner convey the organization's needs and remain faithful to its mission?

2. *Connecting with a library.* Although instructors may seek out community partners, in some cases, the community partner may approach a language teacher with a specific need. A local library reaches out to see if your students can assist with after-school tutoring. Consider how to proceed. What questions will you ask the librarian? Will this opportunity reinforce learning outcomes that you have already identified for your curriculum or allow you to introduce additional learning outcomes? Will it lead students away from the outcomes you have established?

3. *Standards of practice.* Imagine preparing a meeting with a community partner, in which you hope to draw up standards of practice for your partnership. Write a checklist of ten items. Now, reduce it to five items. Here are some examples that you may use for inspiration:

- Meets weekly with partners
- If there is conflict or illness, student will contact partner at least 24 hours in advance and copy professor on message
- Promotes understanding of diversity
- Engages in ethical relationship
- Participates meaningfully in reflection activities
- Cooperates with partners

See *Good to Go: Standards of Practice in Global Service Learning* (Duarte 2014); also see appendix D for a more complete list.

Activities for Students

Mission Statements and Mission Drift. Just as educators craft SLOs, community organizations construct mission statements. This activity directs students to consider how the mission statement of a community organization reflects its internal goals and helps guide its work.

Before class. Students familiarize themselves with Peter Brinckerhoff's work on mission-based management.

1. Website: www.missionbased.com/.
2. *Mission-based Management: Leading Your Not-for-Profit in the 21st Century* (www.wiley.com/WileyCDA/WileyTitle/productCd-0470432071.html).
3. The essentials of mission-based management: http://nnaac.org/wp-content/uploads/2011/09/In-his-book-Mission-Based-Management.docx.

During class. Students visit the website of their community partner organization:

1. Identify the organization's mission (its goals). How does it measure against best practices for mission statements: Is it concise? Is it action-oriented, and does it state what the organization seeks to accomplish? Does it indicate whom it serves? Does it give direction to the whole organization?
2. Next, have students identify the services the organization has listed (what they do). Is there alignment? Or is there "mission drift"?
3. Working with a partner, students consider the following scenarios. They may either provide a written response or take notes for a discussion with the class at large. Remind them to use the mission statement to guide their decisions:
   —The organization functions on a shoestring budget. Imagine the state cuts its budget and donations decrease. The organization must eliminate some of its services. Which two services from their list would you eliminate? Why?
   —The organization is flush with money. Which of the programs in the original list would you enhance and expand with that extra money, and why?
   —A very wealthy community member wants to donate an enormous sum of money to the organization. She is an animal lover, and all you have to do is use the money for a program that involves animals in a prominent way. What should the organization do?
   —Money is very tight. A new Afghan immigrant community is emerging in the town. No one on the organizational staff speaks Pashto or Dari, the two official languages of Afghanistan. No one is familiar with Afghan cultural norms nor with Islam, the religion of the majority of immigrants who have arrived. What should the organization do?

Conclusions: How easy is it for mission drift to occur in an organization? What are the consequences for the organization and their service recipients if mission drift occurs?
(This activity was adapted from a lecture by Annie Abbott, professor at the University of Illinois.)

INTERCULTURAL COMMUNICATIVE COMPETENCE (ICC)

Institutions of higher learning are invested in preparing twenty-first-century students for global citizenship, and many have designed distinct educational pathways to attain this goal. Some schools incorporate training in ICC through targeted workshops, courses, and certificate programs, while others embed these goals in a larger strategic plan. Likewise, some institutions explicitly address the importance of language proficiency in developing ICC, while others do not link the two. ICC and global learning are now common and accepted goals tied to higher learning, from student learning outcomes to educational policy organizations. The International Affairs Office of the US Department of Education (2017) published a "Framework for Developing Global and Cultural Competencies to Advance Equity, Excellence, and Economic Competitiveness" that establishes benchmarks from early learning to postsecondary education. The four categories of this framework include collaboration and communication, world and heritage languages, diverse perspectives, and civic and global engagement. The framework states that globally and culturally competent postsecondary students must be able to work or study in at least one other language. The rationale behind this framework is that "today, more than ever, our students need to be equipped with the critical thinking, communications, socio-emotional and language skills to work collaboratively with their counterparts in the United States and all over the world. Understanding and appreciating other parts of the world, different religions, cultures, and points of view are essential elements of global and cultural competence" (https://sites.ed.gov/international/global-and-cultural-competency/). Although the inclusion of language proficiency in "global and cultural competencies" is explicit in these stated educational goals, it is incorporated inconsistently across US institutions of higher education, which have seen a national decline in world language requirements for graduation. To better explain the relationship of language with ICC, which relates to the primary learning outcomes stated for many CBLL courses, we turn to a historical overview of ICC models.

The field of ICC first emerged in the early 1930s with the Bureau of Intercultural Education (Lal 2004), developing later from research related to the Peace Corps' empirical approach to cross-cultural training. This was followed by a fine-tuning of the concept of cultural training through behavioral approaches, developmental models, multidimensional models (Byram 1997; Risager 2007), and culture-generic approaches (Arasaratnam and Doerfel 2005). Models of ICC generally reference dissonance, designating uncomfortable moments as part of the process of becoming interculturally competent. In the Bennett (1986) scale (figure 2.3), for instance, the stages "denial of difference" and "defense against difference" allude to moments of cultural or linguistic dissonance that one must pass through before learning to accept and integrate difference. Many other ICC models describe these stages as part of a linear process toward "gaining" intercultural competence; but in our experience, this process is more cyclical. In other words, a student may be able to act in culturally competent ways that do not

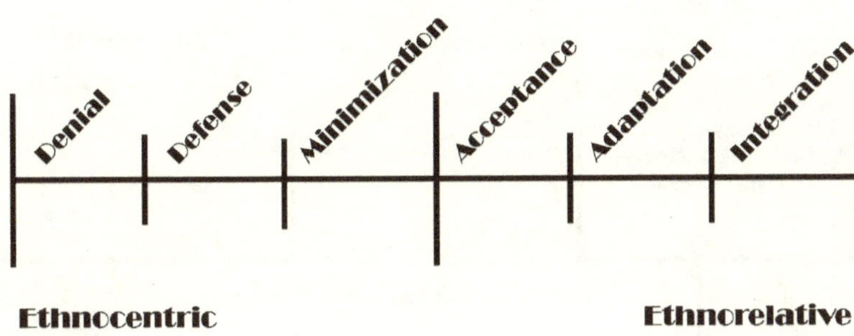

FIGURE 2.3
Source: M. Bennett (1986).

generate resistance one day; but in a subsequent community encounter, he or she may experience conflict or discomfort. Another student might have an opposite reaction to the same events. Deardorff's 2006 framework was the first attempt to theorize a model of ICC, and her process model (figure 2.4; Deardorff 2006, 2009) underscores this nonlinear nature of how a person develops ICC. Rather than imagining ICC as a goal to be achieved or attained, Deardorff showed that ICC is a constant process of learning, one that is—in our experience—often bumpy.

Deardorff's model is widely hailed as a breakthrough in understanding ICC, but it has not silenced the debates about how to define ICC, and new models continue to proliferate. Deardorff recently worked with the Bertelsmann Stiftung German think tank, for instance, to slightly alter the Process Model. A spiral now indicates that the more dimensions a student achieves and the more frequently they pass through them, the greater the degree of learning. This model emphasizes that every experience impacts the students' attitudes, knowledge, skills, and reflection (Bertelsmann Stiftung and Fondazione Cariplo 2008). Current research refers to ICC using over thirty distinct terms, reflecting a growing field that is embraced by an increasing number of disciplines; new terms include *ethnorelativity*, *multiculturalism*, *intercultural cooperation*, and *transcultural communication* (Sinicrope, Norris, and Watanabe 2007). As Fantini (2012) confirms, *intercultural (communicative) competence* has become the preferred term, and it is the one that we use throughout our work here. One commonly cited definition used by the Association of American Colleges and

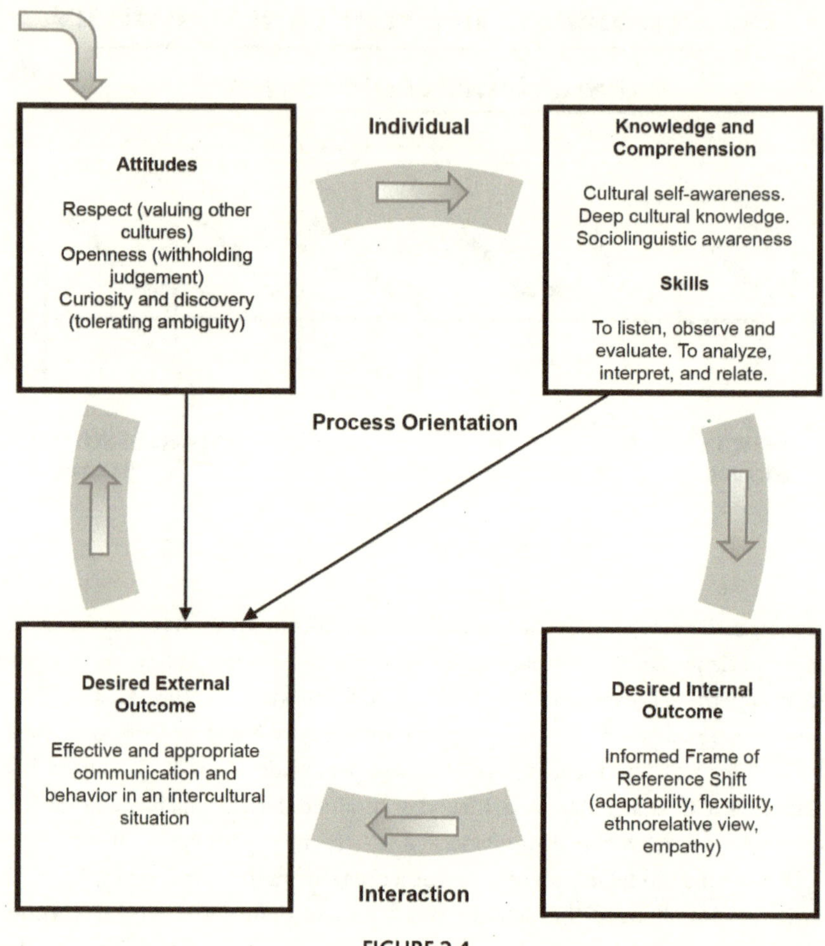

FIGURE 2.4
Source: Deardorff (2009).

Universities draws on both Bennett (2008) and Deardorff (2006) to describe ICC as "a set of cognitive, behavioral, and affective skills and characteristics that support effective and appropriate interaction in a variety of cultural contexts" (Bennett 2008).

Let us consider best practices for guiding students toward ICC by looking at an example of a student engaged in CBL-English. Emily, a college student tutoring English as a second language, works with a group of linguistically and culturally diverse immigrants at a local literacy center. Emily was enrolled in a Spanish course on education, but her weekly community work took place in

English. After just a few tutoring sessions, she began to notice tensions among her students, and decided to explore ways to improve the group dynamic. After conversing with the students, the literacy center staff, and her professor, Emily realized that the tensions stemmed from different cultural norms for classroom behavior. Although some students treated the classroom as a formal space, others arrived late, shouted out their answers with enthusiasm, and chatted with seatmates during class. These unconscious practices—which reflected the cultural norms of the individuals in the room—created bad feelings, with certain students withdrawing their participation and others becoming more aggressive. Soon, there were distinct cliques in the class, divided along ethnic lines. Emily decided to discuss cultural norms with her students, asking her students to share their personal experiences of school in their home country. She then led the class through a process of establishing group norms for their literacy sessions; the students agreed not to interrupt one another and settled on group work strategies that would give them more time to talk. Although she was uncomfortable during the process of taking charge—which she initially did not anticipate as one of her duties—Emily reported significant personal growth as a result of this experience, as well as increases in knowledge and attitudes of ICC. Emily used her skills in ICC to recover from a deteriorating situation. Examining this situation, it is interesting to consider if her studies in Spanish, specifically her role as a language learner, impacted her ability to process the situation. How does language study affect ICC? And how does CBLL build the skills and characteristics necessary for developing ICC, including self-awareness, identity transformation, evaluative orientation, and shifting of worldviews and values?

LANGUAGE AND ICC

Only a few theorists and researchers include explicit references to language proficiency in their definition of intercultural communicative competence. Most notable is Byram (1997), whose Multidimensional Intercultural Competence Model has been integrated into the *Common European Framework of Reference for Languages* (Council of Europe 2001). Byram (1997, 3) suggests that ICC is determined by building relationships and engaging in communication in another language through a process of acquiring attitudes, knowledge, and skills related to ICC. As a language educator, he focuses on the role of the L2 in communication and clarifies that he is not referring to exchanging information or sending messages in another language, but rather to how the L2 is used "to establish and maintain relationships." He defines ICC as "the ability to interact

FIGURE 2.5 Dimensions and Components of ICC
Source: Rico Troncoso (2012).

with people from another country and culture in a foreign language," and he lists five areas of knowledge that language learners must cultivate in order to develop ICC (figure 2.5; Byram 1997, 71):

- *Savoir* / knowledge: Knowledge of self and other; of how interaction occurs; of the relationship of the individual to society.
- *Savoir-être* / attitudes and traits: Knowing how to relativize oneself and value the attitudes and beliefs of the other.
- *Savoir-communiquer* / proficiency: The ability to function linguistically in a second or foreign language.
- *Savoir-faire* / skills: Knowing how to interpret and relate information. The ability to acquire new knowledge of a culture and cultural practices.
- *Savoir-s'engager* / awareness: The ability to critically evaluate perspectives, products, and practices of one's own and others' cultures.

The proficiency area of knowledge in Byram's model highlights the importance of using language appropriately in various contexts; but as evidenced by the five dimensions, L2 proficiency alone does not produce an interculturally competent individual. Let us look at a student, Samantha, who enrolls in an intermediate Arabic language class that puts her in contact with local Arabic speakers through a tutoring program. In her first interactions with her partner, we anticipate that Samantha will activate many of the areas of knowledge identified by Byram. To demonstrate ICC in her community partnership, Samantha should build a certain knowledge of herself and her community partner's culture in order to establish an effective interpersonal relationship. She demonstrates curiosity by researching cultural norms before meeting her partner, and she is able to acquire and interpret new information about the culture. When she learns that modest dress is expected, she forgoes her shorts despite the hot temperatures outside and attends the meeting in a long skirt that reflects respect for her partner's cultural practices. When the family greets her by saying "*As-Salaam alaikum*" (Peace be unto you), she responds in a culturally and linguistically appropriate way. She notices that this ritual linguistic exchange, which carries little literal meaning, is actually quite important culturally. This detail is important because, as Byram and Fleming (1998, 2) write, "Learning a language as it is spoken by a particular group is learning the shared meanings, values and practices of that group as they are embodied in the language." As Samantha gains confidence in her language abilities and cultural knowledge, she and the family build a trusting relationship that furthers their mutual exchange.

As we see through Samantha's experience, knowledge of a second language has a positive impact on student development of ICC. Fantini (2012, 273) states that "it is clear that increased host language proficiency enhances entry possibilities, whereas lack of proficiency constrains entry, adaptation, and understanding of the host culture. Grappling with another language also fosters the development of alternative communication strategies 'on someone else's terms,' a humbling and challenging process." As he underscores, even a minimal level of proficiency gives students the opportunity to increase cultural awareness. He expands on this idea further to say that, "without host language ability, one cannot directly access their [native/HL speakers'] thoughts, their culture, their worldview. One can only learn about these things vicariously and intellectually, but not experientially. L2 completes the whole and provides total access, completely and directly" (Fantini 2012, 276–77). In other words, students who learn many languages gain insights into multiple cultural perspectives that influence how they perceive and interact in the world. Conversely, Fantini (2012, 273) explains, the "lack of an L2—even at a minimal level—constrains one to continue to think about the world and act within it entirely in one's native system, depriving the individual of one of the most valuable aspects of the intercultural experience." Recall the ICC spiral we mentioned above. CBLL interactions allow

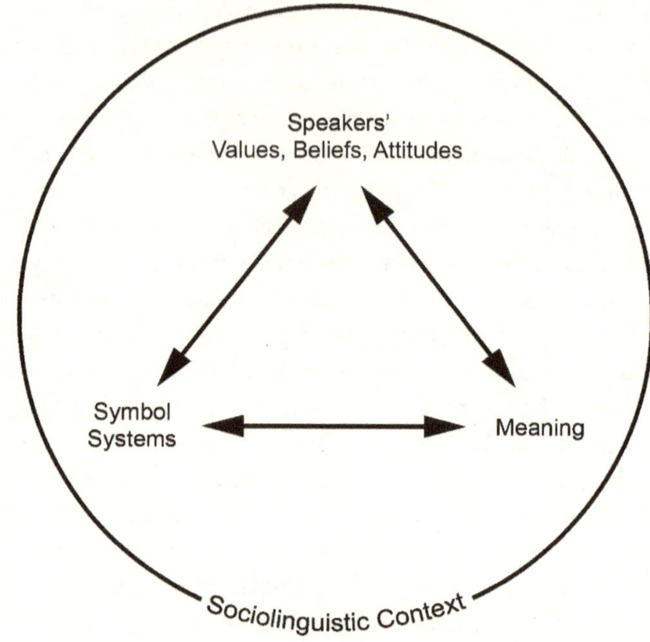

FIGURE 2.6

Source: Jackson (2012). Reproduced by permission of Taylor & Francis Books UK.

students to travel the ICC spiral at an increased pace, offering more opportunities for intercultural learning than CBL-English alone.

Fantini (2012, 266–67) illustrates the relationship among language, culture, and worldview in an interconnected model (see figure 2.6). The "symbol systems" include verbal and nonverbal language. He explains that "each worldview is a cultural-linguistic construct—a way of perceiving, conceptualizing, expressing, and interacting within a sociolinguistic context (represented by the circle)." It is only through knowledge of the relevant language system that variations of worldviews are accessible, and "many cross-cultural challenges are revealed only through access to the host language." Both Fantini (2012) and Byram (1997) conclude that this access to multiple languages plays an important role in developing ICC.

A greater access to the L2 community can also require CBLL students to use the L2 in both familiar and unfamiliar contexts. This unpredictability not only challenges a student's linguistic readiness—if they have never used technical vocabulary in a particular setting, for instance—but also problematizes the construction of a worldview. CBLL students work in locations and in situations that may be unfamiliar or even uncomfortable to them. Their proficiency in a world language offers them access to places they may not have gone before, both physically and metaphorically. One of our students, Sophie, was welcomed into the home of a community member and highly praised for her knowledge of French. Her proficiency gave her a trusted status within the family, and they welcomed her into their fold, sharing meals and playing games. She quickly found that she did not understand many of their cultural references, however, and that despite being "fluent," she still had many moments of confusion that were the result of both lexical errors and cultural misunderstandings. This caused her to question her linguistic ability but also to call on her ability to remain open and tolerant. This example shows both the process-oriented nature of ICC and the significance of an L2 setting for growth in language proficiency. A Spanish language college student, Kanar, reflected about the connection between language and culture: "In one semester, I found a perspective of the world that I had not previously perceived due to my lack of Spanish proficiency. Through the lens of language, I had the opportunity to see a culture that was previously incomprehensible and confusing to my view of the world. I realize that this is what it really means to be 'bilingual'; seeing the world from two points of view" (final reflection translated from Spanish, 2015). By developing relationships in the community, they were able to question, learn, and, ultimately, to expand their worldviews.

Moeller and Nugent (2014, 8) discuss the importance of gauging the readiness of students to engage in activities to build ICC. In order to guide learners toward ICC, world language teachers must pay attention to creating interactive environments that foster exchange of information and knowledge, curiosity and inquiry, and that minimize judgment. They warn that "traditional methods for teaching foreign languages emphasized the importance of students practicing language structure, pronunciation and vocabulary in order to become native-like speakers," noting that this goal is not attainable for many students. They agree with Byram's commitment to creating reciprocal relationships that promote mutual discovery of another language and culture. Such a process allows students to see their own agency in the learning experience and engage more in the practice of considering other perspectives.

When local CBLL partnerships prove complicated to organize, teachers may want to experiment with virtual community partnerships because these also can provide significant stimuli for growth in ICC. Programs like Talk Abroad partner students with trained native speakers in Latin America, West Africa, and East Asia through synchronous video chats. Although many of these companies are fee-based, they offer supported platforms for conversations exclusively in the L2 and allow teachers to later listen to recorded conversations and track student progress toward SLOs. A model of asynchronous exchange is the Cultura program, which was developed by Furstenberg in the late 1990s at the Massachusetts Institute of Technology. In a series of online exchanges between two classrooms in two different countries, students in one country engage with students in another. Over the course of the semester, they each work in their own language, completing sentences ("the best thing parents can do for their children"; "a cool person is . . ."), making word associations ("failure," "money," "family"), and responding to scenarios ("you see a woman in a supermarket slap her child"; "you have been waiting in line 10 minutes; someone cuts in front of you"). Through these exchanges, students offer their own points of view, read new perspectives, and in the process, are challenged to rethink their attitudes, beliefs, and values. This activity engages students in intercultural awareness and language learning, key learning outcomes in CBLL (Furstenberg 2010). The Cultura website (https://cultura.mit.edu/) is rich with past exchanges that also serve as source models for exploring different cultural attitudes; a similar model could also be adapted for and implemented with local communities.

To summarize, in this section we have offered an overview of key definitions of ICC and an explanation of the role of language in ICC. We have explored how proficiency in an L2 enhances ICC learning. We see in the case studies of the CBL-English student and the CBLL Arabic language student that students engage in ICC through community interactions in any language—but, as shown in this chapter, there is added value in using an L2 for ICC learning outcomes. For educators curious about how to assess ICC, it is useful to mention here the Intercultural Knowledge and Competence VALUE Rubric (see appendix C), designed by the Association of American Colleges and Universities (AACU 2009b). Chapter 3 provides an in-depth look into assessment in CBLL, but this particular rubric offers fundamental criteria for measuring ICC across disciplines. The key components include knowledge of cultural self-awareness and cultural worldview frameworks, skills related to empathy and verbal and nonverbal communication, and attitudes of curiosity and openness. These criteria may be adopted as is, or for inspiration for personalized assessment strategies. By acknowledging that there are many different ways "culture" is presented in the classroom, we cement the need to be more proactive as we seek means to better integrate and measure intercultural knowledge and awareness. Looking at how ICC and language are intertwined in CBLL leads us to consider how language acquisition itself becomes an important, if still secondary, SLO of CBLL. In the next section, we examine SLOs in CBLL related to the language acquisition process.

LANGUAGE ACQUISITION

As Byram (1997) and Fantini (2012) underscore, the development of ICC is enhanced by language acquisition. Students who gain proficiency in world languages generally have greater access to individuals and communities than do monolingual English speakers. In addition to ICC-related learning outcomes, then, it is important to explore further how studying and learning an L2 enhances additional SLOs. Students who operate between languages and who interact with the world through multiple lenses demonstrate both translingual and transcultural competencies. As the Modern Language Association states, students of world languages

> are educated to function as informed and capable interlocutors with educated native speakers in the target language. They are also trained to reflect on the world and themselves through the lens of another language and culture. They learn to comprehend speakers of the target language as members of foreign societies and to grasp themselves as Americans—that is, as members of a society that is foreign to others. They also learn to relate to fellow members of their own society who speak languages other than English. (MLA 2007)

Language educators seek ways to build linguistic and cultural competencies, and CBLL provides those opportunities beyond the classroom walls. As we will see, experts in sociolinguistics and L2 acquisition underscore that social interactions with more proficient speakers enhance language learning.

Numerous language acquisition theories indicate that authentic interactions in the L2 improve the process of language acquisition. Vygotsky (1978) shows that the learner acquires language best by interacting with someone who is more proficient than the learner. According to the theories of situated learning (Lave and Wegner 1991) and language socialization (Ochs 2002), "learning is a social, holistic, and emergent process in which the goal is to become a member of a social group rather than merely to master abstract knowledge removed from the context of use" (Nguyen and Kellogg 2010, 57). Nguyen and Kellogg (2010, 70) also underscore the importance of socialization among peers as a powerful learning process that leads to language acquisition. They explore how action-based learning encourages the L2 student to use the language "to fit their own needs and goals, and in so doing, the learner forms new identities." The need to use language in order to be accepted into a group is a strong motivator for many students, and CBLL supports this structure through sustained, meaningful interactions in the L2 with local L2 speakers. Another way of looking at the importance of out-of-classroom exposure to language is through Krashen's (1982) acquisition learning hypothesis. Krashen explains that language is learned through subconscious (repeated exposure to meaningful language) and conscious (formal language learning) dimensions. According to Gass and Mackey (2006), there is greater acquisition of language when students engage in unmediated interactions with individuals with whom they have a communicative need. Through authentic experiences in local language communities, CBLL students are exposed to the L2 subconsciously, through casual interactions with L2 community members, and in day-to-day interactions. Conscious dimensions are accessed through classroom activities and assignments.

Within CBLL, Long (1996) explores the importance of communication and negotiation of input with more proficient speakers of a language. Her research on L2 learners in CBL shows that exposure to language that is more advanced than the student's current level accelerates language acquisition. Because CBLL offers more occasions for genuine interactions between students and community partners, there are more opportunities to build relationships. These relationships reinforce and promote language acquisition, reinforcing the learning spiral of intercultural communicative competence.

Reflections for Instructors

Measuring L2 Acquisition. It is important for both teachers and students to set realistic expectations for language learning in CBLL. Similar to a study-abroad environment, CBLL offers more opportunities for linguistic gains than mere classroom time alone. We must remember, however, that these can occur in spurts, in proportion to the amount of time and effort invested, and in response to particular, sometimes unforeseeable circumstances, much in the same way that a friendship forms. Language learning does not just "happen." What kinds of measurable gains might students be able to attain in the L2 based on their CBLL experiences, and how might these be articulated in SLOs to reflect them?

THE FIVE Cs AND MODES OF COMMUNICATION IN CBLL

Now that we have established that interacting with heritage and native speakers increases language acquisition for CBLL students, let us look more closely at national standards of language learning. The *World Readiness Standards for Learning Languages* (ACTFL 1996, 2016; see figure 2.7) reinforce how CBLL's student learning outcomes align with national standards. As established by ACTFL, the standards focus on five domains: *communication*, *cultures*, *connections*, *comparisons*, and *communities*. In a study of nearly 1,500 students across thirty

WORLD-READINESS STANDARDS FOR LEARNING LANGUAGES

GOAL AREAS	STANDARDS		
COMMUNICATION Communicate effectively in more than one language in order to function in a variety of situations and for multiple purposes	**Interpersonal Communication:** Learners interact and negotiate meaning in spoken, signed, or written conversations to share information, reactions, feelings, and opinions.	**Interpretive Communication:** Learners understand, interpret, and analyze what is heard, read, or viewed on a variety of topics.	**Presentational Communication:** Learners present information, concepts, and ideas to inform, explain, persuade, and narrate on a variety of topics using appropriate media and adapting to various audiences of listeners, readers, or viewers.
CULTURES Interact with cultural competence and understanding	**Relating Cultural Practices to Perspectives:** Learners use the language to investigate, explain, and reflect on the relationship between the practices and perspectives of the cultures studied.	**Relating Cultural Products to Perspectives:** Learners use the language to investigate, explain, and reflect on the relationship between the products and perspectives of the cultures studied.	
CONNECTIONS Connect with other disciplines and acquire information and diverse perspectives in order to use the language to function in academic and career-related situations	**Making Connections:** Learners build, reinforce, and expand their knowledge of other disciplines while using the language to develop critical thinking and to solve problems creatively.	**Acquiring Information and Diverse Perspectives:** Learners access and evaluate information and diverse perspectives that are available through the language and its cultures.	
COMPARISONS Develop insight into the nature of language and culture in order to interact with cultural competence	**Language Comparisons:** Learners use the language to investigate, explain, and reflect on the nature of language through comparisons of the language studied and their own.	**Cultural Comparisons:** Learners use the language to investigate, explain, and reflect on the concept of culture through comparisons of the cultures studied and their own.	
COMMUNITIES Communicate and interact with cultural competence in order to participate in multilingual communities at home and around the world	**School and Global Communities:** Learners use the language both within and beyond the classroom to interact and collaborate in their community and the globalized world.	**Lifelong Learning:** Learners set goals and reflect on their progress in using languages for enjoyment, enrichment, and advancement.	

FIGURE 2.7

Source: "World Readiness Standards for Learning Languages," American Council on the Teaching of Foreign Languages, 2013. https://www.actfl.org/sites/default/files/publications/standards/World-ReadinessStandardsforLearningLanguages.pdf. Accessed May 7, 2018.

different languages, Magnan and others (2012) found that students' learning goals aligned with these standards and that students believed that they could achieve those goals. In this section, we provide lived examples for each domain to clearly articulate how different types of relationships with local L2 speakers complement and enhance varied desired learning outcomes. Although some of the examples provided fit into multiple domains, we focus on the primary one that best captures what the student learned.

Communication

There are many ways that interactions between students and community can be developed to build on the *communication* goal—to "communicate effectively in more than one language in order to function in a variety of situations and for multiple purposes" (ACTFL 1996). Educators should design activities that engage the three modes of communication: interpersonal, interpretive, and presentational. The *interpersonal mode* is two-way communication that requires students to negotiate and build meaning through conversations (both speaking and listening) or written correspondence (both writing and reading) with community members in the L2. Verbal communication can take place in structured settings like tutoring or interviewing, or through a more informal social gathering at a local park or a potluck organized in a community center. The written interpersonal mode might include e-mails or text messages between partners in the L2, a class blog, or a letter to the editor. The *interpretive mode* refers to one-way communication that requires students to interpret written or spoken communication through reading, listening, or viewing. CBLL students regularly read and listen to authentic texts, interviews, and films in class; in the community, they may also participate in similar activities with their partners, such as reading a local newspaper or a school parent–teacher association flyer together or listening to an information session on how to obtain a community identification card. Students must be able to read between the lines and interpret meaning from multiple perspectives, rather than simply comprehend the information. In the *presentational* mode, students present information in oral or written form, with little opportunity to actively negotiate information. Students volunteering in a health care setting might present information on the health care system in the L2 to the community, while others working with local families could write a list of best practices for parent–teacher conferences, highlighting cultural practices that may not be readily obvious to new arrivals. Some activities or projects, such as portfolios or Web projects, will cover two, or even three, modes. These final projects are discussed in more detail in chapter 3.

Reflections for Instructors

1. *Community health assessment.* Identify how interpersonal, interpretive, and presentational modes of communication could be explored through a partnership with the local public health department. Students disseminate the results of a health assessment to a group of Spanish speakers and must prepare and implement various information sessions (table 2.3).

TABLE 2.3

	Which communication modes do students employ in each activity?		
	Interpersonal	**Interpretive**	**Presentational**
Learn about the design and implementation of the health survey			
Prepare PowerPoint presentation			
Prepare handout for community. Translate documents about health assessment			
Identify and invite organizations to host presentations and schedule visits			
Execute presentations			
Meet and converse with community members at events			
Gather and process feedback from the presentation			

2a. *Dual-language tutoring.* Imagine that your student is tutoring Mandarin Chinese at a dual-language elementary school. What types of interactions could you create in order for your student to develop each of the three communication modes? Write a brief description of an activity for each (table 2.4).

TABLE 2.4

Interpersonal	**Interpretive**	**Presentational**

2b. *Spending time with elderly Arabic speakers.* Now imagine that your students are dispersed throughout the community and are visiting the homes of elderly persons who have recently emigrated from Arabic-speaking countries. What types of interactions develop each of the three communication modes? Write a brief description of an activity for each (table 2.5).

TABLE 2.5

Interpersonal	**Interpretive**	**Presentational**

Cultures

The goal area of *cultures*, the ability to "interact with cultural competence and understanding" (ACTFL 1996), invites a more specific treatment of culture than previously identified in ICC. In the standards goal, students are challenged to understand *practices* (patterns of social interactions, e.g., table manners, holiday traditions, and nonverbal communication), *products* (music, literature, political institutions, etc.), and *perspectives* (meanings, attitudes, values, beliefs, etc.). One of the ongoing critiques of a traditional classroom is that it presents cultures in very limited and sometimes stereotyped ways. Galloway identifies this limited way of presenting culture in the classroom as the "4-F Approach," which includes fiestas, folk dances, festivals, and food (Hellebrant and Varona 1999, 2). For example, a textbook might have a dialogue box that describes one specific celebration or historical event with little background or connections to contextualize the practice. To emphasize that this common practice is misguided, many instructors use the image of an iceberg as a tool to recognize the "big C" (Kramsch 2013) cultural products on the surface of the iceberg—such as food, dress, and games—while outlining the "little c" cultural products that are invisible underneath the surface, such as tone of voice, notions of time, and the meaning of friendship. When students go to their tutee family's home, for example, they are sometimes presented with new foods to try. While they eat, they may begin to notice previously unobserved practices related to how food is offered, consumed, and valued. The standards goals outline the importance of understanding practices and products through distinct perspectives; ACTFL has recently expanded the can-do statements to explicitly address intercultural competence outcomes in this area. CBLL offers students ways to extend their cultural understanding by presenting chances to learn how practices and products are intertwined with perspectives. For example, an L2 student who experiences a Chinese New Year celebration with local Mandarin speakers has the unique opportunity to learn about practices and perspectives through personal anecdotes from community members. This contact with the L2 speakers provides increased connections among perspectives, practices, and products, thus offering additional levels of cultural understanding not possible in a classroom presentation or a textbook. We wish to highlight, however, that contact alone does not guarantee meaningful relationships or increased learning. As Allport (1954) has shown, there must be positive, sustained contact in order to reduce stereotypes, prejudice, and discrimination.

Reflections for Instructors

A Halloween Party with Refugee Language Partners. A group of students is paired with refugees from the Democratic Republic of the Congo. The students' objectives are to tutor English to the adults and to assist the children with their schoolwork. Use table 2.6 to brainstorm about how a Halloween party with the refugees might provide opportunities to examine products, practices, and perspectives. Pick one item from the list in the table and describe how to build an activity to support conversations about perspectives.

TABLE 2.6

	Describe how students can explain how one of these products and practices reflects cultural perspectives.
Products • Halloween costumes (skeletons, witches, etc.) • Candy • Jack-o-lantern **Practices** • Pumpkin carving • Trick-or-treating • Playing tricks	

Connections

The learning outcomes of making multidisciplinary *connections* are based on the acquisition of information with the goal of understanding diverse perspectives; connections are defined as how we "connect with other disciplines and acquire information and diverse perspectives in order to use the language to function in academic and career-related situations" (ACTFL 1996). In one example, students worked with a local journalist to develop a series of articles for a Spanish-language newspaper. The journalist coached the students on the selection of topics and reviewed various drafts to mentor them in the appropriate style of the pieces. He praised their high level of language proficiency and yet still had to invest significant time to make revisions related to tone and content appropriate for Latino/a readers. One student, Christina, who had previously only used Spanish for academic essays, commented that she was embarrassed that she had not understood the change in perspective needed for the assignment; she later reported that working with the journalist to reorient the content of the article for the target audience was a profound learning experience for her. Having the opportunity to write and publish a newspaper article shifted the student's understanding of how to use the L2, helping her adopt another perspective.

Reflections for Instructors

Crossing Disciplines. How might you work with colleagues in other disciplines on a CBLL activity? How could you pair your students with the situations given in table 2.7?

TABLE 2.7

An anthropologist studying housekeeping staff at your local institution	
A business faculty researching immigrant-owned entrepreneurial ventures	
A public health researcher interested in vaccination practices among new arrivals	
A public policy researcher conducting focus groups on school choice	
A sociologist interviewing victims of domestic violence	

Comparisons

Students master *comparisons* as they "develop insight into the nature of language and culture in order to interact with cultural competence" (ACTFL 1996). To observe similarities and differences in linguistic patterns and cultural practices, students need exposure to new communities. Through both structured and informal tasks, students investigate, explain, and reflect on their own language and culture in comparison with the target language. In one example, Isabel, an HLL from Mexico, recorded in her weekly blog her initial bewilderment at having encountered a "different Spanish." Her first interaction with a native speaker from Colombia highlighted the large variety of linguistic regionalisms, and as she encountered language variations, she began questioning her ability to understand the language she grew up hearing. Still, she was curious, and after this first encounter she was eager to return to the community center to become more adept at recognizing and interacting with different variants of Spanish. A second example highlights how CBLL can bring students' attention to cultural practices and beliefs. After a conversation with a Nicaraguan woman, one student, Katrina, commented on a profound moment of self-awareness when she learned that her conversation partner had a different opinion of birth control than she did. Katrina wrote, "I surprised myself and I lied to her. Normally I am a very honest woman. But a part of me didn't want to offend her. I said that I agreed with her and that my dad always told me that I shouldn't talk to boys until I was thirty years old. At least the second part of the sentence was true. She nodded her head as a sign that she approved" (blog translated from Spanish, 2015). In that moment, Katrina elected to hide her opinion, in part because the other woman cited her religious beliefs, but when the student reflected on her reaction, she concluded that openly discussing the differences in opinion would have been valuable. Two years after this event, Katrina referenced the importance of this reflection, citing that it changed her understanding of doctor–patient communication and convinced her of the importance of ICC in health care. Knowing that differences exist is distinct from engaging in conversation about these differences—and CBLL provides the direct interactions that create these types of opportunities. With language proficiency and with connections to communities, students form deeper relationships with community mentors and actively make comparisons between distinct life experiences and perspectives. Of course, sometimes these interactions are problematic, and we explore more closely the dissonance that often occurs in these "teachable moments" in chapter 5.

Communities

In the *communities* standard, students "communicate and interact with cultural competence in order to participate in multilingual communities at home and around the world" (ACTFL 1996). By its very definition, CBLL offers multiple opportunities for meeting this standard, placing students in direct contact with native and heritage speakers in their local communities. Magnan and others (2012) found that of the nearly 1,500 students interviewed in a study, 83 percent valued the communities standard the most. Interestingly, however, these students also believed that of the five Cs, they would be least likely to achieve the communities goal. Teachers also find the communities standard to be the most challenging of the standards to implement. In a large-scale ACTFL study of over 2,000 instructors in 2011, teachers attributed this difficulty to a lack of training, resources, and professional development. They also noted that target language communities are "nebulous" and that it is not always feasible to take students into a local community during the semester. The results of these surveys, as well as several others, underscore both the challenge and the promise of CBLL.

CBLL is well poised to enhance and magnify the classroom experience through contact with heritage speakers, immigrants, refugees, and visitors from other regions of the world. The ever-changing nature of authentic community partnerships provides fruitful and demanding opportunities for students to stretch, both linguistically and culturally. In one example, CBLL students became mentors for eighth graders at a local middle school and were challenged to adapt to a new environment that required specific cultural and linguistic knowledge. Usually, the students would all meet together for one hour each week, but when the middle school hosted a Day of the Dead event, the middle school students invited their CBLL partners to attend. The event took place in the evening and required the CBLL students to manage scheduling and transportation logistics. That night, they participated in a community event that was much more complex than their previous interactions with the mentees. As the middle school students introduced the CBLL students to their girlfriends, boyfriends, parents, and teachers in Spanish, the CBLL students had to respond in numerous spontaneous situations in the L2, adjusting their register and language to make small talk in culturally appropriate ways. This event provided a new dimension to the budding relationships among participants.

Reflections for Instructors

The Mariposa Stories Project. As you read the following case study, note the ways in which this project meets the ACTFL World Readiness Standards for Learning (table 2.8):

> A local teacher and the local public school's English as a second language coordinator noted a need for more bilingual materials to support literacy development for their district's Latino/a students. They enlisted the local college's Spanish professor to pair CBLL students with the fourth and fifth graders to read, share, and write stories. The college students collected the stories and then used them to develop a series of bilingual coloring books. The university students edited and illustrated the books, which were then printed and distributed at no cost to the schools. The college students reflected on this project in conversations in class and through written blogs.

TABLE 2.8

Communication	Cultures	Connections	Comparisons	Communities

A SIXTH C

This chapter names many student learning outcomes for CBLL, focusing particularly on how contact with local, native, and heritage language speakers meets linguistic and cultural learning outcomes. CBLL provides multiple opportunities for a variety of learning outcomes, and educators should consider how to identify appropriate SLOs that correspond to curricular, institutional, and community needs. When contemplating outcomes in CBLL, we recommend exploring further how CBLL connects with social justice themes and actions. Trujillo (2009, 379) extends the 5 Cs of the National Standards to include a sixth standard—*consciousness*—which he ties to Freire's critical pedagogy. This sixth standard is the ability to "recognize your role in systems of privilege and promote equity." Trujillo designates two substandards that spell out the connections between language and social justice: (1) "Students recognize the role of language and culture in systems of privilege and oppression," and (2) "students use language and culture to promote equity and social justice." In chapter 4, we explore how to recognize systems of privilege, as well as how to support students as they take in this new awareness.

There are more and more world language educators designing broader learning outcomes for language students that include social issues. As mentioned above, Caldwell (2007) and Zapata (2011) emphasize the role of language as a force for social change. Caldwell (2007, 468) comment on the outcomes of her students, stating, "I attribute the success of this project to this liberatory approach, which promoted self-confidence, motivation, critical thinking, civic engagement, cultural sensitivity, and improved proficiency in the target language." In a recent example, Glynn and Wassall (2014) model the design of social justice "unit plans" for world language educators in their publication *Words and Actions: Teaching Language Through the Lens of Social Justice*. They identify a five-step process to align world readiness standards with social justice objectives. Although they do not address CBLL directly, the examples of how to reconceptualize teaching Spanish, French, and German through the lens of social justice showcase the relationship between language and social change. The broader outcomes of such an approach echo Osborn (2006, 8), who challenges world language educators to embrace a larger set of goals for their students. These include questioning the way we approach language teaching. He writes, "Foreign language educators need to examine the frames of reference within which we have constructed our professional activities. Our endeavors are not apolitical, and our decision making should not stem from the marketplace. I do not mean to suggest that all marketable skills should be banished from the curriculum. Rather, I want to argue that multiple goals are not only advisable, but necessary to maintain an educated democracy." Osborn reminds us that language teaching is not an apolitical act and that expanded learning outcomes related to social issues can be supported in the curriculum. Not only does world language use in the local community support ICC and L2 acquisition; it also empowers educators to develop learning outcomes that can contribute to significant social change.

Recalling Ben's story from the beginning of the chapter, he experiences how a person with limited English proficiency navigates the US legal system. Ben has clearly met his course's ICC and language learning outcomes. We also want to highlight how this CBLL experience provided opportunities for learning outcomes tied to social justice. The community-based learning environment raised Ben's awareness of the barriers to agency stemming from lack of language proficiency, and he was able to use his linguistic and cultural skills to dismantle some of these barriers. His experience reminds us that CBLL learning outcomes extend well beyond scripted parameters. Likewise, Sophie's struggle to understand Central African culture offered her an opportunity to learn more about this refugee family's customs. Instead of ignoring or dismissing what she did not understand, she chose to engage with the family by observing more closely and by asking questions when she was unable to follow conversations. As a result, she gained not only a greater awareness of the family's culture but also a new perspective on her own country's norms. After witnessing the family's difficulty in navigating the US health care system, she decided to volunteer for a refugee health initiative. As we see in these examples, CBLL can play a significant role in supporting our students' consciousness of the world around them, providing them with the tools to question structural inequities and work for change.

When educators intentionally design their CBLL courses to establish clear student learning outcomes, their students gain opportunities to deepen their knowledge in ways that a traditional classroom does not, including aspects of linguistic proficiency, intercultural communicative competence, and social consciousness. In the next chapter, we focus on how to create measurable assessments that can help determine how well students are able reach these desired outcomes.

CHAPTER 3

Assessment Design

By the end of this chapter, readers will be able to:

- Define the roles of various stakeholders in designing assessments
- Explain how critical reflection fits into the continuum of assessment
- Identify assessment strategies based on the three modes of communication
- Recognize appropriate designs of assessments for students, teachers, communities, and programs
- Identify the culture of assessment in higher education

ASSESSING CBLL

The task of assessment requires that we both ask and answer fundamental questions that are central to learning: What do we want our students to learn, and how will we know if they have learned it? In chapter 2, we explored the first question, examining student learning outcomes (SLOs) for CBLL and linking them to linguistic and intercultural competence outcomes. Here we examine the second question, which addresses the role of assessment in our classrooms, at our institutions, and in our communities. This chapter investigates assessment strategies by exploring the ambiguously defined role of critical reflection within the assessment continuum; the various types of assessments needed to support students, teachers, communities, and programs; and the culture of assessment and its impact on teachers. Norris (2006, 582) writes that "assessments are only good insofar as their use does good, in terms of supporting educational efforts and outcomes. . . . Where they do not obviously support the twin goals of helping educators deliver better programs and of helping students achieve valued learning outcomes, assessments should not be used. However, in order to realize these goals fully, assessments must be used." The challenge of designing appropriate assessments is thus squarely linked to the identification of quality assessment models. Throughout this chapter, we explore best practices for creating CBLL assessments that address how all stakeholders, including the community, can be incorporated more systematically into assessment design.

Classroom assessment presents particular challenges to instructors of CBLL, who often lack foundational training. Most teacher training programs focus on L2 student learning outcomes within the classroom but do not address how to adapt L2 learning outcomes to include community-engaged learning. Although some teachers may study or even lead global education programs in target language communities, fewer are familiar with international service learning programs. Language teacher training does not systematically include the study of service-learning frameworks, in which learning manifests at the intersection of community work, academic disciplinary content, and critical reflection. Because many teachers are unable to draw on either personal experience or formal training to design CBLL outcomes that address intercultural communicative competence (ICC) or social justice concerns, they find themselves unprepared for the challenges of working with the local communities. A steep learning curve can leave instructors reticent to engage in CBLL, or can result in feelings of insecurity when engaging in CBLL in the classroom or in the community. Without support, educators may be overwhelmed, or they may not feel comfortable exploring more robust frameworks for assessment. This chapter is in some ways a result of the challenges we have faced as educators, and it responds to these concerns by providing concrete suggestions and practical solutions.

Like many young fields, CBLL has focused its assessment efforts primarily on self-reporting measures. As DeZure (2002, 77) writes, these measures "are relatively easy to develop, administer, score and interpret; are relatively low risk to participants; and can often be disseminated to large groups with consistency, enabling comparisons among cohorts over time." In service learning, for instance, students generate, deepen, and document their learning through critical reflection (Ash and Clayton 2009; Bringle and Hatcher 1999). Students often keep reflective journals about their community partnerships and write papers about how their understanding of the community has evolved during the semester. Reflective writing alone, however, provides limited evidence of SLOs. Although it offers students a way to process their experience and is thus an integral component of service learning that sits squarely on the assessment continuum, it does not by itself provide useful data about student learning; to gather this information, instructors would need to offer structured feedback through rubrics or other mechanisms. Some of the confusion about assessment and reflection may stem from early models of service learning. Bringle and Hatcher's (1996) widely cited definition of service learning presents four stages: preparation, implementation, assessment/reflection, and celebration with demonstration. In some cases, educators will conflate assessment and reflection, assuming that these are one and the same or that reflection is the primary way to assess SLOs. We encourage educators to explore additional measures of critical thinking that assess cognitive skills and insights. A combination of well-designed rubrics, textual analysis, linguistic coding, videotaped interviews, surveys, and focus groups all measure student learning in important ways.

Like the development of student learning outcomes, then, educators should create an *assessment strategy* that addresses these options before the course and integrate them throughout the CBLL experience. The assessment continuum in CBLL thus includes both formative and summative assessment. *Summative assessments* are administered at the end of the CBLL experience or activity and are designed to evaluate SLOs. They include graded work based on standards such as performance tasks or can-do statements. Examples include final projects and integrated performance assessments. *Formative assessments* allow students and educators to learn from feedback given throughout the semester. These are quick checks of student learning that allow teachers to assess student work and offer feedback that can improve and even maximize student learning. They can also help faculty members adjust their lesson plans during the semester to reach unattained goals. As Ash and Clayton (2009, 38) write, "Instructors might review student products critically not only in order to provide helpful feedback to improve students' thinking but also to gauge the effectiveness of their own design (e.g., the clarity of the reflection prompts) and to provide themselves with feedback to improve it." Examples include think-pair-share activities, graphic organizers, and short (reflective) writing tasks that can demonstrate learning.

Although assessment measures focus primarily on student feedback and evaluation, they also can and should include faculty and community feedback. Just as community partners should be consulted in the design of CBLL partnerships, they should also participate in the design of assessments, especially summative projects that may have an impact on the organization. These include assessments of partnerships and programs, as well as course-level evaluations. Unfortunately, community partners have been conspicuously and consistently omitted from both large- and small-scale assessments (Stoecker and Tryon 2009). We therefore urge CBLL educators to include partners in the assessment process, whether they help to create assessments, assess student work, or are the target of assessment themselves. If we wish to move from charity models of service to a standard that emphasizes critical engagement for social change, we must listen to and bring attention to the unheard voices in these organizations. In the next section, we explore these reasons more explicitly, including why we assess.

Reflections for Instructors

1. *Campus assessment.* What does your school, department, or program require for assessment? What kinds of resources related to assessment exist at your school or on your campus? Is there a dedicated specialist at the programmatic level, or a colleague in your department who can become a resource?

2. *Classroom assessment.* What types of assessment do you offer in the classroom? Outside the classroom? How do you envision the relationship between these assessments? Which are summative, and which are formative? Which stakeholders participate in the design of the assessments, and who sees the results? What kinds of assessment models might be used to improve the quality of the CBLL experience for students, teachers, and community members? What are some barriers to implementing new assessments?

WHY WE ASSESS

There are a number of ways to capture student learning in CBLL, and the reasons for doing so are multiple. Although some of this logic will depend on individual goals and objectives, there are basic matters that all instructors need to confirm on a regular basis in order to ensure that learning can take place. At a foundational level, we want to ensure that CBLL partnerships are "going well," and that all parties are *meeting obligations* and *respecting program guidelines.* It is important to check in, both informally and formally, with community partners to assure that students are following standards of practice. Regular communication during the semester about whether students are attending their meetings, being punctual, and the like yields different information than the summative assessment that will gauge overall growth. Likewise, we must ask students during the semester whether community partners are committing the time to train and supervise them adequately. These simple questions can unearth larger issues of whether the partners and students are working together toward a common goal or whether they have diverged from their initial goals. Similarly, we want to monitor how the partnership promotes generative reciprocity, or whether the work has become more one-sided. Even the best laid plans can go awry during the semester, and so we suggest establishing regular check-ins—through e-mail, telephone calls, or in person—to make sure that all participants are adhering to their partnership's basic standards of practice or rules. We discuss additional strategies for evaluating partnerships in chapter 6. Administering a self-report survey at the end of the semester to the community organization and students provides additional information on the partnerships.

We also want to assure that students are *engaging deliberately* in their CBLL work. We hope that students look forward to their engagement, but sometimes they do not, and students may formulate excuses to cancel meetings at the last minute or share in their journal that they dread their weekly visits. Helping students to name their feelings can expose the underlying reasons that they may be avoiding their work, whether this avoidance is physical or emotional. If students cannot see a positive change in their partners, for instance, they may develop a critical sensibility that disengages them from their partner. A sense of disillusionment can creep in, as students sense that they are not learning what they had expected, do not see value in their contribution, or are not making a "big enough" difference. These issues are explored further in chapters 4 and 5. It is helpful to remember that the pendulum of student engagement can swing widely and that community partnerships are often defined by peaks and valleys. Regular and consistent formative assessments encourage students to make important connections between feelings and actions, create opportunities for realignment of relationships, and help instructors better understand the landscape of their students' work.

Most of all, we assess student learning to demonstrate that students are *meeting the determined SLOs* of the course, outcomes that span student development (e.g., leadership skills), linguistic growth (e.g., lexical gains), and cognitive gains (e.g., content knowledge), among others. The evidence we "capture" aligns with our predetermined SLOs and offers proof that students are meeting course goals. To assess oral proficiency skills, for example, instructors may wish to administer presemester and postsemester testing using simulated or modified oral proficiency interviews or similar measurements. Other teachers may focus on performance descriptors and create linguistic tasks for students to perform. These same tasks, such as videotaped interactions, could be assessed for pragmatics. Some teachers might wish to assess lexical gains, a process that could be done through an analysis of writing samples collected over the course of the semester, using a word cloud or linguistic coding program. If desired, instructors can assess aspects of grammar, such as manipulation of verb tenses, through an analysis of student writing samples. Similar types of evaluations can be created to assess cognitive or developmental gains.

Finally, we also wish to address the idea of *transformative learning*, the subject of chapter 5. Mezirow (2000) explains that people reach perspective transformation when they experience significant change in the ways they understand their identity, culture, and behavior. Setting up perspective transformation as an expectation can be problematic, however, because students come into CBLL at many different stages of development. It is problematic if "success" is based on documenting transformation of student perspectives because not all students will grow from the same learning opportunities or they may be in a "down" part of the ICC growth cycle at the time of assessment. Students have differing knowledge of systems of discrimination and socioeconomic structures. CBLL gives them the opportunity to experience architectures of inequality up close, to critically analyze the systemic problems and the conditions they create, and to imagine dismantling structures of injustice. However, we cannot reliably assess transformation because of students' varied developmental pathways, distinct personal backgrounds, and the impossibility of standardizing transformative processes. Although benchmarks are valuable ways to gauge student learning, they cannot be applied to all situations. After considering the broad range of options, then, we suggest implementing an assessment strategy that incorporates different tools, utilizes varied forms, and honors different student perspectives throughout the semester.

THE CONTINUUM OF ASSESSMENT

If reflection is not necessarily assessment, what is reflection? Reflection is an essential component of the CBLL experience, offering a bridge between community work and academic content. According to John Dewey's (1910, 6) pioneering work in the early twentieth century, reflection is "an active, persistent, and careful consideration of any form of knowledge in light of the grounds that support it, and the further conclusions to which it tends." It moves beyond summarizing activities and asks students to process, assess, and understand their work. Although sometimes misunderstood as being touchy-feely (e.g., a student keeping a stream-of-conscious journal), reflection can be structured, guided, and analytical, helping students to deepen and document their learning. As Ash and Clayton (2009, 27) write, "When it is well-designed, reflection promotes significant learning, including problem-solving skills, higher order reasoning, integrative thinking, goal clarification, openness to new ideas, ability to adopt new perspectives, and systemic thinking (Eyler and Giles 1999; Conrad and Hedin 1990)."

We see in Kolb's (1984) Experiential Learning Theory that reflection is foundational in the learning process. The full cycle "integrates the personal and the affective with the intellectual and academic" and depicts how "knowledge and understanding are under continuous construction as we increase our experience, knowledge base, and ideas" (Eyler and Giles 1999, 195). To support the desired learning outcomes, teachers should consider not only that Kolb places reflection immediately after the direct experience because this maximizes effectiveness but also that different learning styles seem to have an impact on the process (McEwen 1996). Of the four learning styles he enumerates (concrete

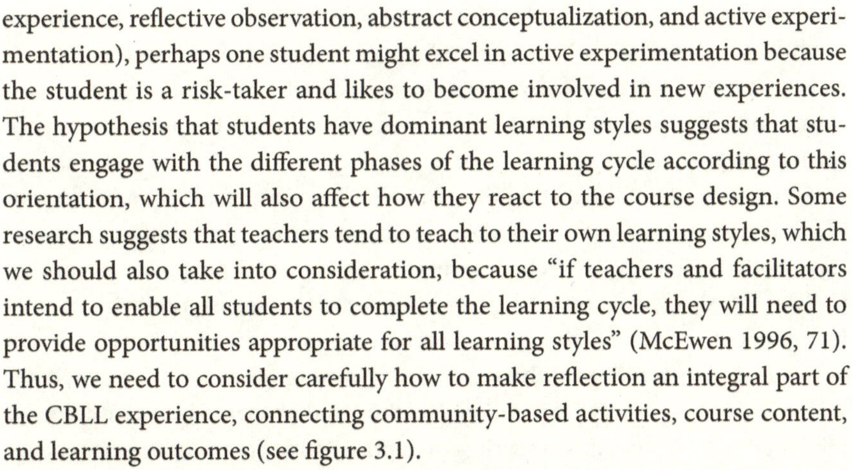

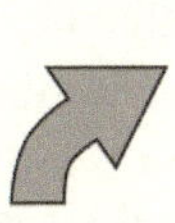

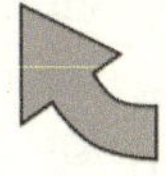

FIGURE 3.1
Source: Kolb (1984).

experience, reflective observation, abstract conceptualization, and active experimentation), perhaps one student might excel in active experimentation because the student is a risk-taker and likes to become involved in new experiences. The hypothesis that students have dominant learning styles suggests that students engage with the different phases of the learning cycle according to this orientation, which will also affect how they react to the course design. Some research suggests that teachers tend to teach to their own learning styles, which we should also take into consideration, because "if teachers and facilitators intend to enable all students to complete the learning cycle, they will need to provide opportunities appropriate for all learning styles" (McEwen 1996, 71). Thus, we need to consider carefully how to make reflection an integral part of the CBLL experience, connecting community-based activities, course content, and learning outcomes (see figure 3.1).

According to Mezirow (1990), critical reflection is an essential step toward transformative learning. It provides a vehicle by which we can engage students in conversation about their work in the field and monitor the types of conclusions that they draw from those experiences. In one example we witnessed, Tomás, an Arabic language student working with a refugee family, was upset by the low-paying jobs that the agency continued to offer the family members. Tomás wrongfully concluded that the job placement agency was not doing enough to help the family and joined the family in bad-mouthing the agency.

He did not grasp the complexity of the situation or understand that limited English proficiency narrowed the kinds of jobs available to family members. Reflection activities helped Tomás think more critically about the structures that create these difficult situations. This, in turn, led to a transformative moment, in which Tomás understood the importance of his role as an English tutor in a new light. He moved beyond disillusionment and into action; we discuss how to support this kind of shift in more detail in chapter 5.

When we present academic content without reflection, critical thought is not stimulated, and entrenched ideas go unquestioned. Without critical reflection, assumptions go unchallenged, knowledge acquisition becomes the sole goal, and students are not prepared to transfer their experiences into habits of mind that include thinking flexibly, managing impulsivity, remaining open to continuous learning, and applying past learning to future situations (Costa and Kallick 2009). Jacoby (2015, 44) states that critical reflection should "lead students to recognize the need and potential for social change, together with their own capacity to effect it." If we do not support students as they process these experiences, service work and interactions in the community can produce problematic results that reinforce existing stereotypes or simplify complex information. For example, a student could be very dedicated to tutoring at underprivileged schools but never "recognize the need to address the root causes of their underachievement or feel empowered to do so." Quite simply, community or experiential work without reflection does not support or enhance the learning process.

Still, it is important to distinguish reflection and assessment, for all reflection is not assessment. In fact, one of the principal criticisms of community engagement is that reflection is rarely optimized for assessment purposes. According to Eyler (2000, 11), self-reporting can confuse student satisfaction with student learning. In her research, she found that more rigorous reflection activities, such as critical reflection, lead to better student learning outcomes. She concludes with a call to create ways for students to show rather than tell us that they are meeting SLOs. A student who writes in depth about a community partnership, for instance, is doing important thought-work that helps give academic and community experiences broader meaning. The teacher may not assess the reflection in a formal way and may not even read it. The reflection becomes part of the student's learning process, but it is not a part of the formal assessment continuum that the instructor must use to gauge whether students are meeting learning outcomes. Likewise, an educator may lead students in a classroom reflection activity in which the class analyzes case studies of crisis moments in community partnership: a child discloses abuse, a student has trouble refusing a partner's request, and a community partner reports being unhappy about a student's work. The primary goal of this activity is to unpack moral and ethical issues so that students come to name and recognize their own values. This formative group activity is rigorous and leads students to think critically about their work and themselves. It also helps the teacher identify concepts or situations that confuse or trouble students. By itself, however, this activity does not offer an assessment of student learning. To assess SLOs in this context, a teacher would need to transform the activity further and have students create a product or perform a task that demonstrates what they have learned, which would then be measured with a rubric. The information collected from student reflections, in both written and oral form, generally provides an excellent source of raw data that can be assessed in a more rigorous and structured way if desired. To summarize: Reflection in itself is not assessment but critical reflection, which, when intentionally designed and assessed, can be a powerful way to guide students to meet learning outcomes. In this chapter, we focus on critical reflection as an intentionally designed product. In chapters 4 and 5, we offer critical reflection activities targeted to specific challenges common to CBLL.

In order to integrate critical reflection into student learning outcomes with purpose, teachers should determine appropriate reflection strategies and mechanisms (Ash and Clayton 2009). To develop a solid *reflection strategy*, we begin by considering the following questions:

1. *When* and how often do we reflect? At what point during the course or project do we reflect? Before, during, and/or after the experience? How can reflection be scaffolded to help build on itself?
2. *Where* do we reflect? Will we stage activities in the classroom, in the community, or in a virtual space? Will we prompt students to reflect in a private or public space?
3. *Who* participates in reflection and who facilitates it? Which groups participate in reflection activities: students, instructors, and/or community partners? Can and should the community partner participate? Should the instructor or someone else (such as a teaching assistant or community member) facilitate reflection with students?
4. *How* will feedback be provided and by whom? Will feedback be written or oral, public or private, in person or virtual? Will it be created by instructors, peers, and/or community partners? Will it evaluated or graded, and how?

A *reflection mechanism* places reflection in a broader context of SLOs. Here, we ask the following questions:

1. To which specific *learning outcomes* do we tie reflection? We design reflection activities to guide students to deepen their learning and eventually reach outcomes. Which reflection activities match the desired SLOs?
2. What *language* will be used? L1 or L2? The literature on using L1 in CBLL is neither conclusive, nor is it vast. Will reflection be done in the L1 or L2? Will feedback be given in the L1 or L2? How does the choice of language affect how students receive the feedback? How will the language used by a student affect his or her ability to communicate thoughts and feelings, or influence how final products are created? Will the chosen language have an impact on the community's participation?
3. What *medium(s)* will be used to guide the reflection activity? There are myriad ways to elicit reflection, including written blogs, photography, oral recordings, drawings, discussions, videos, cognitive maps, and collaborative role-plays.
4. What *products* will be created that demonstrate that outcomes are being met? As Ash and Clayton (2009) note, the product used to demonstrate an SLO may be the same as the medium used to generate it. Products include oral presentations, essays, task-based activities, performances, museum exhibits, and the like. Which will be most effective in achieving SLOs and in addressing multiple modes of communication?
5. What *tools* and *criteria* will be used to assess the learning outcomes? Teachers will need to develop rubrics for student-created products, peer and self-evaluation criteria for role-plays, or a coding strategy for reviewing blog entries. Categories should address form and content, and should be tightly aligned with SLOs.

Together, reflection strategies and mechanisms help us transform reflection into a critical and intellectual process that facilitates, monitors, and demonstrates student learning. As Lear and Abbott (2009, 321) explain, "Guided student reflection enhances student learning and gives the instructor an opportunity to gauge misaligned expectations, language proficiency and cultural misinterpretations." They conclude that though this practice can be time-consuming, its benefits are ultimately rewarding for all participants.

THE DEAL MODEL

To move students into the kind of critical thinking that can develop habits of mind, we must guide them to deeper critical reflection. Rigorous reflection leads to better student outcomes across multiple areas, including critical thinking, complex problem solving, application of subject matter knowledge, and openness to new ideas (Eyler and Giles 1999). Ash and Clayton's (2009, 39–40) DEAL model, based on a multiyear research project involving members of various disciplines, offers a solid tool for promoting development of SLOs. As they explain, "An integrated approach to assessment and reflection includes using the same set of objectives and standards and tools to generate learning (through reflection prompts), to deepen learning (through formative assessment or feedback), and to document learning (through summative assessment or grading and reporting outcomes)." The model can help teachers and students align reflection with SLOs.

The DEAL model leads students through three steps: *D*escribe, *E*xamine, and *A*rticulate *L*earning. In the first step, students objectively *describe* and offer details from an experience or community encounter. When and where did this event take place? What was communicated? Who was there (and who was not)? What did I (the student) do, and what did others do? Students then *examine* the interaction through the lens of SLOs that reflect academic enhancement, personal growth, and civic engagement. What disciplinary, professional, or intellectual skills were applied in this experience, and how did they shape the understanding of it? What materials are relevant to this experience, and how were they utilized (or not) in the experience? In the final step, students *articulate learning*, writing clear statements that respond to the following four prompts: (1) What did I learn? (2) How did I learn it? (3) Why does it matter? and (4) What will I do in light of it? The model guides the students to produce four directed statements of articulated learning.

The DEAL model can also be used for more advanced critical thinking that moves students through the seven steps in the taxonomy developed by Bloom and others (1956, 45). This helps them connect with and begin to take ownership of their learning *while* they are learning, rather than after (Clayton, Ash, and Jameson 2009). In this way, articulated learning is not unlike ACTFL's performance indicators, or "can-do" statements, whereby students chart their own learning. Although the can-do statements offer a checklist (e.g., "I can write some simple paragraphs about events and experiences in various time frames") rather than a generative format for students to self-assess, the goals are similar. We know that when students are engaged in the learning process, they become more intrinsically motivated, and when they set goals, they are also more likely to achieve greater levels of proficiency (figure 3.2).

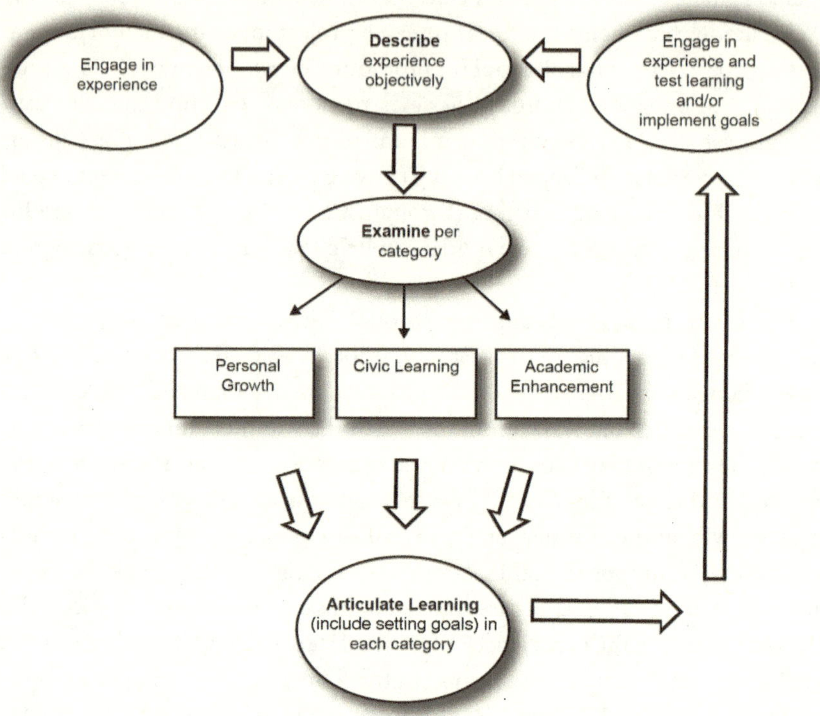

FIGURE 3.2
Source: Ash and Clayton (2009).

The DEAL model has accompanying rubrics that help teachers evaluate student reflection, and thus monitor the achievement of SLOs. One rubric that focuses on critical thinking assigns a score of 1 through 4 in five categories: accuracy, clarity, depth, breadth, and fairness (Paul and Elder 2001; Ash and Clayton 2009). A score of 4 in the category of "depth," for instance, reads, "Thoroughly addresses salient questions that arise from statements being made; avoids oversimplifying when making connections; considers the full complexity of the issue" (Ash and Clayton 2009, 40). Teachers can use this rubric to grade reflections and offer students feedback about their critical thinking. Other versions of the DEAL model's critical thinking rubric include additional categories, such as logic, relevance, precision, significance, and integration (Paul and Elder 2001). Ash and Clayton (2009) have also developed "depth of learning" rubrics based on Bloom's taxonomy. These rubrics are scored on a scale of 1 to 6 and assess learning in a number of categories that include academic enhancement and personal growth.

USING THE DEAL MODEL

Let us look now at an example of how a student might critically reflect about a CBLL experience using the DEAL model. In one CBLL course, instructors and students organized a holiday party to celebrate the relationships they formed over the course of the fall semester. Students invited the immigrant families that they visited weekly to the party. They made colorful flyers with pictures that depicted a group of ethnically diverse children making cookies and happy families holding ornaments. On the back of the flyer were directions to the venue, a building on campus that was adjacent to a city bus stop. A student hand-delivered the invitations on the Thursday before the Sunday event, scheduled from 2 pm to 4 pm. Before the event, students used funds from a small grant to buy arts-and-crafts materials, cookies, and decorations; they also rented an African drum from the local music studio.

By 2 pm on the day of the event, the room was filled with students; only one could not attend, and she had already cleared this with the instructor. By 3 pm, however, no families had arrived. Students called the families and left reminder voice messages, but because no one had showed up, they began to pull out laptops to study for their exams. The instructor could feel the tension rising in the room: Where was everyone? At 3:30 pm, a father from one of the families knocked on the door. The student greeted him and walked him through the various activities, many of them geared to children. At the designated 4 pm ending time, as the students packed up to leave, a mother and her four children burst through the door, apologizing that they were not sure where to park and that they could not find the building. The remaining students showed the children how to decorate the cookies like snowmen, and the father who had arrived earlier began to play on the drum, showing one of the students how to keep a slow beat. At 5 pm, one hour after the official close of the event, the instructor thanked everyone for coming, and the event ended.

After this experience, students were prompted to process the event using the DEAL model in a class discussion. First, they worked as a whole class to *describe* the event, summarizing what happened during planning and execution. As students described the characteristics of the event, the teacher took notes on the board. Then, she broke students into groups to *examine* aspects of the experience, calling on previous readings and discussions about power and privilege. This phase of the process allowed students to express their confusion, and even their hurt that their families did not attend the event. In this collective and reflective space, they explored many reasons that might explain this lack of participation. Some students noted that the choice of venue placed power squarely with the students, who could easily find the building. Others realized that some families might have felt pressured to say "yes" to an invitation, but realistically, they had many other important things to do on Sunday (e.g., cook, clean, shop). When they considered the extent to which the event was successful, some concluded that though the experience offered potential for community building, it did not feel sufficiently structured to be useful for their family partners, which may have contributed to their absence. Others were more positive, noting that despite the low attendance, those who participated enjoyed sharing an experience that did not reinforce power structures. They pointed out that because both the students and the families were positioned to learn or practice a new skill (drumming, cookie decorating) and because there was little need for language, power dynamics were diminished; unlike the weekly visits where students were teaching English, these exchanges felt more balanced, and more joyful. Finally, at the end of the class reflection, students were prompted to work individually to *articulate learning* from the event in writing (in the L2) and to provide suggestions for future activities. One student wrote, "I learned that I still can't always anticipate all of the conflicts that can come up when we plan activities. I realized that I *hope* things will work out, but that I don't always go through all of the steps to assure that they will. In light of this experience, I will be more assertive to make sure my partners can attend" (Nelia, in-class writing, translated from French, fall 2016).

The DEAL model may thus be used as a written reflection, as a way to frame class discussion, or as a hybrid of these activities. The first two directives (describe; examine) help guide the class to critical reflection, which can manifest through articulated learning. Depending on how the teacher structures the application of the model, the educator can participate directly in the conversation, facilitate the in-class conversation among students without offering personal observations, or even apply a rubric to offer written feedback. The structured, yet simple, design of the DEAL model can be productively implemented in many different forms for CBLL programs.

ADDITIONAL MODELS FOR CRITICAL REFLECTION

In addition to the DEAL model, a number of other tools can help students critically reflect upon pivotal CBLL experiences. The ABC Model of Reflection (Welch 1999) is one approach to writing that can be used to critically process challenging moments. In this model, students are first asked to identify a moment of dissonance from a community encounter. They then describe the moment through these three lenses:

- Affect: exploration of feelings and emotions
- Behavior: examination of past actions and projection of future behaviors
- Cognition: connection to course content

By exploring their dissonance in these three ways, students often come away with a broader and deeper understanding of the issue from multiple perspectives.

Deardorff and Deardorff's (2000) OSEE tool ("OSEE" means Open System Engineering Environment) offers a slightly different way to reflect critically. It may be used for a lived experience or to help guide critical reflection about a text or film that students study. This tool is designed to help students self-assess their attitudes toward others and is very effective for developing intercultural communicative competence. The steps are as follows:

O: Observe what is happening
S: State objectively what is happening
E: Explore different explanations for what is happening
E: Evaluate which explanation is the most likely one

The OSEE tool can be used as a writing prompt but also to help guide a conversation with students about a challenging scenario.

Mezirow (1998) writes extensively about the importance of critical reflection in supporting students through transformative learning, arguing that it is essential to question our assumptions. This involves "a critique of a premise upon which the learner has defined a problem" (Mezirow 1998, 186). In the example given above that we analyzed using the DEAL model, one of the "problems" identified by students is that family members did not attend an event that students had planned. Mezirow suggests reframing this problem from two different angles, an *objective reframing* and a *subjective reframing*. An objective reframing of the event breaks it down into narrative ("My family did not attend this event") and action ("I followed up with them to discover why"). A subjective reframing filters these questions through critical self-reflection on assumptions, which involves looking at the event from four angles: narrative ("is this event really a worthwhile use of our time?"), systemic ("is it ethical to ask the family to attend something when they are already so busy?"), therapeutic ("do I really want to attend this event?"), and epistemic ("does this unsuccessful event reflect the nature of my family partnership, and will it have a negative effect?"). Objective reframing examines the assumption of the problem, and subjective reframing considers what caused the assumption to occur. By delving into experiences this way, students examine their worldview through the lens of their own particular belief system. This kind of critical reflection also helps students learn to perform their own diagnostic analyses of problems and assumptions in such CBLL engagement.

REFLECTION IN THE L2

The models we have presented, as well as their accompanying rubrics, were developed for native speakers of English who are reflecting in English. And yet, as language educators, we want to consider having students write in the target language. This practice allows educators access to a product through which they can assess language production in the L2. It also builds on research indicating that reflective writing in the L2 helps build proficiency (Lear and Abbott 2009, 314). Still, an instructor may have concerns about whether a student can articulate the nuances of complex feelings or situations in the L2, or whether L2 outcomes should be prioritized over cognitive or more holistic learning gains. By writing in the target language, for instance, will the student be able to express sophisticated ideas? Bettencourt (2015) explores this challenge in an action-learning study based on a CBLL course in Spanish. Encouraged directly by Ash and Clayton, she translated the DEAL model and its rubric into Spanish and required that her students complete all assignments in Spanish. Her students were at intermediate low to intermediate mid levels of proficiency, and because she was concerned about their ability to communicate effectively, she administered a midterm survey that asked her students which language they preferred to use for the reflections. Although the vast majority of students indicated that they were able to express themselves using the DEAL model in Spanish, the same percentage said it was challenging (91 percent), with a majority of students (66 percent) preferring English. In our experience as well, students can participate in critical reflection in the L2 and report language gains, but they are sometimes frustrated at their inability to accurately express nuanced feelings and observations in the L2. Because of these concerns, some instructors may decide to allow students to reflect in English, at least on occasion, and we have witnessed successful examples produced through the L1. The use of English could also provide a way of reaching a wider community, through a public presentation, a publication, or the invited participation of a community partner.

The literature on using L1 in CBLL environments is not conclusive, nor is it vast. Still, such a choice must be weighed heavily, given not only the possible L2 gains in our SLOs, but also given ACTFL's directive to teach 90 percent of language classes in the target language. When reflection does take place in the L2, teachers should distribute reflection activities across the three modes of communication—presentational, interpersonal, and interpretive—just as they would when planning a balanced lesson plan. Doing so assures a more even use of skills, giving students ample opportunity to develop self-expression through different modes of communication. Moreover, varied reflection models and their accompanying rubrics offer students important opportunities to determine in which domains they need practice in order to move to a higher range of proficiency.

ASSESSMENT DESIGN: INCORPORATING THE THREE MODES OF COMMUNICATION

As outlined in chapter 2, the ACTFL performance guidelines denote three modes of communication—interpersonal, presentational, and interpretive—that reflect the communication goal of world language study. Mode-based tasks are designed to assess different aspects of L2 student learning. Separately, they do not indicate performance or proficiency; but together, they create a holistic picture of language production. Because we seek to assess SLOs along an assessment continuum that incorporates different mediums, we must also actively assess linguistic performance in all three modes.

In this section we explore several assessments that can serve as evidence of SLOs for CBLL. The "assessment products" listed here reflect the variety of opportunities possible when building a continuum of assessment across the semester, one that includes formative, summative, and multimodal assessments. In a language class on refugee resettlement, for instance, students might keep a weekly reflective blog, write case notes to the community partner, research and write a formal analytic reflection, give oral presentations, debate case studies, attend community events and trainings, and present a roundtable discussion with their peers. Although some of these activities are unique to CBLL, most are common in a traditional language curriculum. Many of these products can be used as activities *or* assessments, and so, like reflection activities, there may be some overlap in how an instructor decides to implement these activities in class. We have organized types of activities by mode to highlight the uniqueness of language acquisition SLOs in CBLL, but we acknowledge that many of these assessments can be designed for multiple modes.

Reflections for Instructors

Before we introduce concrete assessment tools, take a moment to recall the SLOs generated in chapter 2 for a CBLL partnership.

1. *The three modes.* Table 3.1 can help strategize how to balance activities in order to distribute them to cover all modes. Identify the communication mode associated with each activity listed in the table by placing an X in the correct box(es).

TABLE 3.1

	Presentational communication	Interpersonal communication	Interpretive communication
Give an oral presentation			
Write reflective blog			
Analyze a text			
Complete a survey			
Read a case study and discuss response with class			
Create a portfolio			
Participate in a class reflection session			
Role-play or improvise a dialogue			
Create a drawing based on the main events in a story			
Enact a scene from a play			
Listen to a newscast and take notes on the topics heard			

2. *Aligning assessment.* Now return to the SLOs, and select three to focus on in table 3.2. What kinds of corresponding assessments might capture student learning? For each student learning outcome, name an assessment in each mode of communication (presentational, interpretive, and interpersonal) that will show mastery of the SLO.

TABLE 3.2

Student learning outcome	Acceptable evidence: Assessment
Exercise: *Students will demonstrate culturally appropriate interpersonal skills related to controversial topics*	Presentational mode: *In-class presentations* Interpretive mode: *Recorded interviews with community partners* Interpersonal mode: *in-class debate*
1.	Presentational mode: Interpretive mode: Interpersonal mode:
2.	Presentational mode: Interpretive mode: Interpersonal mode:
3.	Presentational mode: Interpretive mode: Interpersonal mode:

INTERPERSONAL COMMUNICATION

In the interpersonal mode, students engage in two-way written or oral communication. Oral communication is characterized by negotiation of meaning, with individuals engaging in spontaneous and unrehearsed communication. Written interpersonal communication is also unscripted and is not presented for multiple drafts. Although it is often characterized as informal communication, it can also include formal information exchanges, such as an e-mail to an agency. Language in this mode can be unpolished and will contain more grammatical errors than one would expect to see in the presentation mode. Rubrics should be adjusted accordingly.

Writing

Journals and blogs. We suggest that students keep a weekly journal or blog that documents community meetings. A blog should be at least 250 words in order to ensure a minimal level of engagement by the student. As formative assessments, regular posts help instructors capture the content of weekly meetings and allow educators to see if students are meeting the commitments of their partnerships. More important, however, they provide meaningful opportunities for students to reflect more deeply on their partnerships. Well-designed writing prompts and structured models, such as the DEAL or ABC models, guide students to explore challenging moments or delve into key issues they might otherwise ignore, dismiss, or avoid. In addition to capturing what is happening in the community partnership, where the faculty may or may not be present, reflective writing can provide a platform for measuring student engagement and growth, because it allows educators to track shifts in understanding, in changes, and in action. We want to again underscore that participation in reflection alone does not constitute formal assessment of SLOs and that instructors must develop an appropriate rubric aligned with the SLO in order to assess reflective writing.

Writing prompts. Although it is important for students to contribute freely to their blogs, instructors should also offer students writing prompts to guide their critical thinking. In addition to using the DEAL model, teachers can consider allowing students to use different forms and formats: dialogues, letters to a community partner, poems, songs, short stories, newspaper articles, opinion pieces or op-eds, cartoons, thank-you notes, interviews, and lists. In subsequent chapters, we provide more concrete models of assignments to move students toward transformative learning outcomes. Here are sample writing prompts that may elicit thoughtful responses:

- Describe an event using the prompts: What? So What? Now What?
- Write a letter to yourself in which you describe your goals for the semester.
- What is the difference between service and volunteering? Charity and social change?
- Describe a problem your community partnership (or your team) is experiencing.
- Describe a person you met in the community who is different from you.
- Describe a critical incident or an encounter. Write from a third-person perspective.
- What behaviors have assisted you in your interactions with the community?
- What behaviors have not been utilized, or have been roadblocks?
- What fears do you have that keep you from engaging fully in the community?
- Describe what you think will be the two most important takeaways from your experience (pre-experience) and/or two things that you are taking away from your experience (postexperience).
- Describe a high or low point in your community interactions.
- What are assets that the community brings to this partnership? Describe your own assets for working with the community.

Quotations. Meaningful or provocative quotations and citations often elicit thoughtful responses and can serve as excellent jump-starts for student writing. Instructors can give students a list of quotations before class, asking them to select one that best represents their CBLL experience. Writings could also form part of a personal or class blog, or be transformed into a spontaneous, one-minute paper that then forms the basis for an in-class discussion. When constructing lessons that use quotations, educators should be intentional about selecting prompts that represent diverse perspectives. For instance, take a moment to ensure that prompts include quotations from men and women, or from dominant and nondominant identity groups within a given culture or place—such as:

- "It is better to light one small candle than to curse the darkness." (Confucius)
- "Nothing will ever be attempted, if all possible objections must first be overcome." (Samuel Johnson)
- "We cannot understand ourselves without listening to others, especially to those we have oppressed or have the potential to oppress. Such critical engagement is the beginning of solidarity." (Kwok Pui-Lan)

- "Power is not an institution, and not a structure; neither is it a certain strength we are endowed with; it is the name that one attributes to a complex strategical situation in a particular society."(Michel Foucault)
- "Anyone who speaks for others should only do so out of a concrete analysis of the particular power relations and discursive effects involved." (Linda Alcoff)
- "Reading (or serving) without reflecting is like eating without digesting." (Edmund Burke)
- "When I settle into a place, listening and watching, I don't try to fool myself that the stories of individuals are themselves arguments. I just believe that better arguments, maybe even better policies, get formulated when we know more about ordinary lives." (Katherine Boo)
- "Unless you choose to do great things with it, it makes no difference how much you are rewarded, or how much power you have." (Oprah Winfrey)
- "A different world cannot be built by indifferent people." (Horace Mann)
- "No problem can be solved from the same level of consciousness that created it." (Albert Einstein)
- "One of the biggest misunderstandings you have about us is your belief that our feelings aren't as subtle and complex as yours." (Naoki Higashida)
- "To act is to be committed, and to be committed is to be in danger." (James Baldwin)
- "The difference between the helper and the helped is a line drawn in water." (Kristiina Kumpula)
- "The stranger is not *any-body* that we have failed to recognize, but *some-body* that we have already recognized *as* a stranger, as 'a body out of place.' Hence, the stranger is some-body we know as not knowing, rather than some-body we simply do not know." (Sara Ahmed)

Correspondence. Letter writing is an exercise in interpersonal communication that can take a variety of forms. Students might be asked to write to a relative who has a differing point of view on a particularly controversial topic or to write to a student at another university about the class. Sending a personal thank-you to a community partner, penning a formal letter to an elected official, or texting with partners are all examples of interpersonal writing tasks that demonstrate a student's ability to communicate effectively in the L2. Assessment can revolve around effective messaging, linguistic register, or cultural competence.

Social media. Social media provide equally valid ways to have students practice informal writing. Sometimes these tasks are part of the CBLL work (e.g., creating and maintaining a Facebook page or Instagram account for a community organization), though, in other instances, they may be born of a student's initiative (one student we know created a Twitter feed designed to raise awareness about issues related to immigration law). Students may also participate in online forums in the L2.

Speaking

Whole-class reflection sessions. Setting aside class time to reflect on the CBLL experience provides a supported structure for guiding students through reflection. In these discussions, class time is focused on reflection related to the CBLL experience. Teachers may choose to explore larger questions related to CBLL, taking a broader perspective that asks students to conceptualize what this experience means to them, or what is the place of CBLL at a university. They might also drill down to tackle current challenges students are confronting in their partnerships. Structured scenarios or mini–case studies can help the teacher understand where there might be learning gaps or simple redirects that she can provide in class. A teacher might cull these examples from student journals or blog posts (keeping them anonymous) or may simply use personal experience to relate common challenges. Students might use the DEAL model to engage in perspective taking, helping them develop a sense of distance from their own experience; alone or in pairs, they can talk through and analyze the experience. Small groups of students may work on scenarios that pose challenges: a family whose members continually ask for translation services, although the students are supposed to tutor conversational English; a school that is supposed to provide supportive tutoring services but is never set up when the session is supposed to begin; a situation in which the community and/or students do not seem engaged; a community member who keeps canceling appointments; and so on. In this time for conversation, students often engage in brainstorming solutions and are reassured when they confirm with their peers that sometimes there are no easy answers.

PRESENTATIONAL COMMUNICATION

In the presentation mode, students write or speak in a way that reflects formal preparation and incorporates feedback. These products can be published in a wider venue or presented before an audience. We find that when students know that the audience for their work extends beyond their teacher and their classmates, they invest more, and the content is usually more robust. The type of language and research needed for a formal presentation also pushes students to thoughtfully consider the accuracy and appropriateness of their work. This mode of communication meets SLOs related to personal efficacy, leadership, L2 acquisition, ICC, professional skill development, and critical thinking, among others.

Presentational Writing

In the one-way mode of communication termed presentational writing, students present a product that facilitates interpretation by the audience but does not offer a chance for negotiation. Presentational writing products are generally more polished; they may stem from drafts or incorporate teacher or peer feedback.

Analytic reflection papers. At the end of the CBLL experience, students reflect on their experience in a longer, summative form (three pages or more). Teachers may offer a prompt or series of questions that asks students to document their learning in the community using academic materials studied over the course of the semester. Students who study Foucault's (1978) notions of discourse and power might apply these theories to explore the power of the prison system in the United States, using their community partnerships as evidence. Classes that read Freire's (1970) work on critical pedagogy might apply this critique to a CBLL tutoring placement. A language seminar on global displacement could cite authors of numerous fictional stories to support the struggles they see in the community. These kinds of assessments help guide student reflection by requiring that students integrate academic materials into their community experience, and provide teachers products that document SLOs.

Newspaper articles. Students write and submit newspaper articles to a local or national journal. In one example, students connected with a local journalist, who helped them publish articles in a Spanish-language newspaper. In another example, students published articles in an English-language newspaper.

Directed writings. These assignments require students to base their responsive writing on a written prompt. For example, "Author X writes that there are five models of service learning: charity . . . , transformational. In which model does your current community work fit? Please elaborate with examples." These writings ask students both to apply and critically analyze course content.

Experiential research paper. This writing form uses Kolb's experiential model to zero in on one area of the CBLL experience and develop it. This formal paper requires students to identify a particular experience and analyze it within the broader research context, using about five articles (in L1 or L2) on the subject. Based on research and personal experience, students then write up recommendations for future actions that promote social change. Students can turn in their work or present their findings to the class.

Case studies. Students write case studies of challenging ethical or social dilemmas that they have encountered during the CBLL experience. Students describe the situation that was ethically challenging, including details about who was there, when the moment occurred, and how the dilemma unfolded. They then present it as a case study for the class, or discuss it in small groups. Instructors can assess this assignment for L2 or critical thinking outcomes.

Ethnographic study. Students may enjoy working to answer a specific question about cultural norms or societal roles and behaviors. Qualitative research can be completed through different data collection methods, including interviews, relationships, conversations, and participant observations. Be sure to work with the community to obtain permission for this type of interaction well in advance. Chapter 6 discusses informed consent in more depth.

Field notes. Some students respond well to a more objective approach to mapping the community. Field notes include two types of information: descriptive and reflective. Descriptive information comprises data such as date, time, location, behaviors, actions, and conversations. Reflective information includes descriptions of thoughts and questions as observations are noted.

Creative writing. Forms such as poetry and short stories can be written individually, as a class, or in community partnership. Students might write a short story to parse out an experience, or work together to compile a collection of reflective poetry. Self-publishing offers a more permanent medium for sharing these works with a wider audience.

Presentational Speaking

Like presentational writing, the presentational mode of speaking demonstrates a one-way mode of communication. Presentational speaking calls for increased grammatical accuracy, including use of the formal register. Educators need to adjust rubrics to account for these distinctions.

Oral presentations. Formal presentations can provide excellent documentation that students have met targeted SLOs. Individual students present 10 to 15 minutes to the class, with the aid of slides, images, or handouts. This assignment can be as structured as the teacher wishes. Rubrics can target research, critical thinking, and L2 production, among other SLOs.

Group presentation. Students work in groups of three or four to present a topic. Formal presentation skills are assessed. The audience may include classmates, the community, or both. Ideas for presentations include research-based work, or generative topics based on community work during the semester. In the latter example, students could develop presentations for the community based on a jointly identified need; we have seen excellent work in areas of health and education. One class presented a series of short workshops on health and safety protocol for underserved populations. Another put together a formal presentation on local charter and magnet schools that helped local parents better navigate the school district.

Roundtable discussion. Students work together on a topic, with each presenting one aspect of the topic for 5 minutes and then facilitating discussion with the class. Topics can be presented as a question or general topic. Examples might include: the ethics of service, education policy, English as a second language (ESL) resources in the community, or campus–community relationships.

Guided tour. Using an app or other virtual tool, students record a tour of the city, the campus, or local businesses. Content should match need, so students might consider everything from a guided tour for new arrivals to a literary tour of the city's writers. Recordings could also be organized to broadcast a regular podcast.

Theater production. Students act in a self-authored play that summarizes or reflects upon their work in the course. They might also incorporate Baol's Theatre of the Oppressed and use the production as a vehicle through which the community and students build a teaching tool.

INTERPRETIVE COMMUNICATION

In the interpersonal mode of communication, students demonstrate comprehension of written, oral, and/or visual communication. Unlike the interpersonal mode, they do not have the opportunity to negotiate meaning with the individual who created the message. Watching a film, reading a text, or listening to an interview are all examples of the interpretive mode.

Textual analyses. Students read a text and respond to a prompt. Qualitative analyses of written texts (articles, literature, testimony) can help gauge student growth over the semester. A rubric will help teachers assess critical thinking; repeating the exercise at the beginning and end of the semester will provide a way to analyze deepening of critical thinking skills over the semester. Frequency and type of terms used by students can be assessed as well, by coding or even counting word usage connected to certain topics.

Radio interviews or podcasts. The wide availability of podcasts in multiple world languages broadens our students' understanding by exposing them to distinct ways of seeing the world, of viewing content differently, and of comprehending distinct accents. Many sites have pedagogical features that offer teacher resources.

Personal stories. There are numerous websites with audio and video archives of personal stories from immigrants living in the United States. Students could be assigned to listen to several and then compare and contrast different themes that align with their own life experience, or with another assigned text or guest speaker's narrative. A discussion of personal representation and identity construction could be a productive way to delve into an analysis of the stories.

MULTIMODAL ASSESSMENTS

Integrated performance assessments take students through all three modes of communication. If students are to create a bilingual brochure for their city (presentational mode), they could interview community partners to complete a needs assessment (interpersonal mode). Students then use a rubric to assess the recorded conversations, listening to see if questions were posed or the correct information was elicited. From there, students research websites to locate information to put in their brochures (interpretive mode). The teacher can create a checklist for students to use as they complete their research online; this interpretive assessment asks students to mark off information as it is located, and it helps teachers track student work. When projects are approached in this way, we maximize opportunities for students to use the language. Interrelated tasks strengthen language acquisition and also reinforce CBLL goals. In the following paragraphs, we present a number of summative projects that are made up of multiple modes of communication.

Portfolios. Portfolios can offer a comprehensive overview of student work that supports integrative learning and self-understanding. As Randy Bass (2014) notes, "E-portfolios are at heart a set of *pedagogies and practices* that link learners to learning, curriculum to the co-curriculum, and courses and programs to institutional outcomes." Portfolios can be either paper or digital (e.g., platforms such as Pebble Pad or Weebly). Over the course of the semester, students compile materials relevant to their CBLL experience. Portfolios are not a mere collection of preassigned documents to showcase student work, however, but should be composed of artifacts that document and deepen high-impact learning. Materials might include an analytic paper, a recorded interview, copies of case notes submitted to an organization, photos, a link to a reflective blog, lesson plans for home visits, brochures, handbooks, timesheets documenting service hours, class presentations in the form of PowerPoint slides, handouts, or notes.

A successful portfolio is a vehicle that promotes critical reflection about the CBLL experience. In order to capture this, teachers must create reliable forms of assessment that avoid leading students into the very checkbox mentality we wish to avoid. Carefully constructed rubrics will help determine if an artifact or a group of artifacts meets a set of standards. Educators will also want to explore ways for all stakeholders to provide feedback, including community partners. It is important to make sure that the university can support the portfolio platform and that there is adequate training for teacher and students. Also important are issues of ownership: who owns the portfolio, and what kinds of copyright measures must be considered when sharing materials. If students are including interviews or photos with a community partner, they may need to have completed institutional review board training (IRB) or requested the requisite informed consent and release forms from their partners (see chapter 6). If there are sensitive materials, we recommend protecting portfolios with a passcode.

Capstone reflection. Ask students to save artifacts from their CBLL experience (notes, photos, flyers, journal entries, etc.) that reference a certain observation or feeling of the student at that particular moment in time. As a capstone project, have the students showcase the artifacts (through a digital presentation, poster, show-and-tell format, videorecording, etc.) to their classmates and their community partners. Work with your community partner to develop a rubric that will track the level of critical thought that students are able to incorporate into their presentation. Make sure that the students understand that they need to make connections between their artifacts and discussions from class (based on readings, films, etc.), and also include self-reflection about the experience.

Website production. Multimodal and multilingual websites are an excellent way to showcase SLOs that reflect multiple modes of communication. One such example is Languages in Durham (https://sites.duke.edu/languageindurham/), a website that captures the stories of some heritage and native speakers in Durham, North Carolina. The site is the product of multiple CBLL courses at Duke University in which students interviewed community members in their native languages about their experiences of immigration and resettlement. Students who work with immigrant communities might wish to capture individual stories about moving to the United States, and, with permission, they may publish them on a website, submit them to a local library audio archive, or present them at a live venue such as a conference or community event.

ESL training videos. The Duke HELLO website (www.dukehello.com) was created in response to the English language learning needs of recently arrived refugees to the United States. In consultation with community partners, faculty, and the resettlement center's ESL coordinator, students identified five areas of immediate need: medical appointments, parent–teacher conferences, job interviews, grocery shopping, and driver's education. They then scripted and recorded videos that modeled sample interactions; videos were then subtitled and dubbed in three languages.

Poster session. Poster sessions offer excellent opportunities to combine communication modes. Classes might work with a local organization to put on a community education event about health issues. Research for the poster requires students to consult a number of sources; these can include written texts or individual persons, depending on the subject matter. The writing portion of the work asks students to synthesize information and present it in a concise way that reaches a wide audience. At the poster session, students engage in presentational and interpersonal speaking as they interact with audience members and visitors.

Photography exhibit. Teachers who wish to offer students the opportunity to combine visual or numeric literacy with cognitive skills may be drawn to photography or videography. When photos or videos involve human subjects, they require informed consent and agreements to release images to the public; if this proves to be an obstacle, students might focus on landscapes, apartment complexes, or photos that omit faces, all of which are compelling. Exhibits can be displayed in a community center or at a local library, followed by a reception; they can then be archived in a community engagement office on campus, or even at a state library.

Museum exhibits. More and more museums offer educational institutions a way to display products of teaching and research. A short-term "pop-up" exhibit can allow students the opportunity to cull information for a targeted audience. In one example, students in a CBLL course with refugee partners documented the immigration path of Central Africans to the United States. The exhibit covered history, law, and policy and included personal interviews with the city's residents. A reception after the exhibit brought diverse groups of people together, offered a "meet and greet" opportunity, and provided a space for conversation about the project between participants and the wider public.

ASSESSMENT MEASURES AND FEEDBACK

Assessment design must include quality feedback measures for students. Feedback on formative assessments should be offered soon after the assessment, so both instructors and learners can quickly identify knowledge gaps. These assessments can range from informal checks of understanding, such as having students hold up cards that indicate whether they agree or disagree with a statement, to short quizzes. More lengthy interim assignments, such as written papers or tests, can help identify larger knowledge gaps and give students the opportunity to readjust their learning strategies. Instructors will give the most feedback on these assignments, annotating rubrics and writing or recording more lengthy comments. For summative assessments such as final projects or examinations, teachers generally share less feedback with students, because there is usually little chance to improve learning. In this case, feedback based on a rubric can be sufficient. Whether instructors use ready-made rubrics or create their own, they should share them with students when they introduce the assignment.

By developing a rubric, instructors will also help clarify the goals of the assessment or activity for the students. Good rubrics help students understand how well they have met these goals, and how they can improve their performance. When writing rubrics, instructors may wish to consult *The Keys to Assessing Language Performance: A Teacher's Manual for Measuring Student Progress* (Sandrock 2015, 37), which provides a complete road map for designing rubrics that assess language performance. Sandrock identifies six steps for designing rubrics:

1. Identify what makes a quality performance.
2. Evaluate the qualities against the characteristics of the targeted level of proficiency.
3. Describe the performance that meets your expectations with the specificity and clarity that will focus your instruction and student learning.
4. Describe the performance that exceeds your expectations and the performance that does not meet your expectations.
5. Pilot with students and revise based on students' work and feedback.
6. Determine how you will communicate the assessment results (including using the rubrics in grades and incorporating feedback into your instruction).

From here, instructors can further narrow down characteristics of successful language production according to the three modes of communication. Sandrock breaks down each mode into the following key elements, which provide relevant categories for all levels of language proficiency:

- *Interpretive:* Level of ability, ability to provide a summary, able to use context clues to help comprehension.
- *Interpersonal:* Negotiation of meaning, use of strategies when there is a lack of comprehension, means of asking for clarification, ability to sustain a conversation.
- *Presentational:* Accuracy of vocabulary and structure, organization and flow, impact on the audience, use of clear and supportive examples. (Sandrock 2015, 42)

These elements provide a solid foundation for developing personalized rubrics. The process of designing a rubric can be very beneficial for the instructor because it requires that we closely consider the targeted outcomes, evidence of performance, and feedback mechanism. If educators do not wish to design their own rubrics from scratch, however, there are numerous ready-made templates online that can be adapted or directly implemented. The next paragraphs offer suggestions for implementing rubrics and offering feedback.

For assessing student blogs or critical reflections, the critical thinking rubric from the DEAL model works well. Instructors may also wish to develop a simpler version that includes relevant categories, such as language/conventions, critical thinking, reference to course materials, or organization/development of ideas. We must also consider what kinds of feedback to offer students on journals and blogs. Some teachers may simply circle a number on a rubric, but others will communicate brief written or recorded comments in the L2. Feedback may be shared after every assignment, but some instructors may find it more realistic to check in after students have written several blog posts. Although holistic comments that focus on content and organization are generally most meaningful for students, it is important to be specific; instructors should avoid generic statements like "Great reflection!" or "Interesting!" because comments or questions that refer directly to the content will stimulate more thought. Another strategy is to have students share their blogs. If this is agreed upon in advance, students generally enjoy reading each other's work, from both a linguistic and a content perspective. Seeing how another student approaches a certain topic or knowing that another student is grappling with a similar issue can cultivate greater awareness and compassion.

For spoken presentational communication, such as in-class presentations, it can be effective to engage the listening audience in measures of feedback. Teachers can distribute a rubric that includes one or two open-ended questions that ask the audience to note which aspects of the presentations were particularly effective and which could be improved. The instructor then culls these responses and shares the group's feedback with the presenter in writing, sharing quotations from the audience. The instructor might also include the average score from the audience as a component of the overall grade. This approach engages listeners as they interpret the presentation and helps keep the presenter(s) mindful of the larger audience. The comments are generally well received and can help students view their presentations in new ways.

Instructors will also need to set clear expectations for student language production on assessment products. Because blogs and journals are less formal types of communication, it is common not to require students to "pay attention to" grammar, spelling, and punctuation. This practice can encourage students to take linguistic risks. Still, some instructors may want to encourage students to use the space to practice language structures or reinforce vocabulary. Those teachers should create a rubric category that assesses student L2 production. If linguistic or lexical corrections are included, we suggest focusing on a narrow range of errors (e.g., agreement errors, the past tense, or lexical difficulties), being as specific as possible, and noting these at the end of the paper in a section separate from comments on the content. Research shows that line-editing of student work does not produce better results and can overwhelm students; we therefore suggest a more targeted approach.

Reflections for Instructors

Feedback on Reflections. Consider how you will provide feedback on your students' critical reflections. Jacoby (2015) provides general criteria for assessing service-learning reflection (based on Bradley 1995) that could be used to create useful parameters for student feedback. Of the following questions, which do you find useful for providing feedback to your CBLL students?

1. Does this student explore the situation from an unexamined personal point of view? Interpret evidence that differentiates between personal beliefs and the perspectives of others? Does the student include and value different perspectives? Show multiple factors in decision making and actions?
2. Does the student provide a list of observations? Insight into the reasons behind the observations? Situation-specific or broader context observations?
3. Does the student demonstrate clarity in reasoning? Draw reasonable or sound conclusions?
4. Does the student explain deep connections to the issues encountered in the community or the discipline? Articulate the issues observed in the community and the student's responsibility as part of it?

Are there other questions that you consider fundamental in pushing students to delve more deeply into their reflection about CBLL?

QUANTITATIVE METHODS OF ASSESSMENT

The American Association of Colleges and Universities developed a series of sixteen rubrics designed to assess key learning outcomes for student success in the workplace, in citizenship, and in life. These VALUE (*V*alid *A*ssessment of *L*earning in *U*ndergraduate *E*ducation) rubrics provide tools to assess authentic student work in a variety of situations that address advanced, integrative learning. For the purposes of CBLL, the "Intercultural Knowledge and Competence" rubric is especially useful (see appendix C). This rubric assesses student learning in three central categories: knowledge (cultural self-awareness and knowledge of cultural worldview frameworks), skills (empathy and verbal and nonverbal communication), and attitudes (curiosity and openness). Scores (1–4) are assigned based on whether students meet benchmark skills (1), milestones (2 or 3), or the capstone (4). The VALUE rubric can be used in a variety of ways. From performance-based tasks, such as role-plays or roundtable discussions, to written or oral reflective assignments, VALUE rubrics can support teachers as they evaluate a student's ability to express sophisticated understanding and insights about complex cultural situations.

Likert scales and questionnaires are common measures used to assess projects or courses. They provide a very quick method to gather feedback from students engaged in a group project or from the audience after a student presentation. George and Shams (2007) caution that self-reporting measures such as Likert scales and questionnaires can provide biased data, as students wish to provide desirable responses. For this reason, we suggest varying assessment types to ensure more reliable measures of feedback.

We have thus far explored various approaches to assessing student learning outcomes. In the final section of this chapter, we turn to assessments for teachers and community members. In chapter 6 we explore strategies for building authentic relationships.

Reflections for Instructors

Design a Rubric. Choose one of the multimodal activities presented in this chapter, such as the portfolio, and design a rubric that assesses the learning outcomes that align with the activity. To start, it may be useful to adapt the following dimensions and descriptors from VALUE rubric capstone levels (https://www.aacu.org/value/rubrics/global):

- *Critical thinking:* Explanation of issues: Issue/problem to be considered critically is stated clearly and described comprehensively, delivering all relevant information necessary for full understanding.
- *Evidence:* Information is taken from source(s) with enough interpretation/evaluation to develop a comprehensive analysis or synthesis. Viewpoints of experts are questioned thoroughly.
- *Written communication:* Control of syntax and mechanics: Uses graceful language that skillfully communicates meaning to readers with clarity and fluency, and is virtually error free.
- *Inquiry and analysis:* Existing knowledge, research, and/or views: Synthesizes in-depth information from relevant sources representing various points of view/approaches.
- *Civic engagement:* Diversity of communities and cultures: Demonstrates evidence of adjustment in own attitudes and beliefs because of working within and learning from diversity of communities and cultures. Promotes others' engagement with diversity.
- *Civic identity and commitment:* Provides evidence of experience in civic engagement activities and describes what he or she has learned about himself or herself as it relates to a reinforced and clarified sense of civic identity and continued commitment to public action.
- *Global learning:* Global self-awareness: Effectively addresses significant issues in the natural and human world based on articulating one's identity in a global context.
- *Perspective taking:* Evaluates and applies diverse perspectives to complex subjects within natural and human systems in the face of multiple and even conflicting positions (i.e., cultural, disciplinary, and ethical).

ASSESSMENT FOR TEACHERS

We strongly recommend that teachers find multiple ways to reflect upon their CBLL work with students, communities, and colleagues. There are numerous ways to evaluate teacher reflection, using methods similar to those in the previous section. In the next paragraphs, we suggest formative activities to encourage educators and program coordinators to think critically about CBLL.

Teaching journals. Educators can benefit from keeping a regular journal in which they reflect critically on significant CBLL moments. A structured journal focuses on key values, motivations, and connections made between community interactions and teaching practices. The final journal entry should provide a summary statement that addresses the themes described over the course of the semester, commenting on the extent to which any established goals were attained. This information can be used as fodder for improving the course, or for developing a research project or publication. The CBLL instructor may also seek a mentor with whom to share the journal or could establish a teaching exchange with a peer from within or outside their department.

Structured discussions with community partners. At a minimum, teachers and community organizations should meet three times during the semester: before, during, and after the shared experience. During these conversations, it is helpful to focus on what went well, along with what challenges were faced by all parties. Educators should take these opportunities to reflect on their own communication and organizational skills. It is equally useful to brainstorm recommendations for future iterations of the course.

Surveys. A community engagement office or your department can conduct faculty surveys to deduce which training and support needs are and are not being met. This information can also be collected through informal conversations or focus groups. Surveys help profile best practices among service-learning faculty, particularly when they are administered to faculty who have taught a course over multiple semesters.

Responsive writing. The act of responding to student writing is itself a form of engagement. This process, whether done in writing or in an oral form (recorded or in person), offers faculty an opportunity to listen reflectively, to respond, and to offer support for different stakeholders.

Classroom observations. Observations offer a way to find out how the community is integrated into the academic content of a course. Although some teachers may arrange to have themselves videotaped once a year, or may designate a colleague to observe them, many will find that regular, consistent observations offer the most fruitful information. An observation form, created by the instructor, should focus on a specific area, such as a teaching method utilized, time allotted to discussing community issues, or awareness of community needs. Student comments made in class can also be incorporated into the narrative observation. For a sample form, see Gelmon and others (2001, 68).

Notes on the syllabus. Instructors may also wish to annotate their syllabi. Sometimes we think we will remember what we want to change in a given course; but with our many obligations, these thoughts often slip away. We suggest that at midterm and again at the end of the semester, instructors jot down notes on class meetings, on the organization of activities, and on CBLL experiences. This can be done with much greater frequency as well. A final *syllabus analysis* identifies promising practices that should inform future courses, including objectives, outcomes, selection of materials, reflection opportunities, and assessments.

Model blog posts. The practice of writing sample blog posts for students can offer ways to enhance student writing while also providing opportunities for teachers to reflect and explore their experiences.

Workshops, retreats, and conferences with other CBLL practitioners. Meetings provide opportunities for teachers to collect, assess, and present their results, not only to higher education management but also in conferences related to language acquisition, assessment, service learning, and the scholarship of teaching and learning. Such collaborations stimulate CBLL research and the production of research tools from a grassroots level (Shumer et al. 2000).

ASSESSMENT FOR COMMUNITY PARTNERS

The assessment of and by community partners has been largely absent from research on community-engaged learning. Recent literature in service learning has critiqued this lack of emphasis on community outcomes (Stoecker and Tryon 2009; George and Shams 2007; Cruz and Giles 2000), noting that "despite this seemingly commonsensical notion of evaluating the community impact of service learning, the bias in focus toward student outcomes has continued to this day, producing a voluminous literature" (Stoecker and Tryon 2009). In fact, as Stoecker and Tryon (2009, 4) note, "This inequity in research focus might seem logical from the academic perspective, since faculty are rewarded, administrators are promoted, and funding is provided to both public and private institutions based on the satisfaction of their 'customer base'—the student." Still, the omission of community perspectives gives an incomplete and, we would argue, problematic and even misleading view of the CBLL experience. As Stoecker and Tryon underscore, research has not fully explored how the focus on student and institutional interests might negatively impact the community. If community input is not solicited, for instance, partners may feel "used"; with their needs not met, and their communities exploited as laboratories, some community partners may deny access to both researchers and students (Smith 1999).

We thus strongly encourage instructors to include multiple, varied assessment measures of community partnerships. In addition to implementing assessments from the university point of view, educators should consult with the community organization to see what assessment measures it already has in place. Such an inclusion would result in a more holistic understanding of CBLL that benefits all parties. It would likewise contribute to documenting a distinct perspective of how student work actually affects the community. Gellmon and others (2006, 92) present a matrix for community assessment that includes variables about both the community partner organization and the community–university partnership. Focusing on the latter category, we can learn more about the nature of relationships and interactions, as well as satisfaction and the sustainability of partnerships. Common evaluation measures include interviews, focus groups, and surveys; these may be conducted in person or via a digital platform. Critical incident reports also help community partners focus on key, defining moments during a community partnership, and, combined with other measurements, they provide an understanding of how programmatic issues affect outcomes. These reports follow a simple format—date, nature of event, and why it is critical—and are used in key ways: to identify moments that have helped attain a specific goal, that have created a barrier to that goal, or that have helped the administration overcome a barrier (Gelmon et al. 2006, 122–23). This type of assessment will provide useful information for an internal conversation within the community organization and generate topics to discuss with the instructor and students that will improve the partnership.

Reflections for Instructors

Program Assessment. Distinct from assessing student gains, program assessment focuses on the outcomes of community partnerships and expands on programmatic goals. Faculty members interested in this broader perspective must look at multiple factors, over a period of time, in order to substantiate larger claims of gains and challenges. In some cases, educators will work collectively across multiple courses; in others, this work will be initiated by civic engagement offices, a department, or a university assessment office in an effort to assess and improve existing and future programs. Such evaluations may include an evaluation of syllabi, class observations, community surveys, interviews, and critical incident reports.

A CULTURE OF ASSESSMENT

Assessment plays an increasingly important role in educational settings, and it is integrated throughout our institutions. In order to demonstrate the impact of our programs and ensure their quality for both students and community partners, we must demonstrate their impact and justify the resources that they require. As a result, assessment has become an integral—and vertically integrated—part of the educational landscape. Still, we do not always pause to consider why we are assessing, what concrete effect these assessments have on our workload, and how this push for assessment might engender a certain resistance among our students, our community members, and ourselves. We therefore conclude this chapter by turning to recent trends in US educational policy that have imposed norms and expectations for assessment and evaluation.

The focus on assessment stems in part from a recommendation by the Spellings Commission, stating that "postsecondary education institutions should measure and report meaningful student learning outcomes" (US Department of Education 2006). Although widely criticized by higher education organizations such as the American Association of University Professors, which critiqued the depiction of postsecondary education as a marketplace, the commission's report has had an important impact on higher education. As the authors of *A Culture of Evidence* write, "Today's Higher Education institutions must not only prove their programs' performance; they must also take their programs to the next level, if they are to be able to choose from the most promising applicants, attract prestigious faculty, and secure access to financial support from a competitive financial pool" (Dwyer, Millet, and Payne 2017, 3). At the level of the institution, then, assessment may manifest as reaching goals in a strategic plan, complying with accreditation models, or recording individual student progress through a centralized university database. At the school or department level, assessment can take the form of a yearly review; a department may focus on how well its majors are reaching a set of standards, or a service-learning program may determine how multiple courses reach targeted civic engagement learning outcomes. At the classroom level, teachers assess their students in both formative and summative ways throughout the semester. Students also assess their own learning through rubrics, and end-of-semester evaluations of their teachers. Few aspects of the modern educational institution are immune to assessment.

The neoliberal paradigm that increasingly defines our institutions prefers quantitative assessments that value numbers and statistics. When applied to CBLL programs, such a model will emphasize the monetization of community contact hours over depth of engagement; it may also attempt to quantify CBLL student learning outcomes by statistical analysis alone. Websites such as Independentsector.org offer calculators to help quantify the economic value of service learning for colleges and universities—$24.69 an hour in 2018. Colleges will publish end-of-year reports that showcase how many of their students provided *X* amount of service hours to *Y* number of community members; costly software programs that track service hours have led to a new industry that provides supportive infrastructure for such endeavors. Although we do want our students meeting regularly with their community partners, a focus on numbers alone can be counterproductive, and even misleading. This can also produce sources of tension with community partners. As Mills (2012) has shown, the student focus on service hours (vs. the community organization's focus on student commitment or program outcomes) is one of four principal areas of tension in community partnerships; the other three include the student emphasis on learning versus the organization's emphasis on efficiency, the student emphasis on flexibility versus the organization's emphasis on dependability, and the student emphasis on idealism versus the organization's emphasis on realism. Moreover, though the use of rigorous measurement tools and frameworks can help administrators determine which programs are high performing, programs that cannot demonstrate statistically positive outcomes may be viewed in a less favorable light and may not be able to sustain funding. This model has led to the closure of "low-performing" departments on university campuses across the United States, disproportionately hitting the humanities. Although we will not delve into this issue more deeply here, it is important to be aware that these paradigm shifts have a significant impact on institutions, and one that is not always positive.

The culture of assessment can also take a heavy toll on classroom teachers. Because efforts to measure and assess are often top down, mandated by deans or program chairs, teachers may sometimes resent or even resist efforts to assess their CBLL work. They may not like having to quantify their teaching efforts, or may disagree with the reasons and means for evaluating CBLL. Measuring "student success" broadly defined, for instance, can suggest that the only outcome is "success" (a nebulous and rarely defined concept), whereas we know that there can be other outcomes, including "failure" (e.g., an inability to meet learning goals, partnerships that fall apart, dashed expectations). In both outcomes, students experience growth and learning, making it challenging to track and capture student "success." This is especially true given the cyclical nature of ICC growth and transformative learning, as described in chapters 2 and 5. Perhaps a student is challenged by a disorienting dilemma and consequently does not feel "successful" in that phase of the relationship or project, and yet we know that that dissonance is a key component to learning and "success."

Other instructors may perceive the focus on assessment as an increased burden that impedes their ability to teach effectively. In the K–12 system, mandated state testing creates an environment of seemingly constant student assessment that takes time away from classroom teaching. A 2014 study by the National

Education Association showed that nearly half of all US teachers considered leaving the profession because of standardized testing, with 72 percent replying that they felt "moderate" or "extreme" pressure from both school and district administrators to help students perform on tests (Walker 2014). Although college faculty are not subject to these same pressures, departments that are mandated by accreditation organizations to measure student learning increasingly emphasize a competency-based approach to education that places an additional burden on faculty.

One way to manage any conflicted feelings that arise when we consider the burden of evaluation is to return to the core reasons why we assess. As the authors of *Assessing Service-Learning and Community Engagement* (Gelmon et al. 2006, 8–9) remind us, assessment is an "improvement strategy" that helps educators understand how learning is conducted, how this method can be improved, and how individuals who use this method know whether a change is an improvement. If we hope to arm CBLL students with the skills to address systemic issues of inequality, assessment and reflection must be productive components of the learning cycle. We hope that CBLL practitioners will continue to contribute to this important conversation and share successful assessment models. In the following chapters, we offer additional activities that develop self and group reflection on key issues in CBLL, as well as strategies for building transformational and authentic partnerships.

CHAPTER 4

Identity, Language, and Power

By the end of this chapter, readers will be able to:

- Explore students' personal assumptions about identity
- Problematize categorizations of language communities
- Summarize the historical and political significance of language for US identity
- Explain how different students perceive power relationships
- Include discussions of power and privilege in the CBLL curriculum

IDENTITY

In this chapter we explore the complex interplay of identity and language that unfolds as students work in CBLL environments. "Identity" is a broad term, and a loaded one. Although intangible and relatively impossible to define empirically, it nonetheless occupies an important place in CBLL. For our purposes, we understand identity as a construct that reflects the beliefs, personalities, appearance, or qualities that make a person self-identify or a group identify collectively. These qualities can be cast in both positive and negative ways, rendering the process of identity construction constructive and/or destructive on an individual and/or societal level. In this chapter, we examine how society attempts to create certain categorizations of identity, how individual and group identities have an impact on CBLL, and how educators can make power dynamics more transparent for students.

First, we look at issues of identity construction on a societal level, such as the naming and categorization of L2 speakers in the community, the impact of dominant language policy and linguistic diversity, and the power of voices. We explore how language has an impact on acculturation and access to services, focusing specifically on education and health. How, for instance, do individuals with emerging English skills navigate the public school system, and how do they access and interact with the US health care system or alternative medicines?

What language policies and practices in the United States affect access to the wider society?

Next, we examine issues related to students' identities. Whether they are interacting with peers in the classroom, working with heritage or native speakers in the local community, or reflecting critically on their own history and identity, students must be guided to think critically about how their identities shape the CBLL experience and their understanding of it. Based on their backgrounds, students will experience CBLL differently. Because many CBLL experiences offer students a new perspective on social and economic inequities, class discussions often turn to discussions of racial and ethnic inequities. As students confront these issues, sometimes for the first time, they may bump into a spectrum of feelings, ranging from belonging to unconscious bias to deep-seated trauma. This can be especially startling when students have traditional expectations of what will be taught in a language course. Throughout this chapter, we pay particular attention to the ways that L1 and L2 affect power and privilege in relationships for native or near-native speakers of English, heritage language (HL) speakers, first-generation students, students of color, and white students, to name a few of the many possible identities and intersectionalities of identity. We examine some of these interactions in this chapter as we introduce ways to deconstruct dominant cultural norms and guide reflective activity.

Finally, we consider the role of the educator. As educators, we need to consider our own identities and how these may affect our teaching. When we anticipate discussions about power and access related to language policy, we are better prepared to select course materials that will help students have productive discussions, such as articles and films that explore structural racism or economic inequalities. Instructors should also be prepared to notice and address personal reactions and students' feelings—ranging from joy to dissonance—that might arise. Faculty, too, should be aware of what they themselves bring to the experience. As white middle-class female educators and authors, we recognize that our own positions need to be examined: We question the systems that benefit us, and we seek to engage our students, who are economically and ethnically diverse, with others who are equally if not more diverse. We hope to model this tension throughout this chapter, for as Osborn (2006, 36) gently reminds us, "Confrontation and conflict are by-products of challenging the status quo."

IDENTITY CONSTRUCTION AT THE SOCIETAL LEVEL

Let us consider for a moment what it means to live in a *language community*, also known as a *speech community* or language enclave. Many immigrants will elect to move to an area where they feel comfortable and accepted. This can be an empowering decision. Still, spatial assimilation theories suggest that immigrants are more likely to experience residential segregation due to a variety of factors, including income, family, and cultural preference. In some cases, affordable housing structures group persons of a particular language together; resettlement agencies also engage in this practice. Research shows that ethnic minority neighborhoods—many of which are characterized by L2 usage—are disproportionately affected by environmental health issues, a lack of healthy food options ("food deserts"), increased marketing by alcohol and tobacco companies, and poor access to health services. Unequal educational opportunities are also a marker of ethnic minority communities, which do not usually have access to the resources found in suburban public schools. Poor education leads to fewer economic opportunities and decreased social mobility, creating a cycle of poverty and segregation. Research shows that segregated communities have slower rates of acculturation and, most notably, do not learn English as quickly (Boal 2000). Learning English is arguably the most important marker of acculturation.

An individual's ability to access dominant forms of knowledge is dependent on his or her cultural capital. According to Bourdieu (1991), cultural capital includes knowledge, skills, and other cultural acquisitions, as exemplified by educational or technical qualifications. *Linguistic capital* is one form of cultural capital. One possesses power if one's language is respected. For example, speaking English accords a person power in the United States, but if someone has a pronounced accent when speaking English, this can diminish their capital; though the person's ability to speak and comprehend English does not impede their access to health and educational services, they may not be treated in the same ways that a native speaker of English with little discernible accent would. In other words, not all ways of speaking English are created equal in certain social spaces. Likewise, different accents accord different statuses; a person with a European accent may have greater cultural capital than a person with a South Asian accent. For HL speakers in the US, their linguistic capital can subject them to marginalization, because it differs from that of dominant cultural groups (Osborn 2006, 15). For instance, though Latino/a parents endow their children with linguistic and cultural capital, this knowledge is often devalued in the school system, which prizes and reproduces dominant (white, English-speaking) culture. HL speakers also find themselves inhabiting the linguistic double bind of having social bonding in their home communities via language, and yet that same language is disadvantaged in the linguistic marketplace (Bourdieu 1991, cited by DuBord and Kimball 2016). This is particularly true of Spanish, which offers HL speakers "little economic and cultural capital to achieve success in the middle-class sense, for example, in the form of scholarships, college credits, and belonging in professional discourse communities" (Velásquez 2015, cited by DuBord and Kimball 2016). The opposite is true for L2 learners, who often use the L2 to gain professional capital, but it rarely gains them access to heritage or native speaker communities. Dual language schools provide strong models for bilingualism that contest these systems by leveraging the linguistic capital of both L2 and HL students. Exploring these distinctions is an important part of CBLL's critical pedagogy.

Although linguistic capital can be used to oppress groups, it can also be leveraged for power. As Foucault (1978, 100–101) writes, "Discourse transmits and produces power; it reinforces it, but also undermines and exposes it, renders it fragile and makes it possible to thwart." Discourse is a site of both power and resistance. Power is everywhere; it does not belong to one group or another, but is embodied and enacted through various types of discourse, including silence. Although speech communities experience discrimination, it is also true that some have gained power and influence by using their linguistic capital. The Chicano civil rights movement of the twentieth century, for instance, drew on ethnic and linguistic solidarity to call attention to Chicanos' subordinate status to gain political power. Chinese settlements in the United States have also used linguistic and cultural capital to form powerful political representation in San Francisco. Increasingly, refugee agencies in the United States are developing programs that seek to empower individuals within refugee communities to become politically active and advocate on their own behalf.

Here, we draw attention to the power of defining and *naming a language community*. This polemic can be seen easily in the complexity of the terms associated with "foreign" languages. As Osborn (2000, 161) explains, "As long as American English or any other variety enjoys special status, linguistic diversity in the United States, whether called 'foreign,' 'world,' 'modern,' 'second,' 'heritage,' or otherwise, will continue to be marginalized both in society at large (as education institutions are complicit in cultural reproduction) and in the field. Only by approaching linguistic diversity as a norm, and not an aberration requiring a special approach, will we begin to move toward a form of social justice in language education." Education plays a large role in creating and sustaining hegemony related to identities, and that includes world language education. Osborn (2000, 87) reminds us that the production of knowledge reflects a process of mediation, one in which some forms of knowledge are advanced while others are devalued: "By assuming that all non-English languages are somehow related to that which is foreign, language educational endeavors serve to reinforce a language identity by default." These "hidden curricula" benefit those students whose cultural capital most closely resembles that of a college's or university's dominant culture (Osborn 2000, 15).

As educators, we may be guilty of defining language communities in ways that do not benefit them, and may even do unintentional harm. Throughout this book, we refer to both "language communities" and L2 speakers in an attempt to recognize the diversity of individuals and diverse groups and to avoid creating monolithic and homogeneous characterizations. Still, the term "language community" is in itself problematic, and though we may use it out of convenience, it merits consideration, particularly as we seek to better understand how language shapes identity. Using such a term, despite our best intentions, may actually treat as "others" the very communities with which we seek to build solidarity. Teachers who pair students with Arabic-speaking refugees may refer to these individuals as an "Arabic community," but Arabic speakers might come from six different countries and share little more than their language; and even this shared language is marked by distinct dialects. By grouping them into one language category, we run the risk of further ghettoizing communities that are already disadvantaged. These labels categorize a group of individuals by language alone and do not reflect the diversity of the "group." We see this mirrored when people generalize the assignment of communities to neighborhoods ("geographic fragmentation"), which further isolates speakers of non-English languages by separating them from the American mainstream (Osborn 2006, 120). The designation of a language community, or an area inhabited by native or heritage speakers of a particular language, is often decided by those outside it, so we must also wonder what purposes this naming might serve, in both positive and negative terms. When we hear about "the Latino/a community" in our town, for instance, we should consider not only to whom this term refers but also who uses this term, in what circumstances, and to what ends.

Reflections for Instructors

1. *Language "communities."* Consider the languages spoken in your community. Where do the L2 speakers live? Are there businesses that cater to them? Do they have commonalities beyond language? What might it mean to categorize them as a "language community"? How do they self-identify? Do they identify themselves in the same way that the local government, media, or school identifies them?

2. *Rethinking assessments.* Consider how you develop student reflection prompts and assessments. Do your prompts assume that all students are L2 learners whose first language is English (not heritage or native speakers of L2, not international students studying in the United States learning an additional language)? Have you considered that all your students do not access the dominant culture equally?

Activities for Students

1. *Latinx*. Ask your students to read arguments supporting and rejecting the usage of "Latinx," a term that has emerged in recent years as a gender-neutral or nonbinary alternative to "Latino" or "Latina." You may also wish to explore definitions in different dictionaries. Allow time in class to engage in debate. Supply questions as a foundation for the conversation, such as: Why do people want to use this new term? What roles do power and privilege have in the creation and use of this term? Next, have students identify a range of perspectives (linguistic, political, historical, gender, generational) that might influence point of view. As a last phase in the activity, ask students to write a short essay developing their analysis and recommendations for or against the term's implementation.

2. *The community identification card*. Divide the class into three groups. Assign one of the following identification (ID) card programs to each group:

- FaithAction ID (http://faithaction.org/services/id_initiative/)
- IDNYC (www1.nyc.gov/site/idnyc/index.page)
- SF City ID Card (http://sfgov.org/countyclerk/sf-city-id-card)

Students should review these websites and look for press publications related to the programs. Each group should present the successes and challenges of how these community ID card initiatives were implemented in particular locations. Track the reported information on the board to look for similarities and differences. After each group summarizes its findings, engage in a broader conversation about the initiatives, using questions such as:

- Why is the community ID card useful for immigrants and the police?
- How does the community ID embody how society perceives identity? How systems of power function?
- What other issues related to ID cards have an impact on inclusion and access? (i.e., national IDs, uniform driver licenses guidelines, required ID for voter registration)
- What are the drawbacks of community IDs?
- Does the holder of this ID card have a claim to citizenship?
- What are different ways of defining citizenship? What is your preferred definition?

LANGUAGE POLITICS AND POLICIES

Considering identity issues requires us to problematize our assumptions, to rethink categorizations, and, most important, to understand how language politics and policies in the United States continue to shape economic mobility, access to education and health care, and social stratification. CBLL classes engage with the experiences of the individual whose first language is not English, whether that person was born in the United States or elsewhere. CBLL courses also ask students to consider how they navigate US systems and how L2 community members' experiences differ from those of native English speakers. Students learn to ask why certain norms, politics, and policies are in place.

To answer some of these questions, let us look more closely at the history of language politics in relation to the ever-changing demographics of the United

States. The US was founded on a set of principles based on equality and inalienable rights. Combined with the rule of law, which states that everyone is subject to the same law, the Declaration of Independence clearly states that all Americans are to be treated the same. The US is hailed as a nation of immigrants and refugees, but it has an equally long history of categorizing people along ethnic, religious, and linguistic lines. From its treatment of Native American populations to African slaves to Latino/a and Asian immigrants, the US government uses categories to construct and maintain an ideology of oppression that has effectively "othered" entire groups of people. This focus on difference constructs communities across the United States that are based solely on race, ethnicity, or language. Some community members may elect to live together, but more often governments utilize strategies like gerrymandering and redistricting to reinforce their marginalization. Although frequently described as a melting pot, or even a tossed salad, the United States is experienced by many as a series of compartmentalized groups. White, English-speaking culture dominates, and is considered "American," though a hyphenated identity (e.g., Asian-American, or Asian American—both with the hyphen written out graphically or implied) indicates a hybrid identity within our society. See Baran's (2017) *Language in Immigrant America* for an in-depth exploration of the history of hyphenated and hybrid identities. Linguistic practices are inextricably linked to language politics and should not be ignored; when a person with a "foreign accent" speaks, an interlocutor will commonly ask where the person is "really from." These examples underscore how people often perceive being American as an ethnicity, when "American" is a nationality, one that even those without citizenship can claim. We cannot disconnect national language policy from language use, specifically for our conversation regarding language learning.

Although English continues to be the *dominant language*, the United States has no official language. From its beginnings, the nation has consisted of people from various, distinct linguistic backgrounds; as early as 1646, more than eighteen languages were spoken on the island now called Manhattan (Parillo 2013). To date, although a steady number of bills have been introduced to make English the official language, no federal law has been passed. The American Civil Liberties Union opposes such a proposition, noting that it would unduly disadvantage nonnative speakers of English, who may not be able to access health and education services. Opposing views state that producing documents in just one language would save the US considerable funds (a point that is contradicted by the bilingual Canadian government). Still, some thirty-six US states have English-only laws, almost all of which go unenforced. In courses that focus on language policy and CBLL, students can research the history of language

Activities for Students

1. *Changes in language.* Ask students to review table 4.1 and to write five factual statements that describe changes in language usage in the United States from 2000 to 2013. Then use variations of the following questions to hypothesize why these changes took place. What historical events may explain these changes? How do you see these changes in your own community? How have these changes affected your college or university?

TABLE 4.1 Foreign Languages Spoken at Home, 2000–2013

Language	2000	2010	2013
Spanish	28,101,052	36,995,602	38,417,235
Chinese	2,022,143	2,808,692	3,029,042
Tagalog	1,224,241	1,573,720	1,612,465
Vietnamese	1,009,627	1,381,488	1,428,352
French	1,643,838	1,322,650	1,251,815
Korean	894,063	1,137,325	1,100,881
Arabic	614,582	864,961	1,052,938
German	1,383,442	1,067,651	984,669
Russian	706,242	854,955	895,902
French Creole	453,368	746,702	783,017
Portuguese	564,630	688,326	677,329
Hindi	317,057	609,395	654,101
Italian	1,008,370	725,223	641,267
Polish	667,414	608,333	549,661
Japanese	477,997	443,497	454,997
Urdu	262,900	388,909	439,129
Persian	312,085	381,408	399,048
Gujarati	235,988	356,394	372,104
Greek	365,436	307,178	294,476
Serbo-Croatian	233,865	284,077	255,573

(*continued*)

policies in other countries and provinces; Quebec's, Catalonia's, and Taiwan's desire for independence offer rich case studies of how language and identity are closely tied.

Statistics are invaluable as we explore the changing landscape of the United States. Trends in language usage in the US offer students a larger perspective than the one lived in their immediate community. Recent data from the 2013 American Community Survey and the 2010 US census, for instance, show that one in five "native-born legal Americans" speaks a language other than English at home, a number that has grown by 94 percent since 1990 (Camarota and Zeigler 2014); of those who reported speaking another language at home, 41 percent reported that they spoke English "less than very well." To date, the ten most spoken languages in the US after English are Spanish, Chinese, Tagalog, Vietnamese, French, Korean, Arabic, German, Russian, and French Creole. The greatest language gains have been in Spanish, Chinese, and Arabic (see table 4.1 for exact figures).

TABLE 4.1 *Continued*

Language	2000	2010	2013
Armenian	202,708	240,402	236,580
Hmong	168,063	211,500	228,965
Cambodian	181,889	220,900	220,921
Hebrew	195,374	204,593	210,908
Navajo	178,014	172,873	160,301
Yiddish	178,945	154,763	157,165
Laotian	149,303	158,847	153,062
Thai	120,464	150,885	151,061
Hungarian	117,973	90,453	82,739
All others	2,960,522	4,390,894	4,853,037

Source: Data are from American FactFinder for the American Community Survey and the 2000 US Census (Camarota and Zeigler 2014, 3).

2. *Languages in your community.* Using the MLA Language Map (https://apps.mla.org/map_main), have students identify the most commonly spoken languages in their community. Develop a short discussion about the visibility or invisibility of the different language communities in your area. Ask students to name concrete evidence (businesses, restaurants, etc.) that identifies the presence of specific communities, and ask them to consider how and why different groups might not be visible.

3. *Data collection.* Form small groups and ask students to discuss these questions related to data collection: What are the positive and negative outcomes of collecting racial, ethnic, and linguistic data on citizens? How might access to this information be useful, and how might it be used for harm? How might a lack of data (mis)inform national policies? A variation of this activity might include a homework assignment for students to compare practices in the United States with those in another country. Students report back their observations and research to the class.

THE POWER OF NAMING

A growing number of colleges and universities have elected to change their departmental names from "foreign language departments" to departments of "world languages" or "modern languages" (Jaschik 2011). This change reflects an important shift in thinking about language usage and also identity. A "foreign" language suggests a language that is indigenous to another country. Historically, schools have been the location of foreign language study, in order to understand texts written in another language or to prepare students for travel to another country. In recent years, this term has fallen out of favor and is often contrasted with "second" language, a term that encapsulates the reasons for learning another language, such as practicing it within a community for a particular objective. As Richards and Schmidt (2002, 472) explain, "When contrasted with foreign language, the term refers more narrowly to a language that plays a major role in a particular country or region though it may not be the first language of many people who use it." Given this definition, can Spanish be considered a "foreign" language? We would argue no, citing both history and current practice. Spanish was spoken before English on the North American continent after all, with Spanish settlers setting up a colony in Saint Augustine, Florida, in 1565. To date, Spanish is by far the most widely spoken second language in the US, with over 41 million native speakers, growing at a steady 4 percent rate. There are now more native Spanish speakers in the United States than in Spain.

To understand better how labels such as "foreign" form rather than reflect identity, let us look at how governments racially categorize their citizens and residents because this practice better informs our discussion of the imposed formation of language groups. *Categorization* can serve both discriminatory and well-meaning purposes. The "one-drop rule," for instance, was used to identify black Americans and Native Americans on US birth certificates, resulting in discriminatory practices that began in the nineteenth century and became law in the twentieth century. This law allowed Southern courts in particular to disallow racially mixed marriages well into the 1960s (Kertzer and Arel 2002). After the rise of affirmative action in the 1970s, the US government began employing similar logic to determine racial categories, but for different reasons. For instance, for Native Americans to receive government resources from the Indian Health Service of the Bureau of Indian Affairs, they must prove that at least one of their grandparents (one-quarter by blood) appeared on original tribal rolls. In this example, we see that categorization benefits some Native Americans while also defining them into a narrow category. In some cases, categorization is used for more nefarious purposes. Internal passports and identity cards that indicate categories of ethnicity or race have led to racial segregation and genocide in places like South Africa, Nazi Germany, and Rwanda. Although the practice of collecting racial or ethnic data is relatively widespread, some countries do not collect this information. In France, for instance, questions about ethnicity, language, and religion cannot be asked on the national census.

In the United States, as we will see, categorization mandated by the federal census contributed to *the formation of race and ethnicity*. From 1899 to 1920, US immigration services categorized new arrivals into forty-eight "races or peoples," generally characterized by the languages they spoke rather than their phenotype (Kertzer and Arel 2002). A shift occurred as more non-Europeans began to arrive. In 1930, a new effort was begun to include a "Mexican" race category in a door-to-door long-form census; Mexican, of course, is no more a race than is North Carolinian. Later, the US Census created separate categories for race and ethnicity, asking residents to identify themselves according to terms that have changed over time (from Negro to black to African American, for instance).

According to the census, "These standards generally reflect a social definition of race and ethnicity recognized in this country, and they do not conform to any biological, anthropological, or genetic criteria" (US Census Bureau 2017).

Let us look more closely at the history of the *Hispanic* category in the US census. This category underscores the challenge of identifying national origin or speakers of other languages and offers a robust example of how governments play a role in shaping group identity. Until the late twentieth century, excluding the 1930 Mexican race census experiment, there was no semantic separation of Hispanic residents of the United States from the general population; persons of Puerto Rican, Mexican, or Latin origin were directed to select the "white" category. In 1970, however, the long-form questionnaire asked "Is this person's origin or descent ________," offering the following possibilities: "Mexican, Puerto Rican, Cuban, Central or South American, Other Spanish," and "No, none of these." This question captured inaccurate data, with later research showing that many residents of Southern and Central states selected the category of South or Central American. In 1980, this question was moved to the short form that all residents complete, marking the first time that all US residents participated in this type of self-identification. The question became "Is this person of Spanish/Hispanic origin or descent?" with the following possible responses: "No (not Spanish/Hispanic); Yes, Mexican, Mexican-Amer., Chicano; Yes, Puerto Rican; Yes, Cuban; Yes, other Spanish/Hispanic." Again, a significant number of non Spanish/Hispanic persons circled "Amer.," indicating the unreliability of self-reporting measures. In 1990, the census moved the Hispanic question to place it before the race question, and a reminder was added to answer both the Hispanic question and the race question. In 2000, the term "Latino" was added, so the question read, "Is this person Spanish/Hispanic/Latino?" In 2010, these designations were reversed, with Spanish appearing last, and the word origin was added ("Is this person of Hispanic, Latino, or Spanish origin?"). The Census Bureau is currently piloting a new version that would combine the race and origin questions, rather than separating them.

This discussion merits our interest because it demonstrates how the federal government participates in the construction of identity through naming. It problematizes the different societal forces that shape the defining of categories. In CBLL we must be careful in identifying and naming the communities with which we work. Educators should take time in class to discuss the politics involved in identity construction. To introduce these discussions, it may be useful to imagine alternative scenarios. What if, as McMaken (2016) wonders, the government had created a category of Latin (and not Hispanic) that included individuals of Italian, Spanish, and Portuguese descent? Would Supreme Court justice Antonin Scalia (of Italian descent) be considered representative of a minority group, rather than of the dominant (white) group? What if the United States had created an ethnic group of Slavs that included Polish, Russians, Hungarians, and Czechs? Would we be talking today about whether the US is inclusive of its Slavic minority and offers sufficient representation of individuals in this category?

Perceptions of belonging are intertwined with these data and practices, and they can strongly influence self-identification. The 2010 US Census, for instance, showed that 53 percent of Hispanics identify as white; the American Community Survey in 2012 put this proportion at 63 percent. This significant shift reflects both a change in the way the question was posed (Cohn 2014) and a sense of belonging to the dominant white culture, influenced by levels of educational achievement and economic success. Tafoya (2004), of the Pew Hispanic Center, explains that

> the fact that changeable characteristics such as income help determine racial identification among Latinos, versus permanent markers such as skin color, does not necessarily mean that the color lines in American society are fading. On the contrary, these findings show that color has a broader meaning. The Latino experience demonstrates that whiteness remains an important measure of belonging, stature and acceptance. And, Hispanic views of race also show that half of this ever larger segment of the US population is feeling left out. (3)

Categorizing Hispanics as a minority group, when half of Hispanics do not identify themselves this way, must be examined more closely. As we see here, the concept of whiteness bears strongly on issues of identity and belonging but not just for Hispanic populations. We explore this further later in the chapter, where we share ways to engage students in discussions of whiteness and white privilege.

Reflections for Instructors

Categorization. What is the role of categorization and naming in your program assessments and reflection prompts? Do forms use appropriate, respectful language to describe members of the university community and the local community? How can class discussions and assignments prompt students to reflect on the ways in which categories affect their CBLL experiences?

Activities for Students

Naming Conventions. Form small groups of students to discuss the following questions: What practices of naming or categorizing does your college or university use when describing students? What impact might these categories have on students, professors, and the community at large? How might the power of naming affect your CBLL experience?

STUDENT IDENTITY

Students enter into community interactions with distinct life experiences, varying linguistic abilities, and differing levels of maturity and knowledge. A student from a rural setting begins his or her CBLL work with Latino/a immigrants in a different place than does one who comes from New York City. Perhaps the rural student was raised in a conservative family who refers to undocumented persons as "illegals," or perhaps he or she has Mexican friends at school and has participated in *quinceñera* celebrations. Perhaps these are both true. What we wish to emphasize is that we cannot assume that students fit a certain mold based on origin, hometown, year in school, socioeconomic status, racial or ethnic background, or political leanings. Each student is unique, and therefore each student engages in the CBLL experience in different ways and with varying levels of agency. In some ways, a natural process of maturation and self-actualization influences outcomes; and in other ways, it is a pathology of US history and policy. When we can help students tailor their own learning in a way that addresses their particular knowledge gaps or challenges their assumptions, they can move more deliberately toward transformative learning experiences. In order to do so, however, they must begin to understand who they are, not only as individuals but also as members of and in relation to other groups. CBLL offers students not just a different way of seeing the world but also a different way of being in the world.

Another way of seeing the world is to consider the dominant culture through a new lens. Educators should problematize the power and privilege associated with the dominant culture and dominant language. Through more self-awareness, students and faculty from the dominant culture or language can create more productive and authentic relationships with communities by acknowledging how their agency is tied to privilege and power.

The charity model of service is familiar to many students who have volunteered at a soup kitchen, helped build a Habitat for Humanity house, or participated in a church mission project. In most of these experiences, students do not have to interact in a meaningful or sustained way with the community; they complete the task and can feel good that they helped someone else. Middle- and upper-middle-class white students are particularly lauded for doing this type of service, which correlates with an English monolingual, monocultural identity (Mitchell, Donohue, and Young-Law 2012).

The fact that service learning has been identified in recent years as a "pedagogy of Whiteness" (Butin 2006; Mitchell, Donohue, and Young-Law 2012) requires a parallel inquiry into CBLL practices. Bocci (2015, 5, 8) warns that "by privileging whiteness, *white normativity* in service learning can lead to assimilative, discriminatory, and/or exclusionary practices that reinforce oppressive socioeconomic power dynamics." Bocci explores historical narratives that position whites "as providers and leaders, while people of color are relegated to the role of 'served' or 'needy' (or are ignored completely)." Educators who are white or educators who have a majority of white students should call out dynamics of power and privilege that manifest in CBLL. We do not want to perpetuate or reproduce prejudicial systems of thought and practice, so let us consider more closely how these might materialize in CBLL partnerships.

The term "white privilege" is now part of common parlance, due in part to Peggy McIntosh's (1989) seminal paper, "White Privilege: Unpacking the Invisible Knapsack," which brought attention to the numerous and often invisible ways that whites more easily navigate the world. *Privilege*, in its simplest definition, can be understood as the rights, advantages, and benefits attributed to a person or group of persons that give them an advantage in relation to other persons. McIntosh's article includes a useful checklist of fifty items that can be translated into the L2 and incorporated into a critical reflection activity. Statements such as "If I should need to move, I can be pretty sure of renting or purchasing housing in an area which I can afford and in which I would want to live" and "I do not have to educate my children to be aware of systemic racism for their own daily physical protection" invite students to recognize their privilege in personalized terms. McIntosh's article is not grounded in a biological, genetic, skin-color-based notion of race, but on the lived experience and historical realities of living as a nonwhite person in the United States.

Privilege can be seen through many lenses, including religion, language, gender, sexual orientation, and socioeconomic status. Perhaps a student realizes that in the eyes of the community, he or she benefits from numerous privileges, some visible and some not. This may be the first time that he or she perceives these privileges, and they may challenge his or her self-conception. It will be challenging for the student to process this situation. Most students will simply want these differences to disappear. They may feel shame, guilt, and embarrassment that they have "so much" (material wealth as well as agency stemming from their privilege). Some students will pretend that the differences do not really matter, while others will seem paralyzed by this discovery, unable to engage in their partnerships. Still others will be so uncomfortable that they will resist engaging in the CBLL experience, stop attending appointments, and conjure excuses for their absences. We explore this dissonance in greater detail in the next chapter.

Mitchell and Donahue (2009, 173) remind us that the literature of service learning has historically been about crossing borders, about students connecting across "difference"—a difference that is usually embodied by the target community. Research suggests that CBL provides white and affluent students with transformational learning experiences, challenging their views of race and class because white students encounter difference in the community (Catlett and Proweller 2011; Hayes and Cuban 1997; Robb Jones, Robbins, and LePeau 2011). So how do we support students with different backgrounds who do not see difference in CBLL? Some students will have personally experienced the structural inequities that are encountered in our CBLL courses. Mitchell and Donahue (2009) draw on Dubois's (1903/1989) notion of double consciousness ("an understanding of self including race through the eye of others") and King's (1991, 135) notion of dynconsciousness ("an impaired consciousness or distorted way of thinking about race") to explore ways to address a more diverse student body. For some students of color, for instance, CBLL means "going home," an experience that can be positive for students who want to work with others from similar communities; but for others, who may enjoy being in a different college environment and may not want to "go back," it can be fraught with tension. Students of color from more economically privileged positions may have never even "been there," and though some may be excited to work with others who share their racial identity (but not their same life experience), others may resist associations based solely on their color. Still others may feel "tokenized" by being asked to translate a language or a culture, or to navigate a CBLL experience. It is vital to consider how students think about community interactions. One student, Lena, told us that the time she spent with her refugee partner became like an oasis for her, a way to get away from campus. In her final reflection, she wrote that "I now choose to spend my Friday and Sunday evenings with Mimi and her kids. They have become like a second family for me—I spend more time with them than I do my friends, or in class" (Lena, final reflection, 2016). For Lena, her community partner offered a welcome escape from her campus environment and a way to connect in different ways. Research shows that students of color and first-generation students find belonging through community interactions and, as a result, have higher retention rates in college; those who are connected to the local community are more likely to complete their degree than those who are not engaged in similar experiences.

When considering the behaviors of students who see themselves reflected in the community more than in the campus culture, the case of heritage language learners (HLLs) is telling. DuBord and Kimball (2016, 320) note that although the HLLs in their research study report participating in fewer service hours in their formative years, these figures may not actually be accurate. They wonder whether the service experience of HLLs has been overlooked: "If a student from a Spanish-speaking family acts as a language broker for her parents at the doctor, is this student doing any less service than her peers who do community outreach with new immigrants? What might typically be described as service when it happens outside of one's family or community is just as valuable, if not more so, when done in intimate settings where there is a greater imperative to actively engage in the process." In other words, though HLLs report doing less "formal" service, they may engage in similar activities or have had more robust service experiences within their own communities. Though their experiences do not count as service, they are equally valid. This consideration reminds us that we should pay attention to the language used to define CBLL experiences, because it may unintentionally exclude students of diverse backgrounds.

Another important example of differences that minority students might experience is developed in Mitchell and Donahue's (2009, 176, 180) exploration of the "pressures of identity." These pressures often extend into the classroom, where students of color report feeling responsible for explaining the actions of people in the community. In CBLL, instructors and L2 learners may unconsciously or explicitly rely on certain students to explain community behaviors. This responsibility may seem like a privilege, because he or she has a different kind of access to community, but it can also be a burden. As Mitchell and Donahue (2009, 183–84) explain,

> Feeling forced to fight or defend their communities, feeling silenced by the continuous voicing of unexamined stereotypes and negative labeling, feeling hurt by their peers' lack of awareness and understanding—the classroom for these students became the space where they crossed boundaries and borders. The classroom became the service site over the communities, which were often more comfortable and more familiar. Instead of experiencing the classroom as a site for learning, students of color were too often teaching their white and economically privileged peers.

As educators, we must monitor whose voices are included in discussions and the types of contributions that we expect from all students. It is our responsibility to maintain an atmosphere that does not discriminate, stereotype, tokenize, privilege, or somehow treat students unfairly. Mitchell warns against discussions by the whole class that can become tense (or silent), advocating for one-to-one discussions with students so that they can address their concerns without fear. We provide more strategies for building norms of behavior and creating brave spaces in the classroom in chapter 5.

Reflections for Instructors

1. *Privilege.* Think of the students that make up a typical class at your school. What traits do they share? How do their experiences differ before coming to the university? In what ways might a student exhibit privilege? How might a student's privilege affect his or her community partnership or the relationship with other students?

2. *Materials selection.* What is your selection process for texts, assignments, and assessments? Do your materials showcase a diverse selection of voices? Will these choices create barriers for learning?

Activities for Students

1. *Privilege.* Share McIntosh's article on white privilege with students, and then ask them to consider their own privilege by engaging in this activity: Distribute a container of twenty beads to each student. Either read, or have students read silently, a list of statements. After each individual statement, the student will either pick out or return beads to the container. Possible statements:

If you . . .
are female, take five beads.
are Caucasian, take one bead. Everyone else, give two beads back.
are under eighteen, give two beads back.
have health insurance, take two beads.
are heterosexual, take two beads. Everyone else, give two beads back.
are bisexual, give back three beads.
are transgender, give five beads back.
own a car, take one bead for each car.
have a parent who graduated from college, take one bead for each parent.
have a job, take one bead.
are a member of a university athletic team, take two beads.
were born outside the US, give back two beads.
speak English as a second language, give back two beads.

Reflection can take place as a discussion by the whole class or as an individual writing assignment. Students should consider what it means to have the quantity of beads that they amass from the container. They also can contemplate how they felt while completing the exercise. Can they identify questions or areas of privilege indicators?

2. *Identity labels.* Ask students to describe themselves by making a list of eight to ten labels that represent aspects of their identity. These might include their gender, religion, family relationships, hobbies, or friendships (e.g., I'm a runner, a sister, a friend, a Unitarian, a woman). Next, ask students to note which of these labels are visible to others from the outside (mark with a *v*) and which are invisible (mark with an *i*). If they are comfortable, students can share with partners what they wrote, as well as how it makes them feel to share the parts of themselves that are invisible. Teachers can use this activity to segue into a discussion about perception and stereotyping, which may lead students to view their community partners in new ways.

3. *Branding.* Project photos of students wearing recognizable school apparel. Ask students to explain what the logos mean to them, and what they might mean to the local community. This activity can be expanded by asking students to imagine how they might be seen by their community partners. In a journal or blog post, they can elaborate on which parts of their identities might be noticeable in their community work, which ones they are comfortable sharing, and which ones they might wish to keep to themselves.

THE EDUCATOR'S POWER AND PRIVILEGE

As Osborn (2006, 44) rightly reminds us, educators must also examine their own privilege in the classroom: "Learning to teach a language is a value-laden process—it involves examining one's own privilege and position in terms of language and culture in the global context." As teachers, we are invited to confront the power conferred to us by virtue of our role, as well as the ways in which our own identities may affect student learning and the CBLL experience. Like Green (2003), who calls for greater attention to the diverse socioeconomic and racial backgrounds of both students and educators, we believe we must deliberately engage in critical reflection on these issues. This is not "identity politics," as some might contend, but rather an important step in engaging in the confrontational act that defines the very teaching of world languages. Osborn (2006, 10) calls this practice "macrocontextualization," emphasizing that language learning always occurs within a context, one that takes into account the local, regional, national, and global contexts in which the programs are situated. Because these contexts include social, political, historical, and ethical considerations, they will vary from classroom to classroom, and from teacher to teacher. This shift moves the study of language from the study of the *word* to the study of the *world*, repositioning language as an indispensable and integrated discipline. These observations and discussions regarding curricular reform are foundational to CBLL because they mandate the inclusion of social justice education, critical pedagogy, and language learning in a local and meaningful context. We must contemplate how to best prepare ourselves to effectively and productively engage in this pedagogy.

Although many teachers are interested in working with communities, most have not formally studied experiential pedagogy. As Osborn (2006, 8) notes, "Critical pedagogies have largely failed to recognize the role language education can play in their endeavors," thus compounding the challenge. If we have not had training, this is because there has not been any training to receive. Although we may be part of an HL or immigrant community, rarely have we been shown how to teach students to interact with local language communities and L2 speakers. Essential practices and reflection about CBL in the L2 are not necessarily included in methodology courses or graduate programs. As a result, we teach from our gut, but also from our personal experience. For this reason, it is crucial that we consider our training, our experiences, and the assumptions we make every day when we make our lesson plans, interact with students, and assess their work.

As teachers, we must carefully consider assumptions about who our students are and what experiences they bring with them, assumptions about the communities within which we work, and assumptions about the ways in which a language should be taught. And we also need to consider how a language is—and should be—spoken; what kinds of input students may have already had—and should be exposed to; and what kinds of registers are appropriate in written communication. These beliefs about language proficiency will affect how we assess our students, as will ideas of which students are "good at" the L2. If we want to include HL learners into our classrooms, for instance, we must be more aware and inclusive of linguistic variants. Most of all, we need be honest with ourselves about what we mean when we imagine a successful language learner.

In chapter 2 we explored the student learning outcomes that researchers report for a variety of demographic student groups. In summary, CBLL has benefits for all students. Of particular interest to this conversation is that HLLs experience increased self-esteem and better outcomes than L2 learners in the areas of problem solving and dialogic communication. DuBord and Kimball's (2016, 304) work problematizes the design of CBL in L2 courses that either fail to attract or even actively exclude HLLs. They note that "gains in proficiency, acquired by the privileged English monolingual student, can become instrumentalized, even fetishized rationales for CBL in Spanish that exclude HLLs and perpetuate a white, monolingualist model of educational achievement." HLLs are well positioned to leverage their cultural and linguistic capital in diverse ways. Rather than perpetuating unequal power dynamics in world language education, educators should consider how to design courses to activate appropriate learning outcomes for all students.

In addition to considering who we teach, we must also question what and how we teach. Teaching itself is a value-laden process, and the teaching of and for social justice is especially so. As Ayers (1998, xvii) writes, "Teaching for social justice demands a dialectical stance: one eye firmly fixed on the students—Who are they? What are their hopes, dreams, and aspirations? Their passions and commitments? What skills, abilities, and capacities, does each one bring to the classroom?—and the other eye looking unblinkingly at the concentric circles of context—historical flow, cultural surround, economic reality. Teaching for social justice is teaching that arouses students, engages them in a quest to identify obstacles."

Embarking on a critical pedagogy of social justice in the language classroom is by its very nature a confrontational practice. CBLL's critical pedagogy invites us to identify, problematize, and work toward the dismantling of structures that create and sustain inequality. This confrontational practice can feel disturbing to language educators. It makes us feel vulnerable and opens us up to criticism. Are we speaking for the community rather than including their voices? By advocating for heritage languages, are we being paternalistic? Are we "doing it wrong?" All these questions and more surface in our CBLL work because educators represent voices of authority with power and influence. Working closely with colleagues and being open to problematizing and challenging norms will help ensure evolution in classrooms and even departments. Educators might have a steep learning curve when reconsidering how language curriculum intertwines with social change, but that should not dissuade us from the challenge.

Reflections for Instructors

1. *Instructor privilege.* Examine your own set of privileges. Which are visible, and which are invisible? Can you choose to hide these privileges, or are they visible to the eye? How might these manifest in the classroom, and in community partnerships?

2. *Instructor training.* How did your own teacher training address the role of your identity in the classroom? How might your identity (race, sex, ethnicity, generation, socioeconomic status, sexual orientation, gender identity, religion, etc.) be perceived by your students, both positively and negatively? What resources are and are not available to you because of your identity?

3. *The imaginary ideal student.* What does a successful language student look like to you? Imagine this person. How does he or she look, speak, and write? Consider their accent, and the grammatical accuracy and lexical breadth of their speech. Now consider how this image might affect your expectations and also how each of your students can or cannot fit into this imaginary role.

4. *Macrocontextualization.* How might Osborn's definition of macrocontextualization be implemented in your school? Definition: Language learning always occurs within a context, one that takes into account the local, regional, national, and global contexts in which the programs are situated.

THE POWER OF VOICE

As CBLL educators, we have a responsibility to bring our students' attention to the ways that voices can be uplifted, marginalized, and co-opted. Discussions of how individuals access power through language are critical to understanding the roles that teachers, students, and communities occupy in CBLL environments. Linda Alcoff's (1992, 29) article "The Problem of Speaking for Others" is a useful starting point for such discussions. As she writes, "The practice of speaking for others is often born of a desire for mastery, to privilege oneself as the one who more correctly understands the truth about another's situation

Reflections for Instructors

1. *Inclusion guidelines.* What kinds of guidelines might help teachers and students avoid "speaking for others" and instead include community voices? Consider the scenarios given in table 4.2 and provide concrete examples of how to be proactive in including partners.

TABLE 4.2

Project or practice	Guiding principles for inclusion of voices
Photography exhibit documenting immigration	*Example:* Photos are taken not by students but by local immigrants. *Example:* Reception includes university and community members and asks community members to speak, with translation offered
Roundtable presentation on immigration and law	
Website that features stories of resettlement	
Potluck dinner at retirement home	
Soccer game at local park	

2a. *Pairing students.* An advanced Spanish for Entrepreneurship course with a CBLL component is made up of 50 percent L2 learners and 50 percent HL students. Students work in pairs and are partnered with local Latino/a businesses. They help design websites, translate signage, and consult on marketing. As the course instructor, you need to pair students together on the project. Will you pair HLs with L2 learners, or will you keep the groups separate? Consider the advantages and disadvantages of each scenario.

2b. *Challenges to pairing.* Now that you have chosen your pairings, make a clear list of any challenges that might arise. If you chose L2 + HL pairing, what if your L2 student lets the HL student do all the talking? How might you be able to address this challenge? What kinds of activities can help keep this from happening, or help students process this possible outcome?

or as one who can champion a just cause and thus achieve glory and praise. And the effect of the practice of speaking for others is often, though not always, erasure and a reinscription of sexual, national, and other kinds of hierarchies." Her interrogation of motive also points to the dangerous and unintended consequences of these practices. In the context of CBLL, her words remind us to consider how we represent the work we do in partnership with the community, at the university, and in the community at large. When we plan project-based work in the community, we must consider how we can include our community partners in our work from the beginning. Projects that invite collaboration can offer a voice to others without speaking for them. We explore this idea further in chapter 6.

Activities for Students

1. *Bienvenue (welcome)?* Plantu's 2006 cartoon "Bienvenue" offers a simple, yet profound critique of immigration practices. To develop visual literacy, distribute or project the cartoon. Students should first describe details of what they see (a migrant or refugee), how they know this (he is carrying a suitcase, and his clothes are tattered), and then use these details to build meaning (although the door is open and there is a welcome mat, the wall indicates that the host country may not really be welcoming or that there are structural barriers to entry). This activity can be done as a class discussion or as a writing prompt.

2. *Culture bump* (http://culturebump.com/student-workbook-culture-bumps/). In this activity, students watch a video and think about lifestyle and hospitality in the United States and the Middle East. Ask students to evaluate the effectiveness of their own intercultural and interpersonal interactions. Practice the skills to predict, self-reflect, compare, visualize, evaluate, and synthesize.

3. *Sanctuary and refuge.* Assign students to review media, websites, and testimonials connected to the sanctuary movement. Explore issues of power and identity on your campus by asking students to examine the mission of Every Campus A Refuge (http://everycampusarefuge.net/), an organization that challenges campuses to support the resettlement of at least one refugee family. Ask students to fill in table 4.3 after they research how their campus would embrace this challenge. This activity could be modified to analyze the perspectives of the community at large.

TABLE 4.3

Identify various points of view regarding sanctuary cities/churches/campuses.	
Describe how this program fits (or does not fit) within the values and culture of your campus	
Who has the power of contributing to or enacting this program?	
List possible motivations for participating in or to resisting this program?	

4. *New eyes.* Choose a picture that connects with students' community experience, such as a photograph of businesses on Main Street or a public school campus. Instruct them to look at the picture and write down what they see. Next, ask them to look at the picture again and find something they had not noticed before. Finally, ask them to look again and find something they did not see the first two times. What had they missed at first? Why? How does this relate to what they are learning in their experience? (See https://sites.duke.edu/responsibleengagement/files/2015/04/Reflection-Activities-for-All-Classrooms.pdf.)

5. *Citizenship and naturalization.* Ask students to assume the role of someone going through the naturalization process. Students should study for the English and civics tests by reviewing the information on the US government's citizenship website (www.uscis.gov/citizenship/learners/study-test). In a subsequent class, give students 10 of the questions from the website's 100 civic test questions (www.uscis.gov/citizenship/teachers/educational-products/100-civics-questions-and-answers-mp3-audio-english-version). Students with 6 or more correct answers pass the test.

(*continued*)

Now, ask students to discuss the following questions with a partner:

- Why would someone choose to become a US citizen?
- Is knowledge of both English and civics a necessity for naturalization?
- How does citizenship affect life in the United States? Should identity defined by citizenship have an impact on access to services and protections of human rights?
- What power systems are in play within the naturalization process? Does legislation like Deferred Action for Childhood Arrivals create second-class citizens?

A variation of this activity can include the use of the N-400 Application for Naturalization Form (www.uscis.gov/n-400). After students review the information requested on this form and the oath of allegiance, have them discuss their observations.

6. *English only.* Students read the following excerpt from James Crawford's (2001) article in *The Guardian* about the perceptions of language use in the United States, either in class or as homework:

> As the linguist Einar Haugen observes, "America's profusion of tongues has made her a modern Babel, but a Babel in reverse." There is no reason to think the historic pattern has changed. Although the number of minority language speakers has grown dramatically in recent years, thanks to a liberalisation of immigration laws in 1965, so has their rate of acculturation. Census figures confirm the paradox. While one in seven US residents now speaks a language other than English at home, bilingualism is also on the rise. A century ago the proportion of non–English speakers was nearly five times as large. As the population becomes increasingly diverse, newcomers seem to be acquiring the national language more rapidly than ever before.
>
> The political problem is that many Americans have trouble believing all this. One conservative organisation claims: "Tragically, many immigrants these days refuse to learn English! They never become productive members of society. They remain stuck in a linguistic and economic ghetto, many living off welfare and costing working Americans millions of tax dollars every year."
>
> Such perceptions are not uncommon. Perhaps this is because Americans who came of age before the 1970s had little experience of linguistic diversity. Growing up in a period of tight immigration quotas, they seldom encountered anyone speaking a language other than English, except foreign tourists.

Form small groups and have students either discuss or write down answers to the following questions. Additional research could be conducted by having students review studies from the Pew Research Center (www.pewresearch.org):

- What evidence do you see in your community that the United States is "a Babel in reverse" or that "immigrants refuse to learn English"?
- What are the various points of view regarding the desire to declare English as the official language in the United States?
- How does language affect interactions with the police, schools, and social services (among other public institutions)?
- Where do you encounter people speaking a language other than English? Are there multilingual media sources (newspapers, television, radio) in your area?

Student orientations for CBLL should include these ethical concerns about appropriation of community voice. Students should be reminded not to co-opt personal information about others—not posting photos on social media showing off their "good work," not sharing the personal details of their work in exploitative ways, and being aware of minors and their legal rights. These seemingly inconsequential behaviors not only display disrespect for the individual with whom they have a trusted relationship but also reflect other forms of dominance, which we examine in chapter 6. An example of how this might manifest in CBLL is if students in our refugee partnerships are asked for help in translating documents, writing letters, or scheduling appointments in English. Although it is tempting to help and would certainly save time, this approach is counterproductive because it does not empower the community member's voice. If the goal of working with refugee populations is to help them develop English proficiency and foster independence, then this kind of linguistic "help" does not enable the individual to develop his or her language skills in any meaningful way, especially because the student's commitment concludes at the end of the semester. Such "help" is merely a quick fix that cements an existing power dynamic. In this situation, the student could instead role-play the telephone call with their partner to practice the vocabulary and expressions needed to complete the task successfully. Students can be very successful developing these kinds of activities and generally can lead them independently.

In another example, students of Spanish were partnered with local multigenerational Latino/a families. Rather than interviewing the families only one time and creating an outward-facing deliverable, such as a Web page of recorded histories, students met regularly with the families over the course of the semester, sharing meals and conversation. Families shared stories of their immigration to the United States and photographs of their children and grandchildren. Together, they created an album that was archived in the local library and was also given to the family. In this exchange, we see how the individual is listened to and not spoken for.

We must also consider the many ways that our speech may be interpreted in the community and beyond. Evoking Foucault's reminder that power is diffuse, Alcoff (1992, 26, 32) writes, "One cannot simply look at the location of the speaker or her credentials to speak; nor can one look merely at the propositional content of the speech; one must also look at where the speech goes and what it does there." Given the popularity of community engagement in higher education at this moment, including the ways in which CBL is commodified, we should be especially careful to consider how, as educators, we occupy a very privileged position. This position grants us the immediate status to speak, and though this platform might seem to be a positive way to draw attention to social inequity or health disparities, it may also be at the expense of the individual who is spoken about and who remains silenced. Where we speak (on or off campus) and with whom we speak (campus or local community) will also help us consider Alcoff's final question, one we must ask whenever we speak for others: "Will it [my speaking] enable the empowerment of oppressed peoples?"

CONCLUSION

In this chapter, we have examined the intersectionality of identity, language, and power. By problematizing the categorization of language communities, we highlight the need for educators to consider the social, political, and historical contexts of language use and identity construction. Personal explorations of identity and explicit study of power relationships provide ways for students to deconstruct assumptions about themselves and their communities. Through discussions of power and privilege in the CBLL curriculum, language study can embody themes connected to social change.

CHAPTER 5

Dissonance, Resistance, and Transformative Learning

By the end of this chapter, readers will be able to:

- Explain Mezirow's and Kiely's theories of transformative learning
- Recognize dissonance that leads to transformation
- Examine situations in which unhealthy dissonance endangers students
- Identify common triggers of resistance and dissonance for students and teachers
- Implement strategies for supporting transformative student learning

TRANSFORMATION AND REFLECTION

This chapter examines the student's transformative learning process in CBLL, including various triggers that can spark transformation. Throughout our exploration, we consider the readiness of the individual student to engage in these critical moments. As Sorrells (2016, 234–35) states, "Today the rapid and increasing movement of people; demographic shifts in neighborhoods, schools, and workplaces; as well as local and international events can and do prod people from their comfort zones." He explains that twenty-first-century intercultural competence demands that "individuals and groups are motivated and take the initiative to engage with people who are different from themselves, recognizing both the challenges and benefits of intercultural interactions, relationships, and alliances." Transformative relationships challenge students' moral, political, intellectual, personal, cultural, and spiritual perspectives and lead to transformation in perspectives, one of the primary goals of CBLL (Kiely 2004, 2005; Eyler and Giles 1999).

Student reflections can reveal to us how CBLL transforms their thinking. In the following example, a student who participated in a Spanish language service-learning course explains how her interactions with the community were personally transformative:

> One of the goals of this class was to access, not only academic knowledge, but also gather information outside the realm of what is considered to be conventionally "educational." As I have matured as a person, I have begun to recognize the vast amounts of wisdom that both the individuals around me and their experiences have to offer. The amazing variety of worldviews and experiences is a valuable resource in which no education would be complete without. This class has taught me to transform empathy into social consciousness and action. And as a result these lessons in civics have become apart of my philosophy on life. (Marisa, final reflection essay translated from Spanish, 2006)

This student describes the importance of her experiences in the service site as a way to supplement "conventionally 'educational'" materials. She states that through the CBLL course she was able to consider a different way of thinking about the world and embrace the importance of social consciousness and action. Although not all students are as eloquent in their reflections, many have shared with us similar transformative experiences. This chapter explores how CBLL supports transformative learning through individual growth and relationship-building.

TRANSFORMATIVE LEARNING

Mezirow (2012, 76) defines transformative learning as "the process by which we transform our taken-for-granted frames of reference (meaning perspectives, habits of mind, mind-sets) to make them more inclusive, discriminating, open, emotionally capable of change, and reflective so that they may generate beliefs and opinions that will prove more true or justified to guide action." Mezirow calls this "perspective transformation," relating it to "personal transformation and growth, where the unit of analysis is primarily the individual, with little attention given to the role of context and social change in the transformative experience" (Taylor 2009, 5). This emphasis on critical reflection distinguishes him from Freire, whose understanding of transformation highlights political consciousness and consciousness-raising. For both scholars, however, reflection and dialogue play key roles in the process, although Mezirow goes further in his elaboration of the role of reflection, articulating specific processes that shape transformation (1990, 2009):

1. A disorienting dilemma
2. Self-examination
3. A critical assessment of assumptions
4. Recognition of a connection between one's discontent and the process of transformation
5. Exploration of options for new roles, relationships, and action
6. Planning a course of action
7. Acquiring knowledge and skills for implementing one's plan
8. Provisional trying of new roles
9. Building competence and self-confidence in new roles and relationships
10. A reintegration into one's life on the basis of conditions dictated by one's new perspective

As shown in this list, transformation is a growth process that does not happen overnight. It involves critical thought and consideration of the self, as well as active planning and repeated practice.

According to Mezirow, it is the *disorienting dilemma* that most often serves as the trigger for transformative learning. Kiely (2005, 7) defines the disorienting dilemma as "a critical incident or event that acts as a trigger that can, under certain conditions (i.e., opportunities for reflection and dialogue, openness to change, etc.), lead people to engage in a transformational learning process whereby previously taken-for-granted assumptions, values, beliefs, and lifestyle habits are assessed and, in some cases, radically transformed." The cognitive dissonance that accompanies triggering events can provide the necessary push for intellectual and personal development (Bowman 2011; Bowman and Brandenberger 2012; Diaz and Perrault 2010; Gurin et al. 2002; Hudson and Hunter 2014; Richard et al. 2016). We return to the concept of dissonance later in this chapter.

One critique of Mezirow's framework of transformative learning is that it does not acknowledge the emotional aspects of transformative learning. Grain and Lund (2016, 50) explain that CBL often stirs up strong emotions, stating that "there is little doubt that service-learning has the capacity to be an emotional journey in which participants, including students, community partners, host communities, faculty, staff, and others, may encounter varying types of difference and are necessarily put in position to question their own ontologies, ethics, and ways of knowing."

Educators are sometimes at a loss as to how to unpack the emotions that crop up in CBLL, whether they be surprise, fear, joy, or anger. This may be because the classroom is often understood as an intellectual space of emotional neutrality. Teachers (and students) may believe that emotions belong to the private realm, rather than the public sphere; others may have concerns about conflating education and emotion. The desire to keep emotions at a distance in the classroom may also be tied to "emotional hegemony," defined by the philosopher Allison Jaggar as "the phenomenon by which certain emotions are deemed epistemically valued while others are judged suspect or ineffective" (quoted by Langstraat and Bowden 2011, 5). Because these phenomena are socially constructed and embedded in race, gender, and class politics, it is important to question how we respond to emotion in the classroom. As we bring attention to our comfort level with expressing our own emotions in the classroom, we must also consider our students' reactions. If students perceive that a conversation or a written prompt is "touchy-feely" (e.g., "Please describe a moment when you felt confused or scared in your CBLL experience"), they may resist and avoid exploring or disclosing their feelings. We should therefore consider alternative and varied ways to support students by offering them the opportunity to process difficult feelings through critical reflection.

One part of this conversation is how we define and identify *compassion* and *empathy*. As Langstraat and Bowden (2011, 6–7) have written, too often in service learning, the emotions of empathy and compassion "are under-theorized or uncritically characterized as unmitigated goods and automatic outcomes." The authors present an important distinction between compassion and empathy. Compassion, they write, is "usually more intense and entails both judgment and action, unlike empathy, which may result only in a judgment (e.g., 'I feel bad for that person' vs. 'I feel bad because this is unjust and I am going to act to change that injustice'). Hence, while both compassion and empathy require the capacity for fellow-feeling, compassion demands forms of ethical appraisal and action not necessarily inherent to the feeling of empathy." When discussing service learning, Langstraat and Bowden prefer to use the concept of compassion because it "includes identification with other humans, an evaluation of injustice and suffering, and ethical actions in response to that evaluation." They do warn, however, that compassion can easily mask unequal power relations, so practitioners must be careful. In some cases, for instance, compassion can end up reaffirming ethical or moral superiority of the (privileged) person feeling compassion. A tutor who feels compassion for a struggling student may also feel sorry for them because of their lack of access to resources, reinforcing unstated perceptions of privilege and superiority.

Reflections for Instructors

Disorienting Dilemmas. What kinds of disorienting dilemmas have you or your students encountered (or would imagine encountering) in community-based learning environments? How did you support this situation, if you did? How can critical reflection be used in these cases?

KIELY'S TRANSFORMATIONAL SERVICE-LEARNING PROCESS MODEL

Based on Mezirow's work, Kiely's (2005, 8) Transformational Service-Learning Process Model identifies key triggers for transformative learning, all of which we include in CBLL. In this model, five categories describe how students experience transformative learning within service learning: contextual border crossing, dissonance, personalizing, processing, and connecting. *Contextual border crossing* challenges students' framing of personal, structural, historical, and programmatic factors in service-learning experiences. Robb Jones, Robbins, and LePeau (2011) liken this border crossing to Giroux's (1992, 136) notion of border pedagogy that "decenters as it remaps" (quoted by Robb Jones, Robbins, and LePeau 2011, 35). It is especially important to consider differences in student identity because one student's borders are not necessarily the same as another's, resulting in different reactions and different ways of processing experiences. Students who are not crossing borders—because they belong to the community with which they are interacting—may need to be supported by different reflection prompts than those designed for border crossers (Carracelas-Juncal 2013). Robb Jones, Robbins, and LePeau (2011, 38) suggest that when students engage in this process over a more extended time period, they better navigate the "remapping process." Later in this chapter, we discuss how the length of immersion affects students' experience.

Dissonance, the second category in Kiely's (2005, 8) model, is the "incongruence between participants' prior frame of reference and aspects of the contextual factors that shape the service-learning experience." Kiely distinguishes between the impact of different types of dissonance, observing that low-level dissonance leads to "forms of learning that further adaptation" but intense-level dissonance "continues to instigate ongoing learning and is shaped by both internal factors (the psychological impact) and external forces (dominant cultural ideologies, social relations, and institutional arrangements)" (Kiely 2005, 15).

Unlike Mezirow, Kiely (2005, 15) recognizes the need to anticipate the emotional and cognitive responses of students. He pays particular attention to the emotional side in the process of *personalizing*, which he defines as "how participants individually respond to and learn from different types of dissonance." It is through this emotional reaction that students can assess internal strengths and weaknesses. He underscores the importance of supporting varied emotional responses that are triggered by different types of dissonance (Kiely 2005, 8, 16).

Processing, the fourth process in Kiely's (2005, 8) model, is defined as "an individual reflective learning process and a social, dialogic learning process." Kiely outlines the importance of critical reflection in transformative learning, stating that transformation "is more apt to occur and persist over the long term if there are structured opportunities for participants to engage in reflective (i.e., processing) and nonreflective (i.e., personalizing and connecting) learning processes with peers, faculty, and community members" (Kiely 2005, 17).

Connecting is the learning process "to affectively understand and empathize through relationships with community members, peers, and faculty" (Kiely 2005, 8). It highlights the important role of affect, the body, and emotions in transformative learning (Belenky and Stanton 2000; Kiely 2005; Taylor 2000; Yorks and Kasl 2002). This echoes the previous reference to emotional hegemony and the differences between compassion and empathy. Each educator will need to devise a path by which to incorporate appropriate support for "connecting." Strategies associated with mindfulness, such as yoga and meditation, are possible avenues to explore, as are group meals and other shared experiences.

So how does transformation present in CBLL? Gravatt and Petersen (2009, 107) explain that "to facilitate transformative learning, educators need to create the conditions under which learners are pushed toward their learning edge, where they are challenged and encouraged toward critical reflection." At their learning edge in CBLL, students should learn to dialogue across difference, whether that difference be linguistic, racial, economic, sexual, or otherwise. Here is an excerpt from a final reflection paper written by a student who enrolled in a service-learning course in Spanish and who worked on a research project for a high school ESL coordinator:

> This semester, I have entered a world that I did not understand and I barely knew existed. I decided to take this class because issues in education, particularly, are so near and dear to my heart since as a young Latino male, I realize how lucky I am to have parents that pushed me to be the best I could and I found the right programs with the right resources to get me to where I am today. However, I did not stop to think about the limits of my experience. . . . It was not part of my experience to deal with kids arriving at middle or even high school ages, knowing no English.

> I could not fathom what it would be like to immigrate to a hostile racial environment like [here] with no network similar to that which exists in multiethnic, immigrant-centric cities such as New York, Miami, and Los Angeles. I expected to see similar issues upon entering this course and my service learning project at [the] high school that I had in my life and work in New York City, . . . students with little motivation, young people tempted by gangs and drugs, guys playing dice outside the school, girls who find themselves pregnant at age fourteen, fifteen. I was right—these issues did exist at [this school]. However, what shattered my perception were the other things—fifteen- and sixteen-year-olds who could barely read in Spanish, much less in English; students who had crossed the border just weeks before entering the classroom; a class filled with twenty teenagers with blank stares on their faces—not because they don't understand earth science—but because they can't even understand the language it is being taught in. For the majority of the Latino students at [this] High School—this is reality, and it blindsided me. . . . If it isn't clear enough already, I admit that I gained a tremendous amount from this course and that the experience truly humbled me. . . . For someone as passionate as I am about education and the issues surrounding it, it astounded me to realize how little I really knew. The biggest thing that I experienced and I am so thankful to have seen first hand is the issue of sheltered-content courses and the process of acquiring English as a second language in an American public high school. (Richard, final paper written in English, 2006)

Richard's transformative learning seems to have been shaped by border crossing, dissonance, personalizing, processing, and connecting, which are all present in his reflection.

Still, not all students will experience the kind of transformation that Richard outlines here. In fact, we should not make any assumptions that students will undergo significant transformation during or after one course in CBLL. Although this particular student was strongly impacted by the service-learning component of his course, not all students will be as committed, open, or ready to face the issues that he embraced. Setting high expectations for transformative learning needs to be tempered by the realities of diverse student identities, individual abilities to process the experience, and concepts as seemingly mundane as time. Robb Jones, Robbins, and LePeau (2011) indicate from their own research, and that of Camacho (2004) and Kiely (2004; 2005, 38–39), that "a sustained service-learning experience is needed to produce truly transformative outcomes." In the space of a fifteen-week semester, during which time students are engaged in many other activities, we may need to temper our expectations. These scholars outline the tenuousness of developmental gains given the complexities of maintaining connectedness to the experience, especially once students return to their normal routine or take on other new projects. We must also keep this in mind as we design rubrics to assess our assignments. Success should not be defined as having had a transformative experience but as having engaged in the process.

Reflections for Instructors

Identifying Transformation. Identify the five categories of transformation in Richard's reflection. Where do you see border crossing, dissonance, personalizing, processing, and connecting in his story?

RECOGNIZING DISSONANCE

When students encounter uncomfortable situations in CBLL, they experience dissonance: a conflict or tension that results from their engagement (or lack of engagement) with their peers, their instructor, or their community partners. Dissonance arises when there is tension within a relationship or a clash of viewpoints. It may manifest inwardly, when students feel internally conflicted, and it may arise in relationship, when students do not see eye to eye on an issue, either with their peers, their instructor, or their community partners. It may also be linguistic in nature, reflecting challenges related to register and basic communication (Can the student and community partner understand each other?) or to content-specific word choice (Can parties agree on a shared vocabulary, such as appropriate terms for designating immigration status?). Whatever form the dissonance takes, we want to be clear that dissonance is common, that it is not indicative of a failure, and that it does not mark the end of the relationship. Rather, moments of dissonance offer us opportunities to learn from and engage more deeply with ourselves and our partners. Dissonance is a necessary step in the process of transformative learning. According to Mezirow (2003), disorienting dilemmas can be catalysts for shifting our perspectives, particularly when combined with critical reflection and rational discourse. The disequilibrium that students experience offers an opportunity to rethink assumptions and beliefs and to experience transformation, whether that be incremental or epochal (Mezirow and Associates 2000). Giles (2014), however, questions the claim that high intensity dissonance catalyzes ongoing learning, noting that her students became more entrenched in their original political views when challenged to confront new perspectives. Her findings (Giles 2014, 74), that "students' responses to high intensity dissonance of a political or social nature may depend on their personal biographies, and the social and political views of their support networks," corroborate the work by Baumgartner (2012) and Taylor (2009). This finding reminds us not only that context and relationships have a great impact on transformative learning but also that we need to scaffold appropriate support for the variety of learners in our courses, rather than assuming that dissonance will necessarily lead to transformation.

The following example shows how one student processed the dissonance she experienced after a disorienting dilemma. Judith, a Latina student enrolled in a Spanish service-learning course, worked as a teacher's assistant at a local high school, helping newly arrived Spanish-speaking immigrants adjust to the American educational system. One afternoon when she showed up at her volunteer placement, one of the students was missing. When Judith learned that the student had been deported, she was moved to tears. In her final essay, she described her overall experience in the class, focusing on how this particular moment changed the way she thinks about her life:

> Although I knew exactly what to expect, in retrospect, my experience at [the school] was very humbling. The struggles and obstacles that these kids face before they reach the age of eighteen are things that no teenager should have to go through. Although I have always known that I was one of the fortunate ones that immigrated when I was only seven years old, I never realized how hard it can be for a teenager to suddenly find himself in a new country, and a new culture. My experience at [the school] has personally made me even more grateful that my parents brought me to this country at a very early age. Although the things that my family has gone through, and my personal struggles are extremely hard, they are nothing compared to what some of these kids have already gone through. (Judith, final reflection essay written in English, 2016)

This perspective transformation would not have transpired through in-class activities. It was through CBLL that Judith experienced a disorienting dilemma and was pushed to her learning edge, where she engaged in critical reflection that led her to reconsider her previous understandings. Her relationship with the high school students had an emotional impact on her, and the gratefulness and humility she expressed are an important—and, in our experience, common—part of this process.

ORIGINS OF RESISTANCE AND DISSONANCE

Student resistance will manifest in distinct ways. Different profiles of resistance to service experiences that introduce us to the basic behaviors of this common reaction are presented by Jones, Gilbride-Brown, and Gasiorski (2005); Hill-Jackson and Lewis (2011); and Jacoby (2015). There are students who are very helpful at the service sites, but they fail to engage in the work of critical thinking; they are labeled "passive resisters," "good volunteers," or those involved in "service-*loitering.*" Some of these students prioritize contact with the "served" as a way to feel good about themselves. "Politely frustrated volunteers" recognize some of the external power and privilege issues inherent in CBL, but they remain locked in their own perspectives. Such students are generally passive in their resistance, and they remain unwilling or uninterested in questioning their worldview in a serious manner. "Active resister volunteers," conversely, are confrontational in their resistance. They argue and defend their version of the "truth," often dismissing other perspectives. They might be stuck in the mentality of blaming the victim, believing that the community member is responsible for his or her situation. Jones, Gilbride-Brown, and Gasiorski (2005, 4) suggest using a critical developmental lens that pulls from the theoretical frameworks of self-authorship and critical whiteness (an exploration of socially constructed power of white identifications and interests) to try and break through to those students. Monitoring these behaviors is paramount to maintaining good relationships with the community. When we look specifically at contact with L2 communities and remind students that they are not hegemonic groups but are composed of individuals with differing viewpoints and perspectives, these encounters will inspire divergent responses from students.

Dissonance arises because of challenges to worldviews, behaviors, assumptions, beliefs, and more. Dissonance can even arise when a CBLL student is motivated by earning an A in a course and does not adequately understand the community commitment as a central component of the academic experience. One major source of dissonance is when assumptions are made without knowledge of the cultures in play. For example, when students experience polychronic approaches to time that allow for interruptions and do not value punctuality, they complain that their partner is "late" to their meetings. Or when a partner is not focused on completing an ESL lesson, students express frustration that they are unable to complete their scheduled tasks. Some students who engage in CBLL may experience the equivalent of a reverse culture shock. Although they are not abroad, they experience their country or community in a new way, as they had not seen it before. They may have ignored social inequities, poverty,

Activities for Students

Cultural Differences. Provide the following list of twelve cultural contrast sets to your students. Ask them to write for 5 minutes and identify examples of which cultural differences they might encounter when working with local language communities and L2 speakers. Give them 10 minutes to discuss their ideas in small groups and then debrief as an entire class. In table 5.1, provide examples of these cultural norms before the activity as needed.

TABLE 5.1

INDIVIDUAL Individualism	GROUP Collectivism
COMPETITION Independence	COOPERATION Interdependence
TIME = MONEY Time is limited	TIME = LIFE Time is abundant
TASK-CENTERED Activity/doing	PERSON-CENTERED Relationships/being
FRANKNESS Directness	HARMONY Indirectness
EQUALITY Egalitarian	HIERARCHY Hierarchical
LOW CONTEXT Information given	HIGH CONTEXT Information understood
INFORMALITY Warmth and Equality	FORMALITY Respect for Age and Status
SELF-DETERMINATION Control over life	FATALISM Subject to fate
CHANGE Future oriented	TRADITION Past/history oriented
MATERIALISM Acquisition = success	SPIRITUALITY Success = spiritual growth
YOUTH ORIENTATION Value youth	HONOR ELDERS Respect ancestors and elders

Source: www2.pacific.edu/sis/culture/.

racial discrimination, and language enclaves before the class, or they may not have interrogated the systems that produce them in critical ways. They might find that the individuals with whom they interact in the community hold different values and practices than what they expect. When educators make explicit the different cultural values and behaviors of all stakeholders, they can provide fertile material for critical reflection that helps students unpack these feelings and reactions.

Another important aspect of understanding the origins of resistance and dissonance lies in recognizing what is developmentally appropriate for young adulthood. Because the human brain does not reach maturity until the mid-twenties, many students are still testing boundaries and experimenting with new behaviors and values. The development of critical thinking, emotional regulation, relationships, appreciation for diverse views, risk-taking, decision making, and a greater capacity for self-evaluation are still under way in young adults.

Because dissonance and resistance originate from many different sources, educators must examine explicit curricular content (e.g., readings that may only give one perspective), hidden practices in the classroom that may perpetuate inequalities (e.g., gender or racial bias), and student beliefs about communities (e.g., stereotypes or misconceptions). The role of the educator in the classroom and in the community is complicated. As Jones, Gilbride-Brown, and Gasiorski (2005, 18) remind us, "Given the developmental readiness of many students and the role of external forces in self-authoring, it is important for service-learning educators to remind themselves of the power and responsibility that comes with serving as an authoring figure in students' lives." For these reasons, it is paramount for educators *and* students to practice appropriate critical reflection that examines institutional and social relations and structures. Considering that people usually find it easier to critique other people's behaviors than their own, we suggest developing specific activities aimed at sustained self-reflection.

UNHEALTHY DISSONANCE

This chapter develops many examples of healthy dissonance that provide opportunities for transformative learning. We must acknowledge, however, the existence of unhealthy dissonance. Educators should monitor for dissonance triggered by unsafe situations or inappropriate behaviors. When students are put in dangerous situations, it requires immediate communication and swift intervention. When community partners are put at risk because of inappropriate actions from students, students need to be held accountable. We present specific strategies to establish productive lines of communication between students, faculty, community partners, and community members later in this chapter, but we wish to underscore that clear expectations, guidelines of behaviors, and reporting mechanisms between all parties need to be in place from the beginning of the partnership. Chapter 6 provides more detailed practices for establishing ethical relationships with the community, providing models of necessary conversations that help establish appropriate ground rules and guidelines for behaviors. In order to underscore the need for monitoring these types of problems, let us look at a few examples.

The first example details a harassment situation created by a community member. Alejandra and Frankie, two students enrolled in a CBLL French course, were assigned to assist a newly resettled refugee family with learning English and acclimating to their new community. After several meetings, the male figure in the family began to text inappropriate content to the students (salacious photos and inappropriate language). The students were startled but did not immediately communicate this situation to the professor or the community organization. When they forwarded the content to the professor several weeks later, she spoke directly with the community organization, and the students were told to discontinue the relationship; the organization would follow up with the man. The students explained their hesitation in reporting the incident as not wanting to judge the behavior, not being confident that they understood the motivations of the man, and not wanting to jeopardize the agency's assistance to the family. They were not comfortable drawing the line at unacceptable behavior or even knowing how to advocate for themselves. Other situations in which students encounter risks include navigating unsafe neighborhoods or working unmonitored or without a partner. Educators must discuss appropriate boundaries and safe practices in order to properly guide students. Students should not give rides to community members, provide personal contact information (unless clear boundaries are established), give gifts to community members, or be alone with community members.

This second example shows how inappropriate student behavior can have a negative impact on a community organization. Eric, a student in a service-learning course, showed up at his placement site smelling of marijuana. This would be problematic in any service situation, but because his service site was a drug rehabilitation center, it was particularly egregious. The volunteer coordinator asked him to leave immediately and told him not to return. The professor struggled to decide if this student should be offered another service placement or if Eric should receive no credit for the service-learning component of the course grade. In the end, the professor reassigned the student to another local organization, but a penalty was applied to his grade. The lack of maturity of this one student did not have a lasting negative impact on the partnership between other students and the organization, but obviously trust needed to be rebuilt. The privileged and destructive behaviors of students can damage partnerships, so educators must maintain regular check-ins with community members and organizations in order to promote open communication. Students also need to understand that there are consequences for inappropriate behaviors.

The last example is related to the consequences of learning about child abuse in a family with whom students are interacting. During a family home visit, Malik, a CBLL student, noticed bruises on the arms and torso of one of the children. The child told him that she had been beaten by her uncle. Malik reported the incident immediately to his professor and to the community organization that sponsored assistance to the family. The community organization took the lead on reporting the incident to the proper authorities. Malik continued to work with the family while the case was being investigated by child services. Malik found the experience very unsettling; and at the end of the semester, he said that he would not be continuing with this type of service in the future. Educators should remember that because abuse, harassment, and other criminal behaviors exist in our society students may also encounter them in community interactions. Educators need to identify proper channels for reporting these behaviors to the authorities and for identifying counseling for students. It is recommended that educators discuss with campus officials whether the campus police or local police are the appropriate first responders in these types of situations. Educators, campus officials, and community organizations should work together to provide students with clear guidelines for how to report criminal behavior.

Although we hope that no one is faced with these types of challenges, educators are obligated to communicate that students might encounter unsafe or inappropriate behaviors in the community. Students need to be supervised by the community organization and/or work in pairs, especially if they are not meeting in a public space (e.g., a community member's home). Students do not always understand when to report an incident or know how to advocate for themselves, so it is helpful to offer consistent and varied reporting measures to help catch such situations; we suggest building into the syllabus field notes, journals, blogs, quick in-class check-ins, full in-class conversations, individual conversations, and reflection essays, among other mechanisms. Educators and community organizations can consider signing a memorandum of understanding when they establish their partnership that outlines safety procedures, appropriate behaviors, and proper reporting guidelines. Chapter 6 develops more ideas on how to build productive and ethical relationships with community organizations.

SUPPORTING STUDENTS THROUGH DISSONANCE AND RESISTANCE

Knowing that dissonance is a natural part of the cycle of interacting with the community, it is essential to strategize how to support students in challenging moments. In order to build trust and create an atmosphere of solidarity with partners, students must also learn to see past the issue and to the individual. To do so, they need to understand underlying issues. When working with refugees, for instance, it is important to lay the groundwork for understanding why and how a person becomes a refugee. This involves teaching students about the historical underpinnings of the current crisis: introducing the international human rights doctrine that was signed just after World War II, reviewing the United Nations High Commission on Refugees' policies and reports, and examining the reasons for instability in certain regions of the world (internal wars, postcolonialism, environmental crises, etc.). Likewise, to understand undocumented workers, students must first understand why people migrate and build an understanding that the decision is neither simple nor easy. When students comprehend why individuals have fled their countries, they have a framework for empathizing with their situations. The resulting compassion can diffuse partisan politics and introduce a new way of thinking about societal realities that have an impact on the human condition. When we teach hot-button political issues, such as these two examples, it is imperative that we provide, supplement, or even replace existing biases with facts; we must also question media and public discourse and listen to the voices of those who are most vulnerable.

Still, each student approaches encounters with the community through his or her own perspectives, making it crucial not only to attend to different triggers of discomfort and conflict but also to scaffold support for different stages of student development. Educators need to consider a wide range of strategies for supporting students that spans coaching and training to reflective practice. In the following section, we outline a number of challenging situations that students, teachers, and community partners may encounter while engaging in CBLL. These examples reflect common triggers that we have come across in the classroom and in our community practice and research. We call upon frameworks of transformative learning and models of critical reflection to provide additional activities that are appropriate to help students process dilemmas and move through dissonance.

Reflections for Instructors

Supporting Students. What situations cause the most anxiety for your students? Do you feel more prepared to respond to dissonance related to linguistic, cultural, or social issues? How will you prepare to support students in all types of disorienting dilemmas?

Activities for Students

Communication Checklist. Ask students to develop a list of best practices for how they will communicate in the classroom and in the community. This could be done in small groups that share their lists after 15 minutes, or it could be a full class exercise with someone keeping notes on the board. Establish that students should include verbal and nonverbal practices, states of mind, behaviors, and the like. If useful, provide students with the following list and have them modify it. Another variation is to require students to come up with examples of situations that demonstrate good and poor communication skills, such as those given in this sample communication checklist:

1. Be honest and sincere.
2. Remove/resist distractions.
3. Be patient.
4. Empathize with the other person.
5. Actively listen, pay attention, listen for key ideas, and thus be present.
6. Be open-minded and defer judgment.
7. Avoid interrupting or getting angry.
8. Judge content, not delivery.
9. Ask questions that cannot be answered with yes, no, or one word. Ask why someone believes what he or she believes. Wait for a pause before asking a question.
10. Provide feedback, and respond appropriately.
11. Check to make sure you understand; paraphrase what the other person says to you.
12. Use nonverbal clues to show that you are engaged: Face the speaker, make eye contact, and keep an open body position.
13. Put the other person at ease by allowing personal space.

COMMUNICATION

When language learners explore politics, power, public consciousness, and civic courage, individual ways of communicating can produce disorienting dilemmas. Because many problems arise from miscommunication or inappropriate comments, it is useful to coach students to improve communication both in the classroom and in the community. Language students are generally very focused on grammatical accuracy and vocabulary acquisition, but sometimes students are not as aware of broader communication skills. For example, one community partner shared that a volunteer university student would regularly arrive at the middle school and ignore the students in the classroom. The volunteer would sit in a different part of the room and remain occupied on his phone until the official time his service hours began. Once the facilitator of the session indicated that it was time to begin the session, the university student then greeted the students and began to interact with them. The lack of natural interaction between the volunteer and the middle school students created tension. The fact that the meeting was more of a performance of hours than an authentic relationship required intervention. The university student was surprised at how the partner perceived his behavior and changed it immediately. Nonverbal behaviors, multiple languages, generational differences, and the like create potential for misunderstandings, so it is important to review expectations early in the CBLL experience.

Students should consider how their actions will affect how they are perceived, and what type of dialogue ensues in the classroom and outside it. Role-plays for how students greet and work with the community are invaluable. Some students are more aware of external perceptions and will be able to help facilitate this conversation. To introduce the conversation about broader communication skills, it is helpful to ask students to generate a list of best practices in communication. Additional ideas for how to improve communication and approach deeper dialogue on difficult issues can be gleaned from many different sources. For example, the American Friends Service Committee has published a Respectful Listening and Dialogue Curriculum, which is intended for high school and beyond. The Sustained Dialogue Institute offers additional resources that support productive communication.

CREATING BRAVE SPACES

It is difficult both to have and to facilitate discussions about controversial or sensitive topics. When we enter into the classroom or the community, we want to feel safe. When we try to engage in difficult conversations, many students and faculty members shy away from the discomfort inherently produced by the challenging topic. To tackle this challenge, some educators routinely establish group behavioral norms in order to build a common understanding of appropriate interactions. The group identifies guidelines, and individuals are expected to adhere to the rules of communication. The researchers Arao and Clemens (2013, 139), however, have called into question this reliance on "safe" spaces. Suggesting that we conflate safety with comfort, they write that "authentic learning about social justice often requires the very qualities of risk, difficulty, and controversy that are defined as incompatible with safety." They explain: "Our approach to initiating social justice dialogue should not be to convince participants that we can remove risk from the equation, for this is simply impossible. Rather, we propose revising our language, shifting away from the concept of safety and emphasizing the importance of bravery instead, to help students better understand—and rise to—the challenges of genuine dialogue on diversity and social justice issues" (Arao and Clemens 2013, 136). The insistence on bravery acknowledges the diversity of views present in a classroom and challenges educators to create an environment in which risk-taking is honored. Bravery will be defined differently for each student, according to factors such as positionality, the individual's developmental stage, the comfort level among peers, and more.

Positive encouragement can help students learn to explore new ways of thinking that straddle contradiction. In leading these discussions, instructors will need to monitor the levels of challenge to student perspectives and intervene as needed. Arao and Clemens suggest that when time allows, it is helpful to have participants develop their own ground rules and then to participate in their continued revision during the discussion. Some recommended common ground rules include (1) agree to disagree, (2) do not take things personally, (3) challenge by choice, (4) respect, and (5) no attacks. Still, it is necessary to think critically about how these rules can help or hinder students in dialogue. If students become complacent in dialogue with difference, dissonance will remain, and the student will not be open to exploring new ways of thinking. Educators not only need to work with students to devise ways of supporting bravery, but they also need to reflect on their own commitment to braving new challenges created in CBLL.

CALLING IN, NOT CALLING OUT

When students confront differences in opinion in the classroom or the community, the educator, a community member, or a classmate might "call out" those expressing a different perspective "to convey that an infraction of some sort has occurred, or to challenge the ideas, opinions, or actions of another person" (Bright and Gambrell 2017, 223). The practice of calling out someone can take on an accusatory, hostile, or challenging tenor due to the heated emotions bubbling up in the conversation, and can result in defensive posturing or matching of hostility. Bright and Gambrell (2017, 224) declare that "in many cases, *calling out* leaves little space for human connection, growth, or cross-cultural connections that are healthy and positive." They in turn recommend the practice of "calling in," which "carries the message of growth, kindness, and connection" and is done in private with the goals of fostering "new learning and understandings, for the betterment of all." While calling out aims to shut down someone, calling in is meant as an invitation to dialogue.

To create a continuous cycle of learning and growth, Stanlick and Sell (2016, 82) propose that we engage in "a constant cycle of re-evaluation of our values, mistakes, and triumphs." It is through praxis (the combination of critical reflection, disorientation, and critical thinking) that we "can cultivate a sense of a larger purpose in the world and responsibility to one another" (Stanlick and Sell 2016, 82). If we stifle dialogue or real conversation, then we jeopardize the capacity of genuine exchange to generate challenges. The establishment of brave spaces over safe spaces can create a supportive environment for dialogue and the building of authentic relationships. "If the ground rules for our interactions with one another become so limiting that authenticity is stifled, will not the disorientation required for transformation also be stifled? Rather than tapping the transformative capacities of SLCE [service-learning civic engagement] experiences, are we sheltering our students, our community partners, and ourselves from the 'real' dynamics that could help us become more open to critical conversation and more empowered to relate with one another authentically?" (Stanlick 2015, 117–18).

Because each individual will approach the ground rules from his or her belief system, behavioral norms, and values, it can be daunting to create a dynamic and open exchange of ideas. Stanlick (2015, 117–18) states unequivocally that transformation is "not easy, nor is it supposed to be" and that the process of transformative learning includes critical self-reflection, vulnerability, the ability to "hold tension, critically engage and shift attitudes." Palmer (2011) also acknowledges the importance of holding tension between different beliefs and behaviors for the future of democracy. Stanlick (2015, 118, 120) identifies three parts to a multilevel transformation process among students, community members, faculty and staff: "dialogue, critical reflection, deliberate capacity-building for meaningful interaction across sameness and otherness." She states that these practices can have a "ripple effect" when each stakeholder embraces them and this is how multilevel transformation takes place. Stanlick recounts the success of a storytelling project in which all stakeholders bravely embraced topics like "inequality, privilege, and the ever-changing and diverse American landscape," and in which "disorientation abounds in the midst of cross-cultural and outside-the-comfort zone experiences." Participants were able to traverse the difficult dialogues because the project utilized an asset model, with principles of co-creation, and through a relationship of trust. Educators can design CBLL to incorporate all these values in order to support the dialogic learning process.

Reflections for Instructors

Brave Spaces. What types of norms or guidelines do you want to put in place so that your students interact in a brave space? What types of strategies do you want to develop to monitor microaggressions (indirect, subtle, or unintentional discrimination against members of a marginalized group) and create invitations for growth rather than hostile accusations?

Activities for Students

Ground Rules. Ask students to generate a list of ground rules or norms for their colleagues in class. After working individually for 2 or 3 minutes, students share results in small groups. Instructors elicit answers, noting them on the board, sparking a discussion that culls a set of best practices for CBLL. Post this list in a public way and refer back to it during the semester. Review the list at the end of the semester to see if students want to amend it based on their experiences. In chapter 6, we explore ground rules with community partners.

COMMON TRIGGERS

Many different triggers affect students' behavior and emotions. The following situations highlight challenging scenarios that commonly occur in CBLL. Bringing attention to these can help educators support learning outcomes.

Target Language Use

For many students, a community-based learning experience is the first time that they use the L2 outside the classroom context. Before their first meeting with the community partner, they may experience concern about whether they will be able to "perform" in the language. As one student, Alejandra, wrote before meeting her partner, "My principal concern is linguistic: I fear that my French won't be good enough to communicate with these refugees" (blog translated from French, 2016). Once they have tried to communicate with their partners, some may be surprised to find that even basic communication is hard. The textbook Mandarin they learned in class, for instance, may not match the speech patterns of their host. This leaves students feeling unsteady; and thus unsure of their ability to maintain a conversation exchange, they may retreat into silence.

For students who have had more extensive exposure to the language, the shared L2 may not "sound like" the language they are accustomed to hearing. Regionalisms, dialects, or accents may present challenges to students. Congolese refugees may speak one language at home and another with friends, and they will have learned some of the target language—French—in refugee camps or in school; their mastery of French may be confined to oral production, or may be imperfect, leaving students confused about meaning. For these students, who began the semester feeling confident, they may question their knowledge of the language, feel like they are not getting adequate exposure to their version of the language, or even judge the way the language is spoken ("it's not 'real' French").

For students who are heritage or native speakers, the experience can vary widely. In some cases, these students enthusiastically embrace the language experience in the community. They are excited and feel empowered to practice their mother tongue with native speakers. Other students may be surprised and even bothered by the linguistic variations that they encounter. The Spanish that they hear in the community, for instance, may not sound like their family's speech, or it might have lexical differences that students do not comprehend. A discussion of these different reactions can help students explore questions related to identity and belonging. They also offer educators an important opportunity to discuss linguistic variation and how understanding and addressing these features is challenging, even for "distinguished speakers" of the language. As the 2012 ACTFL guidelines show us, "Distinguished-level listeners comprehend language from within the cultural framework and are able to understand a speaker's use of nuance and subtlety. However, they may still have difficulty fully understanding certain dialects and nonstandard varieties of the language" ("Distinguished" section, para. 3). Sharing this classification structure with students can help assuage their fears that they are not "good enough" at the language.

One interesting student reflection comes from a native speaker of English who began to question the importance of language competency levels in his own life and an immigrant's life. The student, Sanjeev, wrote about how the tutee with whom he was working wanted to be a successful entrepreneur but noted that the community member did not have adequate English abilities. Sanjeev wrote, "At that moment, I realized that this is the truth for me as well—I don't have the ability to speak in Spanish at a professional level. The difference between 'basic competency' and complete fluency, without an accent, is very big. Also, I realized how easy it is to believe that a person is not very intelligent or competent if they can't speak well. In other words, it is very easy to discriminate

Activities for Students

Role-Plays. A role-play is a possible scenario from an interaction with the community or one of these following scenarios. Students should track which moments in the role-play are easy and which make them uncomfortable. Are there gaps in knowledge (both linguistic and cultural)?

- Conducting interviews of community members: Students role-play, asking for permission to conduct the interview.
- Meeting tutees for the first time: Students role-play. breaking the ice and getting to know the tutee.
- Conducting a door-to-door survey: Students role-play the informed consent process.

Reconvene the class and ask follow-up questions, such as: Is there specialized vocabulary needed for this interaction? What types of cultural norms might be unconsciously in play? Do you know where the community member is from and if their accent or vocabulary might be specific to their region or country? Where might there be uncomfortable silences or problems communicating? How can students adapt or ask for help when problems arise?

against a person due to his ability in English" (Sanjeev, blog translated from Spanish, 2016). This reflection is a powerful and productive moment that helps the student both to better understand the power issues connected to language and also to question his or her own level of language competency. In this way, CBLL is a transformative tool that enhances the learning of academic topics while also creating opportunities for personal development.

Lack of Confidence

For some students, an initial encounter with a community partner can be fraught with anxiety. How will I come across? What will we talk about? Will they like me? Spending time off campus—whether in a homeless shelter, a nonprofit agency, or in a person's home—can cause stress because students know neither what to expect nor how to behave in these new environments. In some cases, students lack the confidence to enter into unfamiliar situations related to generational differences, gender orientation, religion, ethnicity, race, politics, socioeconomic status, and so on. Some of our students experience discomfort as they realize that they have more privilege and have had access to different resources than their partners. Or perhaps a student observes greater affinity with community members than with peers, and frustration grows about the university environment. In many cases, however, basic differences in communication styles are a source of recurring tension and anxiety. In an age of smart phones and texting, students have not always had extensive practice "breaking the ice" or engaging in extended face-to-face communication with people outside their social circles. Questions from how to broach introductions to how to create smooth transitions from one meeting to another can preoccupy students throughout the entire experience, taking them out of their comfort zone and creating stress.

Activities for Students

Breaking the Ice. Use class time to give students the opportunity to practice small talk. At the beginning of a class, ask students to introduce themselves to another person in class. They should sustain conversation in the target language for at least 5 minutes. Debrief with students afterward to find out what they talked about. Have them switch partners and repeat. This activity can be modified by having students role-play specific scenarios, by engaging in a similar conversation over the telephone, or by creating a meet-and-greet with another group of students.

Tension About Specific Topics

The socioeconomic, political, and cultural realities of the community interaction may present triggers for some students. In particular, service with a social justice orientation may project a different worldview than the one that their family or community shares; the politics may even be in conflict with their own. CBLL that pairs students with undocumented workers, homeless persons, or refugees may pose particular challenges, as these are hot button, highly mediated, and politicized issues.

Activities for Students

Defending a Point of View. Divide your class into pairs and ask students to face one another. Give one student in each pair a statement to read; the statement should reflect a form of dominant discourse and represent a topic that you want your class to deconstruct or question. Examples might include: "Illegal immigrants should be deported." "Refugees pose a national threat, and we should limit their numbers." "People of color commit more crimes than white people." The designated student reads the card and defends the assigned point of view, while the other student must offer an opposing position, based on prepared materials, lived experience, or other tools. Following up with a discussion by the whole class will help students process their experience.

Frustration with Society

Some students feel discouraged by what they learn about society and the world around them. This growing awareness can provoke frustration and even anger. One student who worked with an adult English language learner wrote, "My first week of [ESL tutoring] made me realize just how difficult it would be to have to try and learn English as an adult. It makes me mad that so many people say 'why can't immigrants just learn English,' and [ESL tutoring] has really opened up my eyes to the difficulties of learning English as an adult" (Andrew, blog translated from Spanish, 2016). This student has begun to question certain social tropes and is struggling to come to terms with the realities of life as an immigrant.

Activities for Students

Reflective Listening. Role-play a conversation between a student and community member based on this quotation from a community member with a disability: "The life here is a little hard for me. Why do I say that? Because I do not work. But then how am I supposed to have money? There are [sewing] machines, but no customers. I like [to sew], that's my profession, but I can't do it. How can I do it? I have to ask others to come to my home to help me. I don't like that. It doesn't work for me" (Justin, interview, 2016). Reconvene the class, and ask follow-up questions, such as: How do you respond to the sadness and frustration expressed by the community member? What strategies can you employ besides active listening to better understand the situation? How do you feel about the community member's situation? Are there comments or questions that are appropriate to share with the community member?

Confronting Complexity

In the face of complicated situations, many students struggle to find and to make meaning. In this example, a student volunteer, Imari, reacts to the complexities surrounding the deportation of undocumented minors. While tutoring, she had gotten to know a high school student, whom she now fears has been deported. Here, Imari relates a conversation she had with the missing student's peers, whom (she assumed) were also undocumented: "I began to tell the student at the table that he does not have to leave, that he just needs to move to a different state and they wouldn't be able to track him. I stopped myself halfway through. Did I really want to encourage these students to hide from the police? To ignore what the judge ordered? To break the law? What type of message was I sending if I said that, and did I really feel that was right?" (Imari, blog, translated from Spanish, 2006). Because of her personal involvement with this undocumented individual, and the compassion she had developed regarding this situation, Imari found herself questioning the legal system and her own belief in the letter of the law. As conversations that were once purely academic become on-the-ground realities, students may see their own views begin to shift. This added complexity can be confusing and stressful.

Managing Privilege

As we explained in chapter 4, many students carry certain privileges, whether they are related to wealth, language, education, health, or even citizenship. Some students are unaware of this, and they can struggle with guilt or disassociation as they come to terms with this understanding. Others already possess an awareness of privilege but can still experience dissonance. In this example, a Latino student reported how seeing a different perspective from local Latino/a high school students affected him. He writes:

> This semester, I have entered a world that I did not understand and I barely knew existed. I decided to take this class because issues in education, particularly, are so near and dear to my heart since as a young Latino male, I realize how lucky I am to have parents that pushed me to be the best I could and I found the right programs with the right resources to get me to where I am today. However, I did not stop to think about the limits of my experience. I, like many . . . people my age, was pigeon-holed inside my own experience, thinking that most people had struggles similar to mine. I did not stop to contemplate what could have happened to me if I had been born in Colombia instead of the United States, and had come over

> without documentation. It was not part of my experience to deal with kids arriving at middle or even high school ages, knowing no English. I could not fathom what it would be like to immigrate to a hostile racial environment, . . . with no network similar to that which exists in multiethnic, immigrant-centric cities such as New York, Miami, and Los Angeles. (Esteban, final reflection essay in English, 2006)

The student discusses his expanding view of reality inspired by CBLL. He contemplates how privilege distinguishes him from other Latinos/as. For some students, dissonance comes from unveiling power structures within the community experience. Their own privilege—associated with education, race, or socioeconomic status—cannot be hidden from their partners; and for some, this is an embarrassment. For others, they see their work as an extension of paternalistic values that reinforce existing hierarchies, and prefer to recede from the service experience, functioning as "active resisters" that perpetuate this system.

In order to promote productive engagement during dissonance, we must consider how to prevent, reduce, and address resistance. Goodman (2011) provides a very useful checklist for addressing resistance to social justice issues from privileged groups. This list might be useful as a tool to guide the educator, or it might be shared with students in order to provide them with ideas on how to interact with peers and community members; see table 5.2.

Consciousness about Racism

Some students from privileged backgrounds see "difference" in the community, while others have experienced the same issues that are being addressed in the service experience (racism, poverty, access to education, etc.). Dissonance may thus arise in the interactions between traditionally underrepresented minorities and their white peers. When students of color and white students reflect on service together, tensions can arise that need to be monitored and processed.

In addition to the impact on classroom dynamics, awareness of race can also create internal conflict or dissonance. A first-generation Latina university student reflected on an encounter in which skin color became the topic of conversation. She describes the exchange with the mentorship coordinator at the school where she was assigned to volunteer: "I told him that I would fit well into this position because I am also an immigrant, a first-generation university student in my family, and I attended public school all of my life. [He] responded: 'Yes, but you have white skin.' At first I was a little offended, but during the semester, I realized how true it was and the difference from the collective experience Latinos have" (Carmen, blog translated from Spanish, 2016). This encounter

TABLE 5.2 Checklist for Addressing Student Resistance

Build relationship and trust	• Get to know participants—develop rapport • Self-disclose appropriately • Build a supportive educational environment • Provide clear structure and expectations
Affirm, validate, and convey respect for individuals	• Affirm participants' self-esteem • Avoid personal blame—emphasize cultural conditioning and the systemic nature of oppression • Acknowledge feelings, experiences, and viewpoints • Discuss common reactions and social identity development • Validate and build on current knowledge • Allow participants to discover information themselves • Provide opportunities for frequent feedback
Heighten investment	• Allow participants to have input into or help design the class/session • Humanize the issue • Frame diversity issue in terms of shared principles and goals • Explore participants' self-interest in social justice and alternatives to systems of domination
Responding to resistance	• Avoid getting hooked • Assess reasons for resistance • Invite exploration of the issue raised • Contain the behavior (e.g., set a time limit, summarize, and move on) • If the group is resistant, go with the flow • Provide a time-out (e.g., journaling, free-writing, reactions in pairs, a break) • Arrange a private meeting

Activities for Students

Microaggressions. After the group establishes a broad definition of microaggressions, ask students to reflect individually on moments when they have witnessed or experienced microaggressions. Watch one or both of the following videos, and ask students to jot down the statements that make them uncomfortable or make them laugh. Have small groups discuss these observations and brainstorm about how reactions might change according to the context and the ethnic/racial/gender mix. Ask students to share ideas about how microaggressions might surface in the community or in the classroom. Use your web browser to explore these resources:

- "If Latinos Said the Stuff White People Say"
- "If Asians Said the Stuff White People Say"

forced Carmen to work through a challenge to her identity, and in the end she acknowledged that she needed to reinterpret her understanding of this issue. In an era when many students strive to maintain political correctness, working with this very personal and politically charged topic requires establishing brave spaces. As educators, we must provide space for students to process these kinds of encounters without imposing or forcing a particular realization.

Dashed Expectations

For some students, the CBLL experience does not match their expectations. They engage with the community, hoping to make a difference in the world; and the more they see and learn, the more they realize that they simply cannot and will not make the "big impact" they had anticipated. As one student wrote in her reflective blog, "I really don't think I'm making a difference. My partner is still struggling with English and basic communication, and he doesn't seem to remember what we practiced last week" (Martina, blog translated from French, 2015). When the children they tutor continue to struggle in school or their conversation partners do not make noticeable headway in English, these dashed expectations can lead to despair. This sense of powerlessness can turn to frustration, eventually manifesting in resistance and retreat.

Other students are able to shift their expectations during the semester. Stephanie reported these observations regarding her and her classmates' reaction to "making a difference":

> My classmates expressed their opinions that they did not have a significant impact on the students they worked with in the classroom, probably due mainly to the fact that they did not have one on one time with them. I feel privileged to have been assigned specifically to [one student] to assist her with biology. Because of the limited amount of time I spent with her each week, I do not feel that I specifically influenced her *success* in the course; however, I know she appreciated my presence. (Stephanie, reflection essay translated from Spanish, 2006)

Stephanie reports having a positive experience, even if she doubts the academic impact of her efforts, which had been her original goal. She explains the dissatisfaction among her peers as a lack of one-to-one relationship, but there could be many factors in play here. Both these observations show the complexities of how students and partners interact, as well as how they interpret these interactions.

Service Fatigue

Service fatigue is a common challenge that usually occurs in the middle of or late in the semester, when a student's academic workload increases and the realities of the time commitment linked to sustained community engagement sink in. Faced with exams and papers, students prioritize their own work and begin to question the time they must dedicate to meeting their partners. They may voice a lack of enthusiasm, cancel appointments, or complain that they do not see any "progress" in their work. The novelty has worn off, and students do not see an easy way to resolve the challenges that they are facing. The "feel good" aspect of their interactions is no longer enough to keep them focused.

Activities for Students

Starfish Throwers. Students watch and analyze the documentary *The Starfish Throwers* (83 minutes), which is available for purchase online. In this film, the director, Jesse Roesler, captures the stories of three people who have committed their lives to supporting their communities: an Indian chef in his mission to feed and shelter those in need, a nine-year-old who advocates for gardens across the country to grow food for the underserved, and a retired teacher who helps people living on the streets by providing food, clothing, and support. This film deftly shows how an individual both can and cannot make an impact on the larger community. Discuss the film in a group setting, and encourage students to problematize service and to consider their role within social justice.

Teacher Burnout

The first time a teacher plans and executes a CBLL experience, there is often a buzz of excitement. Showing students that they can use language in a real-world context is powerful, and student feedback on this aspect of the experience is often quite positive. Likewise, relationships with community partners offer important learning opportunities, for both professional and personal development. Perhaps because the rewards of learning are so great, the challenges are equally daunting. Transportation hassles, last-minute cancellations, conflicts of interest, and the inevitable dissonance students will experience demand considerable time. Being tolerant of change and flexible in spirit can go a long way as partnerships are developed. Yet even seasoned CBLL teachers can experience feelings of frustration as their partnerships hit bump after bump, and the lack of institutional infrastructure takes its toll. Without logistical support, adequate funding structures, and a recognition of innovative pedagogies—in both time invested and in scholarship published—even the most avid believer in CBLL can be dissuaded from believing that the investment is worth the time.

Reflections for Instructors

Supporting CBLL Instructors. Who on your campus or in your community gives you energy and encouragement for work in the community? What practices and habits can you develop that will help sustain your CBLL, this semester and years in the future?

Personal and Political Questions

One question that often arises for teachers is whether they should reveal their own opinions to their students. Donahue (2011) develops this challenge in greater detail as he questions if there are boundaries for certain topics. He states that though service learning should not be used "to support partisan political activity, however, it is still value laden and political. It is value laden in the sense that students learn moral and ethical lessons whether or not they were intended by their instructor." Donahue (2011, 21) purports to believe that service learning is political, but "not in the sense that faculty encourage students to vote a certain way or support some points of view over others, but in the sense that faculty and students engaged in service make choices and learn lessons that have a political dimension." Outlining appropriate objectives within the political arena, Donahue (2011, 24) suggests that "students should not only understand how others frame and reframe political issues, they should gain practice in the framing and reframing process themselves." All these beliefs are applicable to CBLL, and educators can serve as important models to students.

Reflections for Instructors

The Politics of Education. Some say education is political but nonpartisan. What do you think? Have you witnessed successful examples of educators articulating and modeling this?

COMMUNITY DISENGAGEMENT

In some cases, it is the community partners who experience service fatigue or dissonance. Partners who are initially enthusiastic about working with students sometimes feel differently after the first few meetings. Students need to be managed and directed, and this can require time in an organization that may already be understaffed. In some cases, students are not sufficiently experienced, and they need more training. In other situations, generational and worldview gaps can exacerbate working relationships, and partners complain that students are unprofessional—too casually dressed, always on their phones, or disrespectful of the organization's larger mission, resulting in misunderstandings or unproductive dynamics. The resulting frustration is palpable on both sides, and as the goodwill of the organization dissipates, relationships become tense.

Reflections for Instructors

Anticipating Dissonance. How might you prepare your students for community dissonance? What strategies can be used to support this likelihood? How do you plan to facilitate conversation about common triggers?

CONCLUSION

As we can see from these numerous examples—and the many more that crop up in the natural cycle of community engagement—dissonance and resistance are a common part of the CBLL experience. It is helpful to see these challenges as characteristic of the experience for students, community partners, and faculty. But it is equally imperative to uncover unhealthy situations in order to ensure proper responses to inappropriate relationships or dangerous situations. In other words, dissonance and resistance should be anticipated, monitored, and supported. Ideally, CBLL creates opportunities for developing perspective consciousness or "the ability to question one's own stereotypes, interrogate areas of one's own cultural upbringing, and recognize that one's own worldview is not universally shared, nonetheless equally valuable" (Pitre and Bohac Clarke 2017, 91). By learning to understand the triggers of resistance and dissonance when encountering new worldviews, educators will be more prepared to accompany students on their journey of exploration. It is through compassion and maintaining an open mind that students will be able to reflect on these challenges that engage them in transformative learning. In the subsequent and final chapter of this book, we explore strategies for building sustainable relationships from which we can negotiate transformational and ethical partnerships.

CHAPTER 6

Authentic and Ethical Partnerships

By the end of this chapter, readers will be able to:

- Identify best practices of authentic community relationships
- Define transactional and transformational partnerships
- Explain the roles of reciprocity and solidarity in building authentic relationships
- Describe ethical behaviors in partnerships, including compassion and humility
- Plan how to implement ethical practices in partnerships

AUTHENTIC AND ETHICAL PARTNERSHIPS

This chapter explores how to build authentic relationships and ethical partnerships with the community. Before we look at types of partnerships, identifying transactional and transformational characteristics, we consider promising practices for building relationships in general. Here we wish to underscore the important distinction between the terms "relationship" and "partnership." As Jacoby (2003, 315) writes, "Partnerships start with and are built upon personal relationships." A relationship is characterized by "interactions between persons," and a partnership is defined as "a subset of relationships characterized by three qualities: closeness, equity, and integrity" (Clayton et al. 2010, 5). Relationships are established first, and they form the cornerstone of a healthy and thriving sustained partnership.

Skilton-Sylvester and Erwin (2000, 74) conducted a study to delve into the role of relationships in the learning process of students and community members engaged in a tutoring program. They conclude that "the positive benefits of service learning hinge on seeing the building of relationships as central rather than peripheral to the work that is being done." Like service learning, CBLL aims to help students create authentic relationships with communities. By "authentic," we mean relationships that are grounded in meaningful interactions that reflect culturally appropriate social interactions based on respect, transparency, confidentiality, accountability, and respect for diversity. We know that in order to build relationships and partnerships with different language communities and L2 speakers, we must offer opportunities to build authentic relationships, rather than focusing on service interaction. A potluck dinner can be a venue for meaningful conversation and serve as a building block for a budding partnership, yet it does not fall into the service category. As Skilton-Sylvester and Erwin (2000) indicate above, a service-oriented relationship does not stress the relationship but rather the product of the relationship as the central objective. In this chapter we discuss a full range of core characteristics and strategies that apply to a broad range of relationships and partnerships with different community members. There are difficulties in coordinating all participants to form authentic and sustainable partnerships, and therefore it is important to review the ground rules for establishing them.

The SOFAR (*S*tudents, *O*rganizations in the Community, *F*aculty, *A*dministrators on the campus, and *R*esidents in the community) framework (Bringle, Clayton, and Price 2009), shown in figure 6.1, explains the complex nature of how relationships are formed between academic institutions and communities. Clayton and others (2010) identify five stakeholders in this framework: students, administrators, community residents, community organizations, faculty members, and the ten dyadic relationships that exist between them. These authors see the SOFAR framework as a starting point for research analyses related to these relationships. The model clarifies who the stakeholders are in campus–community networks and offers a way to help improve goal setting, to understand impact, and to attain CBLL student learning outcomes. It highlights how individual, group, and network views are important considerations for understanding and assessing relationships. The five nodes in figure 6.1 identify each of the stakeholders, and the arrows indicate possible relationships, underscoring that some relationships might be hidden from certain stakeholders. Community organizations that work exclusively with students and faculty members might not fully understand that faculty have additional administrative responsibilities on campus that may affect their relationship. Likewise, faculty and students may not realize that there are multiple campus entities interacting with "their" community organization. In order to build productive and ethical relationships, we need to acknowledge that each identity is linked to different "perspectives, agendas, cultures, resources, power, and goals" (Clayton et al. 2010, 7). Better communication about these identities and their impact on relationships will ensure a healthier partnership ecosystem.

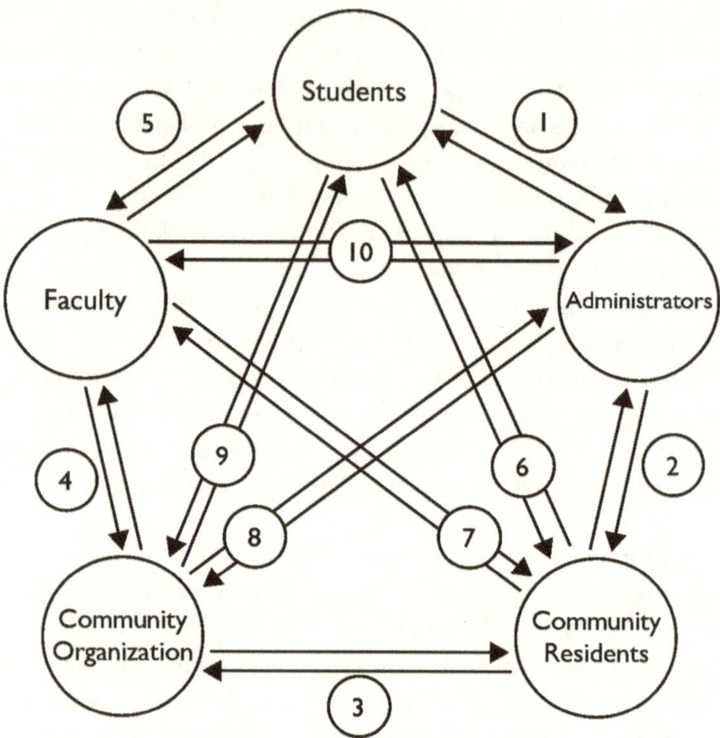

FIGURE 6.1 SOFAR Structural Network
Source: Clayton et al. (2010).

Now that we have established the differences among stakeholders in the campus–community network, let us look at the characteristics of those relationships and consider how various partnerships are formed. Jacoby (2015) identified two foundational guides for creating successful partnerships: *Benchmarks for Campus–Community Partnerships* (Torres 2000) (see table 6.1) and the Guiding Principles of Partnership from the Community–Campus Partnerships for Health (2013). These lists of principles and benchmarks offer promising practices for how to pursue our own partnerships. Within these best practices, commonalities include a clear understanding of mission; a shared vision; a relationship of mutual trust, communication, joint decision making; and regular evaluation. Ethical practices should be of the highest priority, and yet the on-the-ground realities, such as limited time and power differentials between stakeholders, have a direct impact on how partnerships function. As educators, we must commit continuously to matching aspirational goals with concrete practices to inform and sustain authentic relationships and ethical partnerships.

TABLE 6.1 Benchmarks for Campus–Community Partnerships

Stage 1: Defining the partnership	Founded on a shared vision and clearly articulated values. Beneficial to partnering institutions.
Stage 2: Building collaborative relationships	Composed of interpersonal relationships based on trust and mutual respect. Multidimensional: They involve the participation of multiple sectors that act in service of a complex problem. Clearly organized and led with dynamism.
Stage 3: Sustaining partnerships over time	Integrated into the mission and support systems of the partnering institutions. Sustained by a "partnership process" for communication, decision making, and the initiation of change. Evaluated regularly, with a focus on both methods and outcomes.

Source: Torres (2000).

The Guiding Principles of Partnership from the Community–Campus Partnerships for Health (2013) are:

1. The partnership forms to serve a specific purpose and may take on new goals over time.
2. The partnership agrees upon mission, values, goals, measurable outcomes, and processes for accountability.
3. The relationship between partners in the partnership is characterized by mutual trust, respect, genuineness, and commitment.
4. The partnership builds upon identified strengths and assets, but also works to address needs and increase capacity of all partners.
5. The partnership balances power among partners and enables resources among partners to be shared.
6. Partners make clear and open communication an ongoing priority in the partnership by striving to understand each other's needs and self-interests and developing a common language.
7. Principles and processes for the partnership are established with the input and agreement of all partners, especially for decision making and conflict resolution.
8. There is feedback among all stakeholders in the partnership, with the goal of continuously improving the partnership and its outcomes.
9. Partners share the benefits of the partnership's accomplishments.
10. Partnerships can dissolve; and when they do, they need to plan a process for closure.

11. Partnerships consider the nature of the environment within which they exist as a principle of their design, evaluation, and sustainability.
12. The partnership values multiple kinds of knowledge and life experiences.

Reflections for Instructors

1. *Strategies for building partnerships.* In what ways do you consciously build the values of partnership into your relationships? Considering all stakeholders in the SOFAR model, in table 6.2, list your relationships with each and the strategies you use to support them.

TABLE 6.2

Stakeholders	Relationship and Strategies
Students	
Faculty	
University administration	
Community organization	
Community members	

2. *Engaging all parties.* What strategies can be used to engage all stakeholders in the process of building sustainable partnerships, taking into account your particular timeline (e.g., one semester)?

TRANSACTIONAL AND TRANSFORMATIONAL RELATIONSHIPS

Another useful way of assessing community partnerships is to identify and define the type of relationship that partners wish to develop. This approach stems from research in service learning that categorizes relationships on a continuum from transactional to transformative. According to Clayton and others (2010, 7), *transactional relationships* are "instrumental and often designed to complete short-term tasks. Persons come together on the basis of an exchange, each offering something that the other desires." *Transformational relationships* are ones in which "both persons grow and change because of deeper and more sustainable commitments. . . . Persons come together in more open-ended processes of indefinite but longer-term duration and bring a receptiveness—if not an overt intention—to explore emergent possibilities, revisit and revise their own goals and identities, and develop systems they work within beyond the status quo" (Clayton et al. 2010, 7–8). In CBLL, both transactional and transformational relationships contribute to favorable outcomes. An example of a transactional exchange is when students practice their language skills at a workshop sponsored by a local advocacy organization, and the organization receives help with registering clients for community identification cards. A transformational relationship can be seen when Lena, the student mentioned in chapter 4, sought ways to continue to support a refugee family for the remainder of her time at the university, well beyond the one-semester commitment required by her course.

Transformation can occur at different levels and within different entities. The Community–Campus Partnerships for Health's Guiding Principles of Partnership provides a list of outcomes that result from partnerships, including:

- Personal transformation, including self-reflection and heightened political consciousness
- Institutional transformation, including changing policies and systems
- Community transformation, including community capacity building
- Transformation of science and knowledge, including how knowledge is generated, used, and valued; and what constitute "evidence" and "ethical practice"
- Political transformation, including social justice

The variety of transformations—based on personal, institutional, community, knowledge, and/or political identities—shows that the Community–Campus Partnerships for Health outlines not only authentic and ethical partnerships but also *transformative partnerships*. CBLL supports transformation in all these areas. Attention to how all participants in the partnerships interact is paramount to maximizing the relationship, and it underscores the importance of monitoring impact and working toward social change. Critical reflection also plays a role in building personal awareness and political consciousness, and in understanding pathways to social justice and transformation.

How students perceive their partnerships determines in great part the level of possible impact they may have. Educators can be proactive in this arena by supporting students as they build relationships and enter into partnerships. One student, Danielle, observed that "as students with limited responsibility, it seems that what we need more than anything is to somehow comprehend that making a difference requires time, investment, and persistence. We need to learn the importance of being there when the dust settles, of being dependable" (blog translated from Spanish, 2006). Although Danielle notes that students have limited responsibility, she underscores that they can contribute meaningfully in their communities through persistence and dependability. Exploration of the roles of all stakeholders will help make partnerships more transparent and healthier.

Reflections for Instructors

1. *Defining partnerships.* Are your interactions in CBLL (or those observed from your colleagues) mostly transactional or transformational? Which type of partnership fits your learning outcomes? How might you assess your partnership?

2. *Partnership principles.* Name the top five principles of partnership that you want to define your practices. How will you ensure that all stakeholders are actively engaged and fully represented in the partnership? Some of the questions from the checklist in appendix D may be of use.

3. *Needs and assets.* In table 6.3, map the needs and assets that you observe in your CBLL partnership. Which items were easy or difficult to identify? Where do you note gaps in your understanding, and how can you fill them? How will a transactional or transformational relationship be possible in this partnership? (Adapted from Reitenauer et al. 2013)

TABLE 6.3

Stakeholders	Needs	Assets
Students		Exercise: Speaks Arabic
Community partner	Exercise: Arabic speakers to interpret for community members	
Faculty		
University		

4. *The Transformational Relationship Evaluation Scale* (TRES). Clayton and others (2010) provide a way to analyze partnerships by placing them on a longer continuum, TRES, that ranges from exploitative to transactional to transformational; this helps to identify the negative outcomes, benefits, and growth in a given relationship. TRES tracks both the actual and desired dynamics of the relationship by examining nine features: outcomes, common goals, decision making, resources, conflict management, identity formation, power, significance, and satisfaction and change for the better. Access the entire questionnaire through the *Michigan Journal of Community Service-Learning* (https://quod.lib.umich.edu/).

Use these questions (adapted from the TRES survey) to conduct a preliminary review of the transformative potential of your partnership:

1. Are there more costs or benefits for one partner? Do all benefit equally? Do all grow in the partnership?
2. Do we have common goals? Or are we at odds?
3. To what degree have we collaborated? Were decisions made in isolation? Were decisions driven by the interests of one or the other?
4. Who has contributed resources to the work?
5. Do we actively avoid dealing with conflict, or do we openly deal with it?
6. Has this partnership helped or hindered one or both of us do our work? Has it helped both of us define "who I am"?
7. Does one of us have more power than the other? Or is power equally shared?
8. Does what we get and the extent of what we get from the partnership matter? Does the capacity of our partnership to nurture growth matter to us?
9. How satisfied are we in change for the better or change for the worse as a result of this partnership?

RECIPROCITY AND SOLIDARITY

In chapter 1 we introduced the concept of *generative or transformative reciprocity*: "a deep, thick collaboration that holds the possibility for all stakeholders to be transformed by the partnership (Jameson, Clayton, and Jaeger 2010)—and thereby cultivate partnership power dynamics that are just, fair, and inclusive" (Stanlick and Sell 2016, 80). We also explored the role of solidarity for developing authentic and equitable relationships. Here, we wish to reemphasize the importance of these concepts in authentic and ethical relationships and partnerships. Davis, Kliewer, and Nicolaides (2017, 43) state that "generative orientations of reciprocity shape transformative learning by allowing for the possibilities of disorienting dilemmas, reflective thinking and dialogue, shifts in frames of reference, and shifts in actions." We have also proposed that educators consider the role of *solidarity* in CBLL because it makes relationships central to the practice. When working in solidarity, students and communities are not focused primarily on producing something; instead, they are prioritizing building a relationship. Some scholars "conceptualize solidarity as empathy that includes a shared sense of struggle among people across differences in culture and power" (Sleeter and Soriano 2012, 4). If we are vigilant about creating critical consciousness through solidarity, then empathy will not have negative repercussions. It is by building a relationship based on co-creation, shared voice and power, collaborative knowledge, and joint ownership of processes and products that we ensure authentic and democratic relationships (Katz Jameson, Clayton, and Jaeger 2011, 264).

Storytelling and interviewing are useful ways to help students establish authentic relationships. Morton and Bergbauer (2015, 27) explore how sharing real stories can transform abstract ideas into lived experiences. They explain that they promote storytelling because "racism and inequality are not solved in the abstract; we begin by having people share their stories in safe spaces where they can expect to be heard and responded to with compassion, and we determine how to use this to direct future action. We do not learn 'diversity' as an ideological construct; we learn it as a lived experience of relationship building in contexts that require us to negotiate historic and present-day conflicts." This "lived experience of relationship building" is an effective tool for empowering CBLL students. Samantha, a student in a CBLL Spanish language course, reflected on how the experience in the community affected her understanding of solidarity:

> Is it possible to advocate for a community without being part of it? The reality is that we are part of the *same community*. . . . Efforts by Latino

> activists have had the overall goal of solidarity between Hispanic peoples and the rest of the country, recognizing that everyone contributes to our society. Well, my participation as a non-Latina advocate is the expression of the same solidarity, recognizing that our distinct cultures operate within the same community here in [our town] and in the US. (Samantha, blog translated from Spanish, 2016)

Samantha is aware that her voice joins with many other voices to build community, and she values that process of support. Jacoby (2003, 315) suggests that partnerships should be developed together. He writes that "partners can and should learn together, and from each other, about the social issues that most affect them and work as a partnership on behalf of positive social change while dealing with the here and now." Verjee (2010, 11) also explores the need to carefully construct the type of relationship that educators wish to develop with the community. He questions the types of relationships perpetuated in CBL by expressing great concern for charity-based interactions that "usually focus on

Activities for Students

1. *English as a second language on campus.* Read through the following scenario, which describes the challenges of welcoming community members to campus. Next, review proposed strategies for building authentic relationships and consider which one(s) you might adopt:

> On Tuesday and Thursday evenings, students tutor English to community members in an academic building on campus. Community members generally find it challenging to navigate campus, due to lack of parking and the large number of unmarked buildings. For many community members, this is the only contact that they have with local university students; the campus environment is very "foreign" to them. On a given night, tutors arrive at the session and begin to chat with their fellow tutors. The tutors sit together and swap personal stories of campus life. Some of the tutees know each other and also engage in conversations, while other tutees sit quietly and wait for the session to begin. When the leaders of the program officially begin the tutoring session, the tutors move to find their tutees and begin the one-hour session.

Which of the following strategies might you consider promoting in order to make the tutoring environment more welcoming for the community?

- Students practice social interactions, including culturally appropriate small talk.
- The organization sets rules that require tutors to start interacting with the tutees immediately when they walk in the room.
- Once per month, the organization holds a potluck dinner to allow time for the tutors and tutees to socialize.
- The organization holds a workshop to explore ways to make community members more welcome on campus. Discuss town–gown relationships and how different stakeholders might perceive this service.
- Your own proposal ______________________________.

(continued)

the student, with specific attention to their personal, social and learning outcomes, promoting a view of citizenship that involves the transfer of resources and 'doing for' community." He prefers "justice-oriented or transformative programs [that] focus on collaboration with communities or 'doing with,' which underpins the community as a partner in education in actively working for social transformation." This view of community engagement aligns with our belief that CBLL can and should include outcomes related to social change.

ETHICAL BEHAVIOR

Students disposed to engage in transformative learning embody certain understandings of themselves and the world around them. Perhaps it might seem unusual to begin a discussion of ethical behavior with an examination of the role of compassion and humility, but we want to underscore how these practices and values belong at the core of CBLL. In chapter 5 we indicated that *compassion* "includes identification with other humans, an evaluation of injustice and

2. *Checking in.* Ask your students to answer the following questions after two encounters with their community partners. This critical reflection helps push their "learning edge" by encouraging students to think about how they can build authentic relationships. What were the strengths and/or weaknesses of your recent interactions with the community (service- and non-service-oriented interactions)? Did past experiences influence how these interactions played out? What role did privilege play in the interactions? Write one new goal for your next two interactions.

3. *Before and after.* Have your students respond to the following set of questions at the beginning of the semester, and save the responses. At the end of the semester, ask students to respond to the same set of questions. Now return to them their responses from the beginning of the semester and ask them to compare their responses. This activity helps students see changes in beliefs and/or practices and can also generate questions if there was no change. Possible questions:

   1. To what communities do you belong? What defines your membership in these communities (ideologies, race, class, religion, sexual orientation, etc.)? Have you ever engaged in dialogue with a community to which you do not belong? How did you feel?
   2. What three characteristics are most important for building relationships? Do you believe that reciprocity or solidarity is more important for creating authentic relationships? Give an example from a recent experience.
   3. Describe a "border crossing" in which you recently participated. Borders may be defined as physical, cultural, ideological, or institutional. What was the perceived border? How did you adapt to the situation? What skills did you use? How did you feel?

suffering, and ethical actions in response to that evaluation" (Langstraat and Bowden 2011, 7). This combination of judgment and action makes compassion a building block for ethical behavior. If educators want students to avoid the "seduction of empathy," we must remind students to recognize that "spending a relatively small amount of time working with people who are facing difficulties does not equate to facing those difficulties themselves" (Jacoby 2015, 43). This means that we must also thoroughly recognize and support the role of humility in building ethical relationships. Stanlick and Sell (2016, 82) define *humility* as "an intentional acknowledgment of one's modest, humble role in the larger world—[and it] serves as the essential currency of respectful, meaningful partnerships as it inherently places the emphasis on the greater good rather than on personal ego." Humility allows the adoption of "a more democratic form of SLCE [service-learning community engagement] and thereby honoring power sharing, asset recognition, and a shared sense of responsibility to one another for successful and ethical community partnerships" (Stanlick and Sell 2016, 82). These concepts refer directly to issues connected to power and privilege, as discussed in chapter 4. The need for humility is exemplified in this anecdote recounted by a CBLL French student, Maddy, who partnered with a refugee family:

> I arrived at [the] family's house with big ideas. I'd help their children catch up in school, secure the family access to health care, and teach everyone conversational English. I'm happy to say that on those three counts I scored a fail, fail, and fail. This was not because I was too idealistic with my goals. Or slacked off in my responsibilities this semester. The problem was that before meeting this family, I had developed an exaggerated imagination of their needs.
>
> They do not fit the script of the helpless struggling refugee that so often shows up in the news. The most pressing struggles in the mind of a high-school-age daughter, for example, were no different than my high-school-aged cousin's, whose family has lived in the US for four generations. [My classmate] and I spent most of our time at [the family's] apartment with this high-schooler. Sure we helped her with homework once or twice, but the biggest drama we helped her through was one that I knew personally all too well. It was not poverty or American culture shock. Three of her new friends were going to the mall to hang out, and the daughter had to somehow convince mom to let her go hang out all day Saturday. On Friday afternoon, when [we] were over at their apartment, we laughed and we strategized and role-played fake responses that her mom may

> have. We helped out just as friends. This semester we weren't saviors or caseworkers; our most important role was being friends. I look forward to continuing this relationship this upcoming summer and beyond. (Maddy, final reflection translated from French, 2014)

Maddy entered this relationship with lots of assumptions about the needs of the refugee family and how she was supposed to assist them. Because she was open to reassessing her role, putting aside her personal ego and working for the greater good, she was able to grow their relationship. She engaged in active listening and dialogue, strategies that we have identified as key elements for working in CBLL. If Maddy had not been humble in her approach, she would not have built the meaningful relationship that she did with her family.

Having acknowledged the role of compassion and humility in promoting ethical behaviors, let us delve more deeply into other notable practices. In previous chapters we discussed ethical ways to align needs with goals, assess outcomes, build relationships, and manage dissonance. Although we are not able to provide an exhaustive discussion of ethics here, we wish to mention several concerns relevant to CBLL. As we think about if and how we want to develop transactional or transformational relationships, for instance, it is essential to eliminate exploitative behaviors. It is unethical to use the community as a laboratory. Even a question related to an appropriate timeline for social change is relevant to how we engage in ethical partnerships. A false timeline for change is not helpful to anyone and can be perceived as unethical. CBLL participants must assume the mantra of "do no harm" and commit to authentic relationships that prize values of trust, transparency, confidentiality, accountability, equity, inclusion, coeducation, collaboration, respect for diversity, and attention to cultural sensitivity. Practicing these behaviors will help establish ethical relationships. Educators must also consider the importance of *student competence.* We need to closely monitor the types of interactions in which students engage, if they are asked to do something outside their level of knowledge or preparation. Perhaps the student's language level is not appropriate for work in a professional setting, where legal, health, and other sensitive issues are the focus. If a student volunteers at a local health clinic, educators must monitor the type of work the student is asked to do and must discuss any concerns with the students and community partner. One student, Zaina, reported that she was asked by a community member to interpret from English to Arabic during a physical exam, but Zaina was not certified to act as an interpreter at the clinic. Zaina reflected on the tensions caused by the question and wondered whether some assistance was better than no assistance. Zaina came to the conclusion that, ethically, she should not accompany the patient in this role. Sometimes students are asked to translate written documents, such as flyers for school administration or personal documents proving birth or marriage status. In our experience, students are rarely capable of producing accurate written translations independently, and should not be considered for this kind of work unless the educator is willing to oversee and certify the translation. Empowering students to understand how their linguistic range, cultural competence, and relevant knowledge match—or do not match—the situation presented to them is key to enabling them to make ethical choices about their interactions in the community.

Students, community members, faculty members, and community organizations must maintain appropriate personal and professional *boundaries* in their partnerships. Educators should establish rules concerning sexual relationships in order to prevent harassment and abuse. As in the case of Alejandra and Frankie, who received inappropriate texts from a community member (chapter 5), students could receive unwarranted attention; but they might also initiate improper relationships. When university students interact with high school students, they sometimes make poor decisions about what is appropriate behavior for the authority figure (themselves) in the relationship. Students must also observe boundaries in professional settings. Another example concerns a student, Bao, who worked at a health clinic. He observed that the interpreter did not follow the professional guidelines of communicating everything that the doctor said to the patient. Bao was confronted with the dilemma of reporting this breach of behavior, challenging him to weigh the impact of reporting these concerns. In the end, he chose not to report the incident, but he shared it with his professor, who intervened on his behalf and reported it to the clinic's administrators. This example shows that all participants must monitor what transpires during community interactions and policies, such as working in pairs, meeting in public spaces, regularly reporting observations, and guiding reflection on experiences. Examining ethical dilemmas more closely, particularly those that may be triggered by differences in socioeconomic status, provides yet another example. Suzanne, a student assisting a teacher at a local high school, learned that a newly arrived Congolese high school student did not have a bilingual dictionary. During a class discussion, she suggested to her professor that she could purchase the dictionary as a gift. The class debated the pros and cons of gifting something to a mentee and came to the conclusion that Suzanne should not give the student a dictionary. They explained that the relationship that Suzanne had established with the student should be based on their exchange of knowledge and friendship and not based on a transactional exchange that includes gifts. Although there are no hard-and-fast rules for partnerships, participants should stop to reflect on the implications of their actions in order to build an ethical partnership. Issues related to funding activities, purchasing resources, paying community members, reimbursing transportation expenses, and the like need to be evaluated, and clear policies need to be implemented. The convening of an oversight committee or an advisory board made up of different stakeholders could be useful in this and many other instances.

Finally, partnerships might be directly affected by unethical practices initiated by the community organization. It is inconvenient when organizations do not follow through with promises to hold student training sessions or to attend scheduled meetings; but these situations are usually due to staffing or resource shortages and should not be characterized as unethical behaviors. If, however, the organization does not provide proper oversight or monitoring, and this later leads to unsafe conditions for students, then we must categorize these as unethical practices. It is also possible, although uncommon, for a staff member to not follow the rules that have been established by the organization. Regardless of the possible explanation, any unethical decision making or inappropriate behavior by an organization's staff members requires immediate intervention. Clear policies and procedures, agreed upon at the beginning of the semester, provide the necessary steps to avoid these types of situations. Policies should therefore include conditions for terminating a partnership because this will sometimes be the ethical decision.

Reflections for Instructors

Observing Ethics. What activities or prompts might work well to guide students to explore ethical behaviors in CBLL? What concerns do you have about unethical or inappropriate behaviors? Have you observed false promises in community–campus partnerships? If you formed an advisory board, who would you invite to participate?

Activities for Students

An Ethical Dilemma in a Legal Office. Ask students to review this scenario and then discuss the different ways to address the dilemma. What is the ethical choice for the student, professor, and lawyer? Why should each stakeholder resolve the dilemma in the way that you suggest?

> Deandre, a student in a Spanish CBLL class, was assigned to help in a legal aid office. A lawyer presented her with the task of translating various letters written in Spanish that the lawyer wanted to include in a case file. Both the professor and the lawyer had screened Deandre before her placement in the office and had deemed her skills appropriate for the work. Deandre, however, did not feel that she was sufficiently proficient in Spanish to complete the translation task, even though the lawyer was planning to double-check her work. Deandre refused the task.

Providing a regular channel for conversation between partners—including different combinations of students, faculty members, campus administrators, community members, and community organizations—is an ethical practice that produces sustainable partnerships between the university and the wider community.

ETHICAL REPRESENTATION

It is important to consider how to avoid exploiting community members by misrepresenting or appropriating their voices. As Bright and Gambrell (2017, 220) write, "Oppression is best understood from the perspectives and experiences of the oppressed." We must therefore "defer . . . to a range of more organic forms of expression, such as narrative, anecdotes, allegories, parables, illustration, sarcasm, and forms of first-person storytelling as a means to challenge, expose, and deconstruct racial social constructs." When students collaborate on projects that seek to showcase marginalized voices, they should first receive training on the limits of publishing identities or likenesses through written, visual, and audio projects in the public domain. As noted in chapter 4, projects that incorporate photography, voice recordings, video recordings, or writings that reveal personal or compromising information about a member of a vulnerable population must be closely monitored. An Arabic CBLL class working with refugees planned to create a pop-up museum exhibit about refugee resettlement. The students wanted to include photographs of some of the refugee families; but when they asked the families, several seemed reticent about being photographed for the project. One woman cited concern for her children's safety, and another woman simply did not want her image to be displayed in public. Students who had built a trusted relationship with their family realized that by requesting this of their partners, they might have jeopardized their partnership. Following a class discussion, the project was modified to include only two photographs with consenting community members, and to instead concentrate on written stories that community members had approved for distribution.

Community partner organizations often have standards regarding issues such as publishing names or images of minors as well, so educators should be sure to research and adhere to their guidelines. They should also talk to the organizations about whether the planned project or activity accurately reflects the organization's mission. In one example, the students in a French CBLL class were planning to publish a series of articles about their community partnership in the local newspaper. Although the newspaper had agreed, and the families had shown interest, the community partner organization's staff members wanted to approve each article before it went to press. They cited concerns about how the organization might be represented and about whether students might inadvertently reveal sensitive information about the organization's clients. By working together and sharing ethical concerns, however, the organization, the families, the newspaper editor, the educator, and the students all gained a greater awareness of each other's perspectives. The resulting articles were well received by all stakeholders. As we see in this example, the desire to "lift up" the community in a public way needs to be balanced with the appropriateness of disseminating projects to a wider public. Working with a model like SOFAR can help those involved anticipate the motivations and interests of the different stakeholders so that no one is exploited or put at risk because a photo or legal status was made public.

We suggest that educators establish clear permission guidelines with community partners. There are three different stages to the process of obtaining permissions: the invitation, the informed consent, and the release form. The invitation can be issued in oral or written form, keeping in mind the literacy levels of the community, the L2, and what is culturally appropriate. Informed consent is a process of communication that allows the partner to make an educated decision about their willingness to participate. Requesting consent means asking for permission to make images or recordings that will be owned and used in public ways (on the internet, at an exhibit, etc.). The consent should include a clear description of what the participant will be asked to do, any risks or benefits inherent in the process, any confidentiality procedures, contact information in case the participant has questions, any compensation, and how the product (e.g., photo, recording) will be utilized. This information may be provided in written or oral form. Finally, participants must consent to a release that allows the student or educator to use the information collected in public ways. The basic components of a release are:

1. The student's name and academic institution affiliation
2. A title for the research that is sufficiently descriptive to identify the project
3. A description of the material to be released
4. A list of ways you want to use the material
5. A statement that signing the release is voluntary. In other words, subjects may decide that, although they gave you permission to photograph or tape them, they don't want you to use their images or tapes after all.
6. The subject's agreement: written, recorded, or oral, depending upon the circumstances
7. Parental permission if the subjects are minors
8. Child assent if the subjects are minors
   (adapted from Duke University Campus Institutional Review Board 2018)

Reflections for Instructors

1. *Ethics of representation.* Use table 6.4 to examine the ethics of representation. Brainstorm how to apply best practices to ensure ethical behavior that will promote authentic relationships. Consider what types of interactions will be necessary between students and communities to produce each of these projects. Consider also who has control over the arch of the storyline.

TABLE 6.4

	Informed Consent:	**Control of Representation:**	**Authentic Relationships:**
	What negative repercussions could result from this project? Who might object and utilize these stories in a negative way? Is this project exposing a vulnerable population to increased risk?	How can students capture the story of a community member without influencing how they tell their story? Are personal stories being appropriated?	Does this activity build authentic relationships? What are the power dynamics? Does this create a mutually beneficial relationship? What are the effects of this project?
Students work with community members to record (audio) personal stories and post them on a public website.			
Photography exhibit in local library: students take photos of community members and write a short biography.			
Students select a local business leader and create a documentary about his life. The film is shown at the local community center and archived at the university library.			

(*continued*)

Educators should look for resources to guide the design of this informed consent and release process within their own institution or communities. Most universities will have an institutional review board and will be able to provide guidelines or training modules for students.

2. *Partnerships in your community.* Brainstorm potential organizations or community members with whom to partner in CBLL. Use this list to generate ideas:

- Legal aid office, immigration law office
- Domestic violence prevention/support center
- Homeless shelter, thrift shop
- Food shuttle, food bank
- Immigration advocacy group
- Community garden
- Community organizing group
- Churches/synagogues/mosques/temples
- Heritage language schools
- Public schools, college, universities, community colleges
- After-school program
- Parent–teacher association
- Public health department
- Social services department
- Housing authority, public housing
- Recreation and community center
- English as a second language and literacy centers
- Public library
- Chamber of commerce
- Parks and recreations center
- Welcome baby (new mother's support), parent support group
- Detention center, penitentiary
- 4-H, cooperative extension center
- National Association of Latino Elected and Appointed Officials, citizenship workshop sponsors
- Refugee resettlement organizations
- Health clinic
- Museums

CONCLUSION

Contemplating beginning a CBLL course can be exciting and daunting; maintaining a current CBLL partnership is both challenging and rewarding. The time commitment involved in the identification of partnerships, maintenance of relationships, and design of curriculum and assessments, among other aspects of the partnership, is quite manageable, but it does require additional effort. The rewards of getting to know local communities and providing experiential learning opportunities for students are key motivating factors in getting involved in CBLL. Building a sustained partnership that actually generates change for all stakeholders is the ultimate reward.

Depending on the diversity of the local community, educators might need to be creative in how they locate and reach out to different community organizations and L2 community members. We have used examples of interactions with native and heritage speakers in the community throughout this book, but we know that not all communities will have this diversity of L2 speakers. Online synchronous videoconferencing can be a productive alternative for interacting with native speakers. We have also seen thoughtful partnerships with International Baccalaureate and dual immersion schools that bring L2 students from the university in contact with L2 learners in K–12. These examples will not altogether parallel the work that we have outlined in this book, but we encourage educators to embrace community-engaged teaching as a window into new ways of thinking about language and language instruction, including reimagining curricular and departmental structures. Language education and language use can be tools of social change. The dynamic nature of global and local landscapes requires educators to become more proactive and to deepen and diversify how world languages are used and language curricula are developed to discuss inequalities, privileges, power, identity, and inclusion in all communities.

Appendix A: A Backward Design Approach to CBLL

This table draws on Wiggins and McTeague's (1998) design approach to illustrate how to plan a CBLL experience.

APPENDIX TABLE The Big Picture of a Design Approach

Key Question	Consideration	Criteria	Accomplishment (What the final design uncovers)
Stage 1: What is worth and requiring of understanding?	ACTFL standards. Availability of local language communities. Teacher expertise and interest.	Enduring ideas. Opportunities for authentic, discipline-based work. Engaging.	Unit is framed around enduring understandings and essential questions.
Stage 2: What is evidence of that understanding?	Continuum of assessment types (informal checks, observations, quizzes, writing prompts, project).	Valid, reliable, sufficient, engaging, authentic, feasible, student friendly.	Unit is anchored in credible and educationally vital evidence of the desired understandings.
Stage 3: What learning experiences and teaching promote understanding, interest, and excellence?	Research-based repertoire of learning and teaching experiences. Essential and enabling knowledge and skill.	Where is it going? Hook the students. Explore and quip. Rethink and revise. Exhibit and evaluate.	Coherent learning experiences and teaching that will evoke and develop the desired understandings, promote interest, and make excellent more likely.

Source: Wiggins and McTeague (1998), www.fitnyc.edu/files/pdfs/Backward_design.pdf.

Appendix B: Academic Learning Objectives

Learning Objective (LO) Level	Academic Enhancement Learning Objectives	Associated Guiding Questions
LO 1: Identify and Describe	Identify and describe a specific academic concept that you now understand better as a result of reflection on your service-learning experience.	1.1 Identify an academic concept that relates to your service-learning experience. AND 1.2 Describe the academic concept that relates to your service-learning experience
LO 2: Apply	Apply the academic concept in the context of these experiences.	2.1 How does the academic concept apply to/emerge in your service-learning experience? (e.g., How did you or someone else use the material? When did you see it?)
LO 3: Analyze	Analyze the relationship between the academic material* (and/or your prior understanding of it) and the experience.	3.1 Compare and contrast the academic material and your experience: In what specific ways are the academic material (and/or your prior understanding of it) and the experience the same and in what specific ways are they different? AND 3.2 What are the possible reasons for the difference(s) between the material (and/or your prior understanding of it) and your experience? (e.g., bias/assumptions/agendas/lack of information on the part of the author/scientist or on your part.) AND 3.3 In light of this analysis, what complexities (subtleties, nuances, new dimensions) do you now see in the material that were not addressed or that you had not been aware of before?
LO 4: Evaluate	Evaluate the adequacy of the material (and/or your prior understanding of it) and develop a strategy for improved action.	Based on the analysis above: 4.1 How specifically might the material (and/or your prior understanding of it) need to be revised? AND 4.2 If applicable, what additional questions need to be answered and/or evidence gathered in order for you to make a more informed judgment regarding the adequacy/accuracy/appropriateness of the material (and/or your prior understanding of it)? AND 4.3 What should you and/or your service organization do differently in the future (or have done differently in the past) AND what are the associated benefits and risks/challenges?

*Note: "Academic material" includes the concept itself and its presentation (in class, in readings).

Source: Ash, Clayton, and Atkinson (2005, 61).

Appendix C: The Intercultural Knowledge and Competence VALUE Rubric

Intercultural Knowledge and Competence VALUE Rubric

for more information, please contact value@aacu.org

Association of American Colleges and Universities

The VALUE rubrics were developed by teams of faculty experts representing colleges and universities across the United States through a process that examined many existing campus rubrics and related documents for each learning outcome and incorporated additional feedback from faculty. The rubrics articulate fundamental criteria for each learning outcome, with performance descriptors demonstrating progressively more sophisticated levels of attainment. The rubrics are intended for institutional-level use in evaluating and discussing student learning, not for grading. The core expectations articulated in all 15 of the VALUE rubrics can and should be translated into the language of individual campuses, disciplines, and even courses. The utility of the VALUE rubrics is to position learning at all undergraduate levels within a basic framework of expectations such that evidence of learning can by shared nationally through a common dialog and understanding of student success.

Definition

Intercultural Knowledge and Competence is "a set of cognitive, affective, and behavioral skills and characteristics that support effective and appropriate interaction in a variety of cultural contexts." (Bennett, J. M. 2008. Transformative training: Designing programs for culture learning. In *Contemporary leadership and intercultural competence: Understanding and utilizing cultural diversity to build successful organizations*, ed. M. A. Moodian, 95-110. Thousand Oaks, CA: Sage.)

Framing Language

The call to integrate intercultural knowledge and competence into the heart of education is an imperative born of seeing ourselves as members of a world community, knowing that we share the future with others. Beyond mere exposure to culturally different others, the campus community requires the capacity to: meaningfully engage those others, place social justice in historical and political context, and put culture at the core of transformative learning. The intercultural knowledge and competence rubric suggests a systematic way to measure our capacity to identify our own cultural patterns, compare and contrast them with others, and adapt empathically and flexibly to unfamiliar ways of being.

The levels of this rubric are informed in part by M. Bennett's Developmental Model of Intercultural Sensitivity (Bennett, M.J. 1993. Towards ethnorelativism: A developmental model of intercultural sensitity. In *Education for the intercultural experience*, ed. R. M. Paige, 22-71. Yarmouth, ME: Intercultural Press). In addition, the criteria in this rubric are informed in part by D.K. Deardorff's intercultural framework which is the first research-based consensus model of intercultural competence (Deardorff, D.K. 2006. The identification and assessment of intercultural competence as a student outcome of internationalization. *Journal of Studies in International Education* 10(3): 241-266). It is also important to understand that intercultural knowledge and competence is more complex than what is reflected in this rubric. This rubric identifies six of the key components of intercultural knowledge and competence, but there are other components as identified in the Deardorff model and in other research.

Glossary

The definitions that follow were developed to clarify terms and concepts used in this rubric only.

- Culture: All knowledge and values shared by a group.
- Cultural rules and biases: Boundaries within which an individual operates in order to feel a sense of belonging to a society or group, based on the values shared by that society or group.
- Empathy: "Empathy is the imaginary participation in another person's experience, including emotional and intellectual dimensions, by imagining his or her perspective (not by assuming the person's position)". Bennett, J. 1998. Transition shock: Putting culture shock in perspective. In *Basic concepts of intercultural communication*, ed. M. Bennett, 215-224. Yarmouth, ME: Intercultural Press.
- Intercultural experience: The experience of an interaction with an individual or groups of people whose culture is different from your own.
- Intercultural/cultural differences: The differences in rules, behaviors, communication and biases, based on cultural values that are different from one's own culture.
- Suspends judgment in valuing their interactions with culturally different others: Postpones assessment or evaluation (positive or negative) of interactions with people culturally different from one self. Disconnecting from the process of automatic judgment and taking time to reflect on possibly multiple meanings.
- Worldview: Worldview is the cognitive and affective lens through which people construe their experiences and make sense of the world around them.

(continued)

Intercultural Knowledge and Competence VALUE Rubric

for more information, please contact value@aacu.org

Definition

Intercultural Knowledge and Competence is "a set of cognitive, affective, and behavioral skills and characteristics that support effective and appropriate interaction in a variety of cultural contexts." (Bennett, J. M. 2008. Transformative training: Designing programs for culture learning. In *Contemporary leadership and intercultural competence: Understanding and utilizing cultural diversity to build successful organizations*, ed. M. A. Moodian, 95-110. Thousand Oaks, CA: Sage.)

Evaluators are encouraged to assign a zero to any work sample or collection of work that does not meet benchmark (cell one) level performance.

	Capstone 4	**Milestones** 3	2	**Benchmark** 1
Knowledge *Cultural self- awareness*	Articulates insights into own cultural rules and biases (e.g. seeking complexity; aware of how her/his experiences have shaped these rules, and how to recognize and respond to cultural biases, resulting in a shift in self-description.)	Recognizes new perspectives about own cultural rules and biases (e.g. not looking for sameness; comfortable with the complexities that new perspectives offer.)	Identifies own cultural rules and biases (e.g. with a strong preference for those rules shared with own cultural group and seeks the same in others.)	Shows minimal awareness of own cultural rules and biases (even those shared with own cultural group(s)) (e.g. uncomfortable with identifying possible cultural differences with others.)
Knowledge *Knowledge of cultural worldview frameworks*	Demonstrates sophisticated understanding of the complexity of elements important to members of another culture in relation to its history, values, politics, communication styles, economy, or beliefs and practices.	Demonstrates adequate understanding of the complexity of elements important to members of another culture in relation to its history, values, politics, communication styles, economy, or beliefs and practices.	Demonstrates partial understanding of the complexity of elements important to members of another culture in relation to its history, values, politics, communication styles, economy, or beliefs and practices.	Demonstrates surface understanding of the complexity of elements important to members of another culture in relation to its history, values, politics, communication styles, economy, or beliefs and practices.
Skills *Empathy*	Interprets intercultural experience from the perspectives of own and more than one worldview and demonstrates ability to act in a supportive manner that recognizes the feelings of another cultural group.	Recognizes intellectual and emotional dimensions of more than one worldview and sometimes uses more than one worldview in interactions.	Identifies components of other cultural perspectives but responds in all situations with own worldview.	Views the experience of others but does so through own cultural worldview.
Skills *Verbal and nonverbal communication*	Articulates a complex understanding of cultural differences in verbal and nonverbal communication (e.g., demonstrates understanding of the degree to which people use physical contact while communicating in different cultures or use direct/indirect and explicit/implicit meanings) and is able to skillfully negotiate a shared understanding based on those differences.	Recognizes and participates in cultural differences in verbal and nonverbal communication and begins to negotiate a shared understanding based on those differences.	Identifies some cultural differences in verbal and nonverbal communication and is aware that misunderstandings can occur based on those differences but is still unable to negotiate a shared understanding.	Has a minimal level of understanding of cultural differences in verbal and nonverbal communication; is unable to negotiate a shared understanding.
Attitudes *Curiosity*	Asks complex questions about other cultures, seeks out and articulates answers to these questions that reflect multiple cultural perspectives.	Asks deeper questions about other cultures and seeks out answers to these questions.	Asks simple or surface questions about other cultures.	States minimal interest in learning more about other cultures.
Attitudes *Openness*	Initiates and develops interactions with culturally different others. Suspends judgment in valuing her/his interactions with culturally different others.	Begins to initiate and develop interactions with culturally different others. Begins to suspend judgment in valuing her/his interactions with culturally different others.	Expresses openness to most, if not all, interactions with culturally different others. Has difficulty suspending any judgment in her/his interactions with culturally different others, and is aware of own judgment and expresses a willingness to change.	Receptive to interacting with culturally different others. Has difficulty suspending any judgment in her/his interactions with culturally different others, but is unaware of own judgment.

Appendix D: Sample Checklists for Community Partners, Faculty Members, and Students

Checklist for Community Partners:

____ Partner agencies define their needs and are included in planning for the course.

____ Preparation for the service includes discussion of student orientation, clarification of responsibilities and risk management issues.

____ Facilitate signing and activation of the Bolton School's Agency Agreement.

____ Before the service begins, students are oriented to the partner agency mission and goals so they understand their role within the agency/project, including issues to be addressed.

____ Assist in developing opportunities for at least an 8-hour activity that is significant and challenging to the student and builds on the student's abilities and skills.

____ Discuss and sign the Student Project Plan form (appendix A).

____ Provide training, supervision, feedback, and resources for the student to succeed in the service; thus, service is connected to the course through project readings and class presentations.

____ Maintain a safe work environment and reasonable hours for the student to complete the agreed-upon activity.

____ Facilitate ongoing reflection on the community experience that includes dialogue about community issues and the need for the service.

____ Students, faculty, and community representatives participate in the evaluation process provided.

Checklist for Faculty Members:

____ Become acquainted with the community partner agency—understanding the mission, clientele, location, and student role to define their needs and plan for the course. Orient relevant agency staff to the course.

____ Preparation for the service addresses student orientation, clarification of responsibilities and risk management issues.

____ The syllabus is developed and revised to incorporate the service experience into the teaching and learning objectives of the course.

____ Students are oriented to a partner agency before the service begins, including known needs.

____ Students are involved in at least 8 hours of agency contact for each course with a Community Engagement component.

____ Academic credit is awarded for the learning evidenced (project developed) through the experience, not for the service itself.

____ The community experience is connected to the course objectives through readings and class presentations.

____ Reflection on the community experience is ongoing and includes dialogue about community issues and the need for the service.

____ Students, faculty, and community representatives participate in the evaluation provided.

____ Describe the Community Engagement Through Service-Learning activity and its relation to course objectives on the first day of class in reviewing the course syllabus.

____ Maintain regular contact with the service sites and monitor student progress through discussions, journal assignments, progress reports or individual check-ins.

____ Provide an opportunity for informed consent for new participants to enable publication of evaluation findings.

____ Provide opportunities for students to reflect on what they are learning from the experience.

____ Participate in at least one CBLL continuing education program, workshop, or event each year

____ Provide the CBLL coordinator with a copy of any news article featuring their service-learning course and inform them of significant events related to the students or the course.

Checklist for Students:

____ Be oriented to the partner agency before the service begins, including issues to be addressed.

____ Be prompt and respectful in working with their community partner.

____ Arrange at least 8 contact hours with the community partner during the first 2 weeks of class or as directed

____ Design their activity based on abilities and skills and the goals identified by the agency.

____ Complete the Student Project Form within the first four weeks of class; submit to the instructor.

____ Fulfill all agreed-upon duties and responsibilities at the community site; academic credit will be awarded for the learning evidenced (project developed) through the experience, not for service itself.

____ Provide feedback about the service experience and its relevancy to the course material—participate in course discussions.

____ Reflection on the community experience is ongoing and includes dialogue about community issues and the need for the service.

____ Be sensitive to cultures and lifestyles different than their own.
____ Speak with their community partner or faculty if uncomfortable or uncertain about project
____ Respect the confidentiality of the agency and people served.
____ Participate in the evaluation process along with faculty and community representatives.

Source: Case Western Reserve University (2001).

Appendix E: Additional Resources

Barnga: A Simulation Game on Cultural Clashes. Places players in the confounding situation of a silent card game, in which the rules are different for different players. See www.amazon.com/Barnga-Simulation-Cultural-Clashes-Anniversary/dp/1931930309.

Case Studies on Diversity and Social Justice Education (Southern Poverty Law Center, www.tolerance.org/case-studies). Thirty-five school- and classroom-based scenarios that address a variety of issues related to identity and diversity.

Cult of Pedagogy, Social Justice Resource Collection (www.cultofpedagogy.com/social-justice-resources). Especially useful tips on teaching for social justice, plus a whole array of additional websites.

Generator School Network (https://gsn.nylc.org/). An online community with more than 5,000 members who share service-learning and social justice lessons and professional development opportunities.

Global Oneness Project (www.globalonenessproject.org). Provides free multicultural stories and accompanying lesson plans that explore cultural, social, and environmental issues with a humanistic lens.

IWitness (http://iwitness.usc.edu/SFI/Default.aspx). An education website with multimedia life histories and testimonies related to genocide around the world.

NAFSA Association of International Educators Intercultural Activity Toolkit (www.nafsa.org/findresources/Default.aspx?id=8568). Provides hands-on resources that can be easily duplicated and utilized by individuals and groups seeking to internationalize the campus.

Peace Corps Educator Resources (www.peacecorps.gov/educators/resources/?topics=3).

Perspectives for a Diverse America: A Literacy-Based Antibias Curriculum (http://perspectives.tolerance.org).

Pushing the Edge (http://pushingtheedge.org).

Racism No Way (www.racismnoway.com.au). Provides especially useful lesson plans and resources to challenge racism and to promote inclusion.

Teaching Tolerance (www.tolerance.org). A literacy-based curriculum that combines antibias social justice content with the Common Core State Standards. This organization continually produces top-quality lesson plans and resources on social justice issues.

What's Up with Culture? (www.nafsa.org/Professional_Resources/Browse_by_Interest/Internationalizing_Higher_Education/Network_Resources/Teaching,_Learning,_and_Scholarship/What_s_Up_with_Culture_/). NAFSA's resource guide for study abroad.

References

AACU (Association of American Colleges and Universities). 2009a. "Inquiry and Analysis VALUE Rubric." www.aacu.org/value/rubrics/inquiry-analysis.

———. 2009b. "Intercultural Knowledge and Competence VALUE Rubric." www.aacu.org/value/rubrics/inquiry-analysis.

Abbott, Annie, and Darcy Lear. 2010. "The Connections Goal Area in Spanish Community Service-Learning: Possibilities and Limitations." *Foreign Language Annals* 43: 231–45.

ACTFL (American Council on the Teaching of Foreign Languages). 1996. "Standards Summary." www.actfl.org/publications/all/world-readiness-standards-learning-languages/standards-summary.

———. 2012. "ACTFL Proficiency Guidelines 2012: Listening." www.actfl.org/publications/guidelines-and-manuals/actfl-proficiency-guidelines-2012/english/listening.

———. 2016. *World-Readiness Standards for Learning Languages.* http://www.actfl.org/publications/all/world-readiness-standards-learning-languages.

Adams, Maurianne. 2016. "Pedagogical Foundations for Social Justice Education." In *Teaching for Diversity and Social Justice / Edition 3*, edited by Adams and Lee Anne Bell. New York: Routledge.

Alcoff, Linda. 1992. "The Problem of Speaking for Others." *Cultural Critique* 20 (Winter): 5–32. www.jstor.org/stable/1354221?seq=1#page_scan_tab_contents.

Allport, Gordon. 1954. *The Nature of Prejudice.* Reading, MA: Addison-Wesley.

Arao, Brian, and Kristi Clemens. 2013. "From Safe Spaces to Brave Spaces: A New Way to Frame Dialogue Around Diversity and Social Justice." In *The Art of Effective Facilitation: Reflections from Social Justice Educators*, edited by Lisa Landreman. Sterling, VA: Stylus.

Arasaratnam, Lily. A., and Marya L. Doerfel. 2005. "Intercultural Communication Competence: Identifying Key Components from Multicultural Perspectives." *International Journal of Intercultural Relations* 29, no. 2: 137–63.

Arries, Jonathan F. 1999. "Critical Pedagogy and Service-Learning in Spanish: Crossing Borders in the Freshman Seminar." In *Construyendo Puentes (Building Bridges): Concepts and Models for Service-Learning in Spanish*, edited by Josef Hellebrant and Lucía Varona. Sterling, VA: Stylus.

Ash, Sarah L., and Patti Clayton. 2004. "The Articulated Learning: An Approach to Reflection and Assessment." *Innovative Higher Education* 29: 137–54.

———. 2009. "Generating, Deepening and Documenting Learning: The Power of Critical Reflection in Applied Learning." *Journal of Applied Learning in Higher Education* 1 (Fall): 25–48.

Ash, Sarah L., Patti Clayton, and Maxine P. Atkinson. 2005. "Integrating Reflection and Assessment to Capture and Improve Student Learning." *Michigan Journal of Community Service Learning* 11, no. 2: 49–60.

Ayers, William. 1998. "Foreword: Popular Education—Teaching for Social Justice." In *Teaching For Social Justice*, edited by William Ayers, Jee Anne Hunt, and Therese Quinn. New York: New Press and Teachers College Press.

Baran, Dominika. 2017. *Language in Immigrant America*. New York: Cambridge University Press.

Barreneche, Gabriel Ignacio. 2011. "Language Learners as Teachers: Integrating Service-Learning and the Advanced Language Course." *Hispania* 94, no. 1: 103–20.

Barreneche, Gabriel Ignacio, and Hector Ramos-Flores. 2013. "Integrated or Isolated Experiences? Considering the Role of Service-Learning in the Spanish Language Curriculum." *Hispania* 96, no. 2: 215–28.

Bass, Randy. 2014. "The Next Whole Thing in Higher Education." *Peer Review* 16, no. 1. www.aacu.org/publications-research/periodicals/next-whole-thing-higher-education.

Baumgartner, Lisa M. 2012. "Mezirow's Theory of Transformative Learning from 1975 to the Present." In *The Handbook of Transformative Learning: Theory, Research, and Practice*, edited by Edward W. Taylor, Patricia Cranton, and Associates. San Francisco: Jossey-Bass.

Beebe, Rose Marie, and Elena de Costa. 1993. "Teaching Beyond the Classroom: The Santa Clara Eastside Project Community Service and the Spanish Classroom." *Hispania* 76, no. 4: 884–91.

Belenky, Mary Field, and Ann V. Stanton. 2000. "Inequality, Development, and Connected Knowing." In *Learning as Transformation: Critical Perspectives on a Theory in Progress*, edited by Jack Mezirow and Associates. San Francisco: Jossey-Bass.

Bennett, Janet M. 2008. "Transformative Training: Designing Programs for Culture Learning." In *Contemporary Leadership and Intercultural Competence: Understanding and Utilizing Cultural Diversity to Build Successful Organizations*, edited by Michael A. Moodian. Thousand Oaks, CA: Sage.

Bennett, M. 2018. "Constructivist Intercultural Communication; Developmental Model of Intercultural Sensitivity." Entry in Kim, Young Yun, ed. *Encyclopedia of Intercultural Communication*. Wiley-Blackwell.

Bennett, Milton J. 1986. "Towards Ethnorelativism: A Developmental Model of Intercultural Sensitivity." In *Cross-Cultural Orientation: New Conceptualizations and Applications*, edited by R. M. Paige. New York: University Press of America.

Bertelsmann Stiftung and Fondazione Cariplo. 2008. *Intercultural Competence: The Key Competence in the 21st Century.* Theses by the Bertelsmann Stiftung based on the models of intercultural competence of Dr. Darla K. Deardorff. www.ngobg.info/bg/documents/49/726bertelsmanninterculturalcompetences.pdf.

Bertucio, Brett. 2017. "The Cartesian Heritage of Bloom's Taxonomy." *Studies in Philosophy and Education* 36, no. 4: 477–97.

Bettencourt, Michelle. 2015. "Supporting Student Learning Outcomes Through Service Learning." *Foreign Language Annals* 48, no. 3: 473–90.

Bloom, B. S., M. D. Engelhart, E. J. Furst, W. H. Hill, and D. R. Krathwohl. 1956. *Taxonomy of Educational Objectives: The Classification of Educational Goals—Handbook I: Cognitive Domain*. New York: David McKay. (Rev. ed. pub. 2001.)

Boal, Augusto. 2000. *Theater of the Oppressed*. London: Pluto Press.

Bocci, Melissa. 2015. "Service-Learning and White Normativity: Racial Representation in Service-Learning's Historical Narrative." *Michigan Journal of Community Service Learning* 22, no. 1: 5–17.

Bourdieu, Pierre. 1984. *Distinction: A Social Critique of the Judgment of Taste*. Cambridge, MA: Harvard University Press.

———. 1991. *Language & Symbolic Power*. Cambridge, MA: Harvard University Press.

Bowman, Nicholas A. 2011. "Promoting Participation in a Diverse Democracy: A Meta-analysis of College Diversity Experiences and Civic Engagement." *Review of Educational Research* 81, no. 1: 29–68.

Bowman, N. A., and J. W. Brandenberger. 2012. "Experiencing the Unexpected: Toward a Model of College Diversity Experiences and Attitude Change." *Review of Higher Education* 35, no. 2: 179–205.

Boyle, J. Patrick, and Denise Overfield. 1999. "Community-Based Language Learning: Integrating Language and Service." In *Construyendo Puentes (Building Bridges): Concepts and Models for Service-Learning in Spanish*, edited by Josef Hellebrant and Lucía Varona. Sterling, VA: Stylus.

Bradley, James. 1995. "A Model for Evaluating Student Learning in Academically Based Service." In *Connecting Cognition and Action: Evaluation of Student Performance in Service-Learning Courses*, edited by Marie Troppe. Providence: Campus Compact.

Bright, Anita, and James Gambrell. 2017. "Calling In, Not Calling Out: A Critical Race Framework for Nurturing Cross-Cultural Alliances in Teacher Candidates." *Handbook of Research on Promoting Cross-Cultural Competence and Social Justice in Teacher Education*, edited by J. Keengwe. Hershey, PA: IGI Global.

Bringle, Robert G., and Patti H. Clayton. 2012. "Civic Education through Service-Learning: What, How, and Why?" In *Higher Education and Civic Engagement: Comparative Perspectives*, edited by Lorraine McIlrath, Ann Lyons, and Ronaldo Munck. New York: Palgrave.

Bringle, Robert G., and Julie A. Hatcher. 1999. "Reflection in Service Learning: Making Meaning of Experience." *Educational Horizons* 23: 179–85.

———. 2011. "International Service Learning." In *International Service Learning: Conceptual Frameworks and Research*, edited by Robert G. Bringle, Julie A. Hatcher, and Steven G. Jones. Sterling, VA: Stylus.

Butin, Dan W. 2003. "Of What Use Is It? Multiple Conceptualizations of Service Learning Within Education." *Teachers College Record* 105, no. 9: 1674–92. https://academic.macewan.ca/csl/files/2014/04/Of-What-Use-Is-It-Multiple-Conceptualizations-of-Service-Learning-Within-Education.pdf.

———. 2006. "The Limits of Service-Learning in Higher Education." *Review of Higher Education* 29: 473–98.

——. 2007. "Justice-Learning: Service-Learning as Justice-Oriented Education." *Equity & Excellence in Education* 40: 177–83. www.danbutin.net/uploads/1/3/9/6/13968007/butin_justice_learning.pdf.

Byram, Michael. 1997. *Teaching and Assessing Intercultural Communicative Competence.* Bristol: Multilingual Matters.

Byram, Michael, and Michael Fleming. 1998. *Language Learning in Intercultural Perspective: Approaches through Drama and Ethnography.* Cambridge: Cambridge University Press.

Caldwell, Wendy. 2007. "Taking Spanish Outside the Box: A Model for Integrating Service Learning into Foreign Language Study." *Foreign Languages Annals* 40, no. 3: 463–71.

Camacho, Michelle Madsen. 2004. "Power and Privilege: Community Service Learning in Tijuana." *Michigan Journal of Community Service Learning* 10, no. 3: 31–42.

Camarota, Steven A., and Karen Zeigler. 2014. "One in Five U.S. Residents Speaks Foreign Language at Home, Record 61.8 Million." Center for Immigration Studies. https://cis.org/One-Five-US-Residents-Speaks-Foreign-Language-Home-Record-618-million.

Carney, Terry. 2004. "Reaching Beyond Borders Through Service Learning." *Journal of Latinos and Education* 5, no. 4: 267–71.

Carnegie Classifications. 2018. "Carnegie Classification of Institutions of Higher Education." www.carnegieclassifications.iu.edu/.

Carracelas-Juncal, Carmen. 2013. "When Service-Learning Is Not a 'Border-Crossing Experience': Outcomes of a Graduate Spanish Online Course." *Hispania* 96, no. 2: 295–309.

Case Western Reserve University. 2001. *Community Engagement through Service Learning Manual.* Frances Payne Bolton School of Nursing, Community-Based Care Project. Cleveland: Case Western Reserve University. https://depts.washington.edu/ccph/pdf_files/CETSLmanual4.pdf.

Catlett, Beth S., and Amira Proweller. 2011. "College Students' Negotiation of Privilege in a Community-Based Violence Prevention Project." *Michigan Journal of Community Service Learning*, Fall, 34–48.

Clayton, Patti H., Sarah L. Ash, and Jessica Katz Jameson. 2009. "Assessing Critical Thinking and Higher-Order Reasoning in Service-Learning-Enhanced Courses and Course Sequences." In *Planning, Implementing, and Sustaining Assessment: Principles and Profiles of Good Practice*, edited by T. Banta, B. Jones, and K. Black. San Francisco: Jossey-Bass.

Clayton, Patti H., Robert G. Bringle, Bryanne Senor, Jenny Huq, and Mary Morrison. 2010. "Differentiating and Assessing Relationships in Service-Learning and Civic Engagement: Exploitative, Transactional, or Transformational." *Michigan Journal of Community Service Learning* 16, no. 2: 5–22.

Cohn, Nate. 2014. "Pinpointing Another Reason that More Hispanics Are Identifying as White." *New York Times*, June 3. www.nytimes.com/2014/06/03/upshot/pinpointing-another-reason-that-more-hispanics-are-identifying-as-white.html?_r=1.

Community Campus Partnerships for Health. 2013. "Position Statement on Authentic Partnerships: Guiding Principles of Partnership." https://ccph.memberclicks.net/principles-of-partnership.

Conrad, Daniel, and Diane Hedin. 1990. "Learning from Service: Experience Is the Best Teacher—or Is It?" In *Combining Service and Learning I*, edited by Jane Kendall and Associates. Raleigh, NC: National Society for Internships and Experiential Education.

Costa, Arthur L., and Bena Kallick. 2009. *Habits of Mind across the Curriculum: Practical and Creative Strategies for Teachers*. Alexandria, VA: ASCD.

Council of Europe. 2001. *Common European Framework of Reference for Languages: Learning, Teaching, Assessment*. Cambridge: Cambridge University Press.

Crawford, James. 2001. "A Nation Divided by One Language." *The Guardian*, March 8. www.theguardian.com/theguardian/2001/mar/08/guardianweekly.guardianweekly11.

Cress, Christine, Cathy Burack, Dwight Giles, Julie Elkins, and Margaret Carnes Stevens. 2010. *A Promising Connection: Increasing College Access and Success through Civic Engagement*. Boston: Campus Compact. www.compact.org/wp-content/uploads/2009/01/A-Promising-Connection-corrected.pdf.

Cruz, Nadinne I., and Dwight E. Giles Jr. 2000. "Where's the Community in Service-Learning Research?" *Michigan Journal of Community Service Learning* (special issue), Fall, 28–34.

Davis, Katherine L., Brandon W. Kliewer, and Aliki Nicolaides. 2017. "Power and Reciprocity in Partnerships: Deliberative Civic Engagement and Transformative Learning in Community-Engaged Scholarship." *Journal of Higher Education Outreach and Engagement* 21, no. 1: 30–54.

Deans, Thomas. 1999. "Service-Learning in Two Keys: Paulo Freire's Critical Pedagogy in Relation to John Dewey's Pragmatism." *Michigan Journal of Community Service Learning* 6, no. 1: 15–29.

Deardorff, Darla K. 2006. "The Identification and Assessment of Intercultural Competence as a Student Outcome of Internationalization at Institutions of Higher Education in the United States." *Journal of Studies in International Education* 10, no. 3: 241–66.

———. 2009. *The SAGE Handbook of Intercultural Competence*. Thousand Oaks, CA: Sage.

Deardorff, D. K., and D. L. Deardorff. 2000. "OSEE Tool." Presentation at North Carolina State University, Raleigh.

Dees, Gregory. 2001. "The Meaning of 'Social Entrepreneurship.'" https://entrepreneurship.duke.edu/news-item/the-meaning-of-social-entrepreneurship/.

Dewey, John. 1910. *How We Think*. Boston: D. C. Heath.

DeZure, Deborah. 2002. "Essay Review: Assessing Service-Learning and Civic Engagement—Principles and Techniques." *Michigan Journal of Community Service Learning* 8, no. 2: 75–78.

Diaz, A., and R. Perrault. 2010. "Sustained Dialogue and Civic Life: Post-College Impacts." *Michigan Journal of Community Service Learning* 17, no. 1: 32–43.

Donahue, Donald M. 2011. "The Nature of Teaching and Learning Dilemmas: Democracy in the Making. In *Democratic Dilemmas of Teaching Service-Learning: Curricular Strategies for Success*, edited by Christine M. Cress, David M. Donahue, and Associates. Sterling, VA: Stylus.

Dostillo, L., S. Brackmann, K. Edwards, B. Harrison, B. Kliewer, and P. Clayton. 2012. "Reciprocity: Saying What We Mean and Meaning What We Say." *Michigan Journal of Community Service Learning* 19, no. 1: 17–32.

Duarte, Gonzalo. 2014. "Good to Go: Standards of Practice in Global Service Learning." Master's Capstone Research Report, Carleton University, Ottawa.

Du Bois, W. E. B. 1989. "The Souls of Black Folk." In *W. E. B. Du Bois: Writings*. New York: Library of America. (Orig. pub. 1903.)

DuBord, Elise, and Elizabeth Kimball. 2016. "Cross-Language Community Engagement: Assessing the Strengths of Heritage Learners." *Heritage Language Journal* 13, no. 3: 298–330.

Duke University Campus Institutional Review Board. 2018. "Releases for Images and Recordings." https://campusirb.duke.edu/resources/guides/releases-images-and-recordings.

Dwyer, Carol, Catherine Millet, and David Payne. 2017. *A Culture of Evidence: Postsecondary Assessment and Learning Outcomes*. Princeton, NJ: Educational Testing Service. https://pdfs.semanticscholar.org/df21/434e9f3b05c8e85fceca7a482d0ed8b4cd9b.pdf.

Elorriaga, Margarita. 2007. "College Students as Tutors: Learning from the Latino Community of Adams County." *Hispania* 90, no. 3: 533–2.

Eyler, Janet S. 2000. "What Do We Most Need to Know About the Impact of Service-Learning on Student Learning?" *Michigan Journal of Community Service Learning* (special issue), Fall, 11–17.

Eyler, Janet, and Dwight Giles. 1999. *Where's the Learning in Service-Learning?* San Francisco: Jossey-Bass.

Eyler, Janet, Dwight Giles, and Angela Schmiede. 1996. *A Practitioner's Guide to Reflection in Service-Learning: Student Voices and Reflections*. Nashville: Vanderbilt University Press.

Fantini, Alvino. 2012. "Language: An Essential Component of Intercultural Communicative Competence." In *The Routledge Handbook of Language and Intercultural Communication*, edited by Jane Jackson. New York: Routledge.

Foucault, Michel. 1978. *The History of Sexuality*. 4 vols. New York: Pantheon Books.

Freire, Paulo. 1970. *Pedagogy of the Oppressed*. New York: Herder & Herder.

Furstenberg, Gilberte. 2010. "A Dynamic, Web-Based Methodology for Developing Intercultural Understanding." In *Proceedings of the 3rd International Conference on Intercultural Collaboration*, edited by Pamela Hinds, Anne-Marie Søderberg, and Ravi Vatrapu. New York: ACM Digital Library. https://dl.acm.org/citation.cfm?id=1841853&picked=prox.

Gascoigne Lally, Carolyn. 2001. "Service/Community Learning and Foreign Language Teaching Methods—An Application." *Active Learning in Higher Education* 2: 53–63.

Gass, Susan M., and Alison Mackey. 2006. "Input, Interaction and Output: An Overview." *AILA Review* 19: 3–17.

Gelmon, Sherril, Baraba Hollard, Amy Driscoll, Amy Spring, and Seanna Kerrigan. 2006. *Assessing Service-Learning and Civic Engagement*. Providence: Campus Compact.

George, Camille, and Ashley Shams. 2007. "The Challenge of Including Customer Satisfaction in the Assessment Criteria of Overseas Service Learning Projects." *International Journal for Service Learning in Engineering* 2, no. 2: 64–75.

Giles, Hollyce C. 2014. "Risky Epistemology: Connecting with Others and Dissonance in Community-Based Research." *Michigan Journal of Community Service Learning* 20, no. 2 (Spring): 65–78.

Giles, Janet, Dwight Eyler, Christine Stenson, and Charlene Gray. 2001. *At A Glance: What We Know About the Effects of Service-Learning on College Students, Faculty, Institutions, and Communities, 1993–2000—Third Edition.* Nashville: Vanderbilt University. www.compact.org/wp-content/uploads/resources/downloads/aag.pdf.

Giroux, Henry. 1992. *Border Crossing: Cultural Workers and the Politics of Education.* New York: Routledge.

———. 2010. "Bare Pedagogy and the Scourge of Neoliberalism: Rethinking Higher Education as a Democratic Public Sphere." *Educational Forum* 74, no. 3: 184–96. https://s3.amazonaws.com/arena-attachments/74852/Rethinking_higher_ed_-_Henry_A._Giroux.pdf.

———. 2011. *On Critical Pedagogy.* London: Bloomsbury Academic.

Giroux, Henry A., and Searls Giroux. 2004. *Take Back Higher Education.* New York: Palgrave.

Glynn, Pamela Wesely, and Beth Wassell. 2014. *Words and Actions: Teaching Languages Through the Lens of Social Justice.* Alexandria, VA: American Council on the Teaching of Foreign Languages.

Goodman, Diane J. 2011. *Promoting Diversity and Social Justice: Educating People from Privileged Groups.* New York: Routledge.

Grain, Kari M., and Darren E. Lund. 2016. "The Social Justice Turn: Cultivating 'Critical Hope' in an Age of Despair." *Michigan Journal of Community Service Learning,* 23, no. 1 (Fall): 45–59.

Grassi, Elizabeth, Daniel Hanley, and Daniel Liston. 2004. "Service-Learning: An Innovative Approach for Second Language Learners." *Journal of Experiential Education* 27, no. 1: 87–110.

Gravatt, Sarah, and Nadine Petersen. 2009. "Promoting Dialogic Teaching among Higher Education Faculty in South Africa." In *Transformative Learning in Practice: Insights from Community, Workplace, and Higher Education,* edited by Jack Mezirow, Edward W. Taylor, and Associates. San Francisco: Jossey-Bass.

Green, Ann E. 2003. "Difficult Stories: Service-Learning, Race, Class, and Whiteness." *College Composition and Communication,* 276–301.

Grim, Frédérique. 2010. "Giving Authentic Opportunities to Second Language Learners: A Look at a French Service-Learning Project." *Foreign Language Annals* 43, no. 4: 605–23.

———. 2011. "Socio-Cultural Sensitivities and Service-Learning." *Modern Journal of Language Teaching Methods* 1, no. 1: 15–19.

Guillén, Felisa. 2010. "Including Latino Communities in the Learning Process: Curricular and Pedagogical Reforms in Undergraduate Spanish Programs." *Journal of Community Engagement and Scholarship* 3, no. 2: 41–53.

Gurin, Patricia, Eric L. Dey, Sylvia Hurtado, and Gerald Gurin. 2002. "Diversity in Higher Education: Theory and Impact on Educational Outcomes." *Harvard Educational Review* 72, no. 3: 330–66.

Hale, Aileen. 1999. "Service-Learning and Spanish: A Missing Link." In *Construyendo Puentes (Building Bridges): Concepts and Models for Service-Learning in Spanish*, edited by Josef Hellebrant and Lucía Varona. Sterling, VA: Stylus. (Rev. ed. pub. 2005.)

Hayes, Elisabeth, and Sondra Cuban. 1997. "Border Pedagogy: A Critical Framework for Service Learning." *Michigan Journal of Community Service Learning* 4, no. 1: 72–80.

Hellebrandt, Josef, Jonathan Arries, and Lucía T. Varona, eds. 2003. *Juntos: Community Partnerships in Spanish and Portuguese*. Boston: Thomson/Heinle.

Hellebrandt, Josef, and Ethel Jorge. 2013. "The Scholarship of Community Engagement: Advancing Partnerships in Spanish and Portuguese." *Hispania* 96, no. 2: 203–14.

Hellebrandt, Josef, and Lucía T. Varona, eds. 1999. *Construyendo Puentes (Building Bridges): Concepts and Models for Service-Learning in Spanish*. Sterling, VA: Stylus.

Hill-Jackson, Valerie, and Chance W. Lewis. 2011. "Service Loitering: White Pre-service Teachers Preparing for Diversity in an Underserved Community." In *Problematizing Service-Learning: Critical Reflections for Development and Action*, edited by Trae Stewart and Nicole Webster. Charlotte: Information Age.

Himley, Margaret. 2004. "Facing (Up to) "the Stranger" in Community Service Learning." *College Composition and Communication* 55, no. 3: 416–38.

Hudson, Monika, and Keith O. Hunter. 2014. "Positive Effects of Peer-Led Reflection on Undergraduates' Concept Integration and Synthesis During Service-Learning." *International Journal of Teaching and Learning in Higher Education* 26, no. 1: 12–25.

International Affairs Office of US Department of Education. 2017. "Framework for Developing Global and Cultural Competencies to Advance Equity, Excellence, and Economic Competitiveness." https://sites.ed.gov/international/global-and-cultural-competency/.

Jackson, Jane, ed. 2012. *Routledge Handbook of Language and Intercultural Communication*. Abingdon, UK: Routledge.

Jacoby, Barbara. 2003. "Building Service-Learning Partnerships for the Future." In *Building Partnerships for Service-Learning*, edited by Barbara Jacoby and Associates. San Francisco: Jossey-Bass.

———. 2015. *Service-Learning Essentials: Questions, Answers, and Lessons Learned*. San Francisco: Jossey-Bass.

Jaschick, Scott. 2011. "Not So Foreign Languages." *Inside Higher Ed*. www.insidehighered.com/news/2011/10/05/colleges_are_replacing_foreign_language_departments_with_world_language_departments.

Jones, Susan, Jen Gilbride-Brown, and Anna Gasiorski. 2005. "Getting Inside the 'Underside' of Service-Learning: Student Resistance and Possibilities." In *Service-Learning in Higher Education: Critical Issues and Directions*, edited by Dan Butin. New York: Palgrave Macmillan.

Kajner, T., D. Chovanec, M. Underwood, and A. Mian. 2013. "Critical Community Service Learning: Combining Critical Classroom Pedagogy with Activist Community Placements." *Michigan Journal of Community Service Learning* 19, no. 2: 36–48.

Kasl, Elizabeth, and Lyle Yorks. 2012. "Learning to Be What We Know: The Pivotal Role of Presentational Knowing in Transformative Learning." In *The Handbook of Transformative Learning: Theory, Research, and Practice*, edited by Edward W. Taylor, Patricia Cranton, and Associates. San Francisco: Jossey-Bass.

Katz Jameson, Jessica, Patti H. Clayton, and Audrey Jaeger. 2011. "Community Engaged Scholarship as Mutually Transformative Partnerships." In *Participatory Partnerships for Social Action and Research*, edited by L. Harter, J. Millesen, and J. Hamel-Lambert. Dubuque, IA: Kendall Hunt.

Kellogg Commission. 1999. "Returning to Our Roots: The Engaged Institution." Vol. 3. Kellogg Commission on the Future of State and Land-Grant Universities, National Association of State Universities and Land-Grant Colleges, Office of Public Affairs.

Kertzer, David I., and Dominique Arel. 2002. *Census and Identity: the Politics of Race, Ethnicity, and Language in National Census.* Cambridge: Cambridge University Press.

Kiely, Richard. 2004. "A Chameleon with a Complex: Searching for Transformation in International Service Learning." *Michigan Journal of Community Service Learning* 10, no. 2: 5–20.

———. 2005. "A Transformative Learning Model for Service-Learning: A Longitudinal Case Study." *Michigan Journal of Community Service Learning* 12, no. 1: 5–22.

King, Joyce E. 1991. "Dysconscious Racism: Ideology, Identity, and the Miseducation of Teachers." *Journal of Negro Education* 60, no. 2: 133–46.

Kolb, David A. 1984. *Experiential Learning: Experience as the Source of Learning and Development*. Englewood Cliffs, NJ: Prentice Hall.

Kramsch, Claire. 2013. "Culture in Foreign Language Teaching." *Iranian Journal of Language Teaching Research* 1, no. 1: 57–78.

Krashen, Stephen. 1982. *Principles and Practice in Second Language Acquisition*. Oxford: Pergamon Press.

Kubota, Ryuko. 2014. "We Must Look at Both Sides"—But a Denial of Genocide Too? Difficult Moments on Controversial Issues in the Classroom." *Critical Inquiry in Language Studies* 11, no. 4: 225–51.

Lal, Shafali. 2004. "1930s Multiculturalism: Rachel Davis DuBois and the Bureau for Intercultural Education." *Radical Teacher* 69: 18–22. www.jstor.org/stable/20710241.

Langstraat, Lisa, and Melody Bowden. 2011. "Service-Learning and Critical Emotion Studies: On the Perils of Empathy and the Politics of Compassion." *Michigan Journal of Community Service Learning* 17, no. 2 (Spring): 5–14.

Lave, Jean, and Etienne Wenger. 1991. *Situated Learning: Legitimate Peripheral Participation*. New York: Cambridge University Press.

Lear, Darcie, and Annie Abbott. 2009. "Aligning Expectations for Mutually Beneficial Community Service-Learning: The Case of Spanish Language Proficiency, Cultural Knowledge, and Professional Skills." *Hispania* 92: 312–23.

Leeman, Rabin, and Esperanza Ramón-Mendoza. 2011. "Identity and Activism in Heritage Language Education." *Modern Language Journal* 95, no. 4: 481–95.

Long, Donna Reseigh. 2003. "Spanish in the Community: Students Reflect on Hispanic Cultures in the United States." *Foreign Language Annals* 36: 223–32.

Long, Michael. 1996. "The Role of the Linguistic Environment in Second Language Acquisition." In *Handbook of Second Language Acquisition*, edited by Ritchie and Tej Bhatia. New York: Academic Press.

López, Lourdes Sánchez. 2015. "An Analysis of the Integration of Service Learning in Undergraduate Spanish for Specific Purposes Programs in Higher Education in the United States." *Cuadernos de ALDEEU* 28, no. 1: 155–70.

Magnan, Sally S., Dianna Murphy, Narek Sahakyan, and Suyeon Kim. 2012. "Student Goals, Expectations, and the Standards for Foreign Language Learning." *Foreign Language Annals* 45, no. 2: 170–92.

Malkin, Fran. 2010. "The Effects of Service Learning Participation in Foreign Language Classes on Students' Attitudes towards the Spanish Language and Culture and their Language Proficiency." PhD diss., New York University.

McEwen, Marylu K. 1996. "Enhancing Student Learning and Development Through Service-Learning." In *Service-Learning in Higher Education: Concepts and Practices*, edited by Jacoby & Associates. San Francisco: Jossey-Bass.

McGivern, Laura. 2010. "Political, Not Partisan: Service-Learning as Social Justice Education." *Vermont Connection* 31: 60–71.

McIntosh, Peggy. 1989. "White Privilege: Unpacking the Invisible Knapsack." *Peace and Freedom Magazine*, July–August, 10–12. Philadelphia: Women's International League for Peace and Freedom. https://nationalseedproject.org/white-privilege-unpacking-the-invisible-knapsack.

———. 2010. *Some Notes for Facilitators on Presenting My White Privilege Papers*. Wellesley, MA: Wellesley Center for Women.

McMaken, Ryan. 2016. "How the Census Bureau Invented 'Hispanics.'" Ludwig von Mises Institute for Austrian Economics. https://mises.org/wire/how-census-bureau-invented-hispanics.

Mezirow, Jack. 1990. "How Critical Reflection Triggers Transformative Learning." In *Fostering Critical Reflection in Adulthood*. www.ln.edu.hk/osl/conference2011/output/breakout/4.4%20[ref]How%20Critical%20Reflection%20triggers%20Transformative%20Learning%20-%20Mezirow.pdf.

———. 1998. "On Critical Reflection." *Adult Learning Quarterly* 48, no. 3: 185–98.

———. 2000. "Learning to Think Like an Adult: Core Concepts of Transformation Theory." In *Learning as Transformation: Critical Perspectives on a Theory in Progress*, edited by Jack Mezirow and Associates. San Francisco: Jossey-Bass.

———. 2003. "Transformative Learning as Discourse." *Journal of Transformative Education* 1, no. 1: 58–63.

———. 2009. "Transformative Learning Theory." In *Transformative Learning in Practice: Insights from Community, Workplace, and Higher Education*, edited by Jack Mezirow, Edward W. Taylor, and Associates. San Francisco: Jossey-Bass.

———. 2012. "Learning to Think Like an Adult: Core Concepts of Transformation Theory." In *The Handbook of Transformative Learning: Theory, Research, and Practice*, edited by Edward W. Taylor, Patricia Cranton, and Associates. San Francisco: Jossey-Bass.

Mezirow, Jack, and Associates, eds. 2000. *Learning as Transformation: Critical Perspectives on a Theory in Progress*. San Francisco: Jossey-Bass.

Mills, Steven. 2012. "The Four Furies: Primary Tensions between Service-Learners and Host Agencies." *Michigan Journal of Community Service Learning* 19, no. 1: 33–43.

Mitchell, Tania. 2008. "Traditional vs. Critical Service-Learning: Engaging the Literature to Differentiate Two Models." *Michigan Journal of Community Service Learning* 14, no. 2: 50–65. http://hdl.handle.net/2027/spo.3239521.0014.205.

———. 2015. "Using a Critical Service-Learning Approach to Facilitate Civic Identity Development." *Theory Into Practice* 54: 20–28.

Mitchell, Tania D., and David M. Donahue. 2009. "I Do More Service in This Class Than I Ever Do at My Site: Paying Attention to the Reflections of Students of Color in Service-Learning." In *The Future of Service-Learning: New Solutions for Sustaining and Improving Practice*, edited by Jean R. Strait and Marybeth Lima. Sterling, VA: Stylus.

Mitchell, Tania D., David M. Donahue, and Courtney Young-Law. 2012. "Service Learning as a Pedagogy of Whiteness." *Equity & Excellence in Education* 45, no. 4: 612–29. doi: 10.1080/ 10665684.2012.715534.

MLA (Modern Language Association). 2017. "Foreign Languages and Higher Education: New Structures for a Changed World—MLA Ad Hoc Committee on Foreign Languages." www.jstor.org/stable/pdf/25595871.pdf.

———. No date. "MLA Language Maps." https://apps.mla.org/map_about#m01.

Moeller, Aledeine K., and Kristen Nugent. 2014. "Building Intercultural Competence in the Language Classroom." In *Unlock the Gateway to Communication*, edited by Stephanie Donahue. Eau Claire, WI: Crown Prints. www.csctfl.org/documents/2014Report/Chapter_1_Moeller.pdf.

Monbiot, George. 2016. "Neoliberalism: The Ideology at the Root of All of Our Problems." *The Guardian*, April 15. www.theguardian.com/books/2016/apr/15/neoliberalism-ideology-problem-george-monbiot.

Mooney, Linda A., and Bob Edwards. 2001. "Experiential Learning in Sociology." *Teaching Sociology* 9, no. 2: 181–94.

Morris, Frank. 2001. "Serving the Community and Learning a Foreign Language: Evaluating a Service-Learning Programme." *Language, Culture, and Curriculum* 14, no. 3: 244–55.

Morton, Keith, and Samantha Bergbauer. 2015. "A Case for Community: Starting with Relationships and Prioritizing Community as Method in Service-Learning." *Michigan Journal of Community Service Learning* 22, no. 1: 18–32.

Nelson, Ardis L., and Jessica L. Scott. 2008. "Applied Spanish in the University Curriculum: A Successful Model for Community-Based Service-Learning." *Hispania* 91, no. 2: 446–60.

Nguyen, H. T., and G. Kellogg. 2010. "I Had a Stereotype that Americans Were 'Fat': Becoming a Speaker of Culture in a Second Language." *Modern Language Journal* 94, no. 1: 56–73.

Norris, John M. 2006. "The Why of Assessing Student Learning Outcomes in College Foreign Language Programs." *Modern Language Journal* 90, no. 40: 576–83.

Ochs, Elinor. 2002. "Becoming a Speaker of Culture." In *Language Acquisition and Language Socialization*, edited by Claire Kramsch. London: Continuum.

O'Connor, Anne. 2012. "Beyond the Four Walls: Community-Based Learning and Languages." *Language Learning Journal* 40, no. 3: 307–20. DOI: 10.1080/09571736.2011.585402.

O'Connor, K., L. McEwan, D. Owen, K. Lynch, and S. Hill. 2011. "Literature Review: Embedding Community Engagement in the Curriculum—An Example of University-Public Engagement." National Coordinating Centre for Public Engagement. www.publicengagement.ac.uk/sites/default/files/publication/cbl_literature_review.pdf.

Osborn, Terry. 2000. *Critical Reflection and the Foreign Language Classroom*. Westport, CT: Bergin & Garvey.

———. 2006. *Teaching World Languages for Social Justice: A Sourcebook of Principles and Practices*. Mahwah, NJ: Lawrence Erlbaum Associates.

Pak, Chin-Sook. 2007. "The Service-Learning Classroom and Motivational Strategies for Learning Spanish: Discoveries from Two Interdisciplinary, Community-Centered Seminars." In *Learning the Language of Global Citizenship: Service-Learning in Applied Linguistics*, edited by Adrian Wurr and Josef Hellebrandt. Boston: Anker.

———. 2013. "Service Learning for Students of Intermediate Spanish: Examining Multiple Roles of Foreign Language Study." In *Multitasks, Multiskills, Multiconnections: Selected Papers from the 2013 Central States Conference on the Teaching of Foreign Languages*, edited by Stephanie Dhonau. Milwaukee: Central States Conference on the Teaching of Foreign Languages. www.csctfl.org/documents/2013Report/2013ReportWeb.pdf.

Palmer, Parker. 2011. "Higher Education and Habits of the Heart: Restoring Democracy's Infrastructure." *Journal of College and Character* 12, no. 3: 1–6.

Parrillo, Vincent N. 2013. *Strangers to These Shores: Race and Ethnic Relations in the United States*. Boston: Houghton Mifflin.

Pascual y Cabo, Diego, Josh Prada, and Kelly Lowther Pereira. 2017. "Effects of Community Service-Learning on Heritage Language Learners' Attitudes toward Their Language and Culture." *Foreign Language Annals* 50, no. 1: 71–83.

Paul, Richard, and Linda Elder. 2001. *The Miniature Guide to Critical Thinking: The Foundation for Critical Thinking*. Santa Rosa, CA: Foundation for Critical Thinking. www.criticalthinking.org/files/Concepts_Tools.pdf.

Pellettieri, Jill. 2011. "Measuring Language-Related Outcomes of Community-Based Learning in Intermediate Spanish Courses." *Hispania* 94, no. 2: 285–302.

Petrov, Lisa Amor. 2013. "A Pilot Study of Service-Learning in a Spanish Heritage Speaker Course: Community Engagement, Identity, and Language in the Chicago Area." *Hispania* 96, no. 2: 310–27.

Pitre, Natalie J., and Veronica Bohac Clarke. 2017. "Cultural Self-Study as a Tool for Critical Reflection and Learning: Integral Analysis and Implications for Pre-Service Teacher Education Programs." In *Handbook of Research on Promoting Cross-Cultural Competence and Social Justice in Teacher Education*, edited by J. Keengwe. Hershey, PA: IGI Global.

Plann, Susan. 2002. "Latinos and Literacy: An Upper-Division Spanish Course with Service Learning." *Hispania* 85, no. 2: 330–38.

Potowski, Kim. 2002. "Experiences of Spanish Heritage Speakers in University Foreign Language Courses and Implications for Teacher Training." *ADFL Bulletin* 33, no. 3: 35–42.

Raddon, Mary-Beth, and Barbara Harrison. 2015. "Is Service-Learning the Kind Face of the Neo-Liberal University?" *Canadian Journal of Higher Education* 45, no. 2: 134–53.

Reitenauer, Vicki L., Amy Spring, Kevin Kecskes, Seanna M. Kerrigan, Christine M. Cress, and Peter J. Collier. 2013. "Building and Maintaining Community Partnerships." In

Learning Through Serving: A Student Guidebook for Service-Learning and Civic Engagement across Academic Disciplines and Cultural Communities, edited by Christine M. Cress, Peter J. Collier, Vicki L. Reitenauer, and Associates. Sterling, VA: Stylus.

Richard, Dan, Cheryl Keen, Julie A. Hatcher, and Heather A. Pease. 2016. "Pathways to Adult Civic Engagement: Benefits of Reflection and Dialogue across Difference in Higher Education Service-Learning Programs." *Michigan Journal of Community Service Learning* 23, no. 1: 60–74.

Richards, Jack C., and Richard Schmidt, eds. 2002. *Longman Dictionary of Language Teaching and Applied Linguistics, 3rd edition*. London: Longman.

Risager, Karen. 2007. *Language and Culture Pedagogy: From a National to a Transnational Paradigm*. Clevedon, UK: Multilingual Matters.

Rico Troncoso, Carlos. 2012. "Language Teaching Materials as Mediators for ICC Development: A Challenge for Materials Developers." *Signo y Pensamiento* 31, no. 60.

Robb Jones, Susan, Claire K. Robbins, Lucy A. LePeau. 2011. "Negotiating Border Crossing: Influences of Social Identity on Service-Learning Outcomes." *Michigan Journal of Community Service Learning* 17, no. 2: 27–42.

Rosengrant, Sandra. 1997. "Applied Russian at Portland State University: An Experiment in Community-Based Learning." *AATSEEL Newsletter* 40: 14–17.

Sandrock, Paul. 2015. *The Keys to Assessing Language Performance: A Teacher's Manual for Measuring Student Progress*. Alexandria, VA: American Council on the Teaching of Foreign Languages.

Schapiro, Stephen A., Ilene L. Wasserman, and Placida V. Gallegos. 2012. "Group Work and Dialogue: Spaces and Processes for Transformative Learning in Relationships." In *The Handbook of Transformative Learning: Theory, Research, and Practice*, edited by Edward W. Taylor, Patricia Cranton, and Associates. San Francisco: Jossey-Bass.

Shumer, Pat, Pat Duttweiler, Andrew Furco, Madeline Hengel, and Gwen Willems. 2000. "Shumer's Self-Assessment for Service-Learning." Center for Experiential and Service-Learning, University of Minnesota.

Sinicrope, Castle, John Norris, and Yukiko Watanabe. 2007. "Understanding and Assessing Intercultural Competence: A Summary of Theory, Research, and Practice." *Second Language Studies* 26, no. 1: 1–58.

Skilton-Sylvester, Ellen, and Eileen K. Erwin. 2000. "Creating Reciprocal Learning Relationships across Socially Constructed Borders." *Michigan Journal of Community Service Learning* 7, no. 1: 65–75.

Sleeter, Christine E., and Encarnación Soriano. 2012. "Introduction." In *Creating Solidarity Across Diverse Communities: International Perspectives in Education*, edited by C. E. Sleeter and E. Soriano. New York: Teachers College Press.

Smith, Linda Tuhiwai. 1999. *Decolonising Methodologies: Research and Indigenous Peoples*. London: Zed Books.

Sorrells, Kathryn. 2016. *Intercultural Communication: Globalization and Social Justice*, 2nd ed. Thousand Oaks, CA: Sage.

Stanlick, Sarah. 2015. "Getting 'Real' About Transformation: The Role of Brave Spaces in Creating Disorientation and Transformation." *Michigan Journal of Community Service Learning* 22, no. 1: 117–21.

Stanlick, Sarah, and Marla Sell. 2016. "Beyond Superheroes and Sidekicks: Empowerment, Efficacy, and Education in Community Partnerships." *Michigan Journal of Community Service Learning* 23, no. 1: 80–84.

Stoecker, Randy, and Elizabeth A. Tryon, eds. 2009. With Amy Hilgendorf. *The Unheard Voices: Community Organizations and Service Learning*. Philadelphia: Temple University Press.

Tafoya, Sonia. 2004. *Shades of Belonging*. Pew Hispanic Center. www.pewhispanic.org/2004/12/06/shades-of-belonging/.

Tapia, Maria. 2012. "Academic Excellence and Community Engagement: Reflections on the Latin American Experience." In *Higher Education and Civic Engagement: Comparative Perspectives*, edited by L. McIlrath, A. Lyons, and R. Munck. New York: Palgrave Macmillan.

Taylor, Edward W. 2000. "Analyzing Research on Transformative Learning Theory." In *Learning as Transformation: Critical Perspectives on a Theory in Progress*, edited by Jack Mezirow and Associates. San Francisco: Jossey Bass.

———. 2009. "Fostering Transformative Learning." In *Transformative Learning in Practice: Insights from Community, Workplace, and Higher Education*, edited by Jack Mezirow, Edward W. Taylor, and Associates. San Francisco: Jossey-Bass.

Thompson, Gregory. 2012. *Intersection of Service and Learning: Research and Practice in the Second Language Classroom*. Charlotte: Information Age.

———. 2015. "Community Engagement: Implementation and Success of Service-Learning Programs with Heritage and Foreign Language Students of Spanish." In *Service-Learning Pedagogy: How Does It Measure Up?* edited by Virginia Jagla, Andrew Furco, and Jean Straight. Charlotte: Information Age.

Tilley-Lubbs, Gresilda, Richard Raschio, Ethel Jorge, and Silvia López. 2005. "Service-Learning: Taking Language Learning into the Real World." *Hispania* 88, no. 1: 160–67.

Torres, Jan. 2000. *Benchmarks for Campus/Community Partnerships*. Providence: Campus Compact.

Trujillo, Juan Antonio. 2009. "*Con Todos*: Using Learning Communities to Promote Intellectual and Social Engagement in the Spanish Curriculum." In *Español en Estados Unidos y otros contextos de contacto: Sociolingüística, ideología y pedagogía*, edited by Manel Lacorte and Jennifer Leeman. Madrid: Iberoamericana.

US Census Bureau. 2017. "Hispanic Origin." www.census.gov/topics/population/hispanic-origin/about.html.

US Department of Education. 2006. *A Test of Leadership: Charting the Future of US Higher Education*. Report of the Commission Appointed by Secretary of Education Margaret Spellings. Washington, DC: US Department of Education. www.ed.gov/about/bdscomm/list/hiedfuture/reports.html.

Varona, Lucía T. 1999. "La comunidad en el aula y el aula en la comunidad: Un modelo." *Hispania* 82, no. 4: 806–16.

Velázquez, Isabel. 2015. "On Relevance: Sociolinguistic Inquiry and the Teaching of US Varieties of Spanish." Paper presented at the 25th Conference on Spanish in the United States, City College of New York, New York.

Verjee, Begum. 2010. "Service-Learning: Charity-Based or Transformative?" *Transformative Dialogues: Teaching & Learning Journal* 4, no. 2: 1–13.

Vygotsky, Lev S. 1978. *Mind in Society: The Development of Higher Psychological Processes*. Cambridge, MA: Harvard University Press.

Walker, Tim. 2014. "NEA Survey: Nearly Half of Teachers Consider Leaving Profession Due to Standardized Testing." *NEA Today*, November 2. http://neatoday.org/2014/11/02/nea-survey-nearly-half-of-teachers-consider-leaving-profession-due-to-standardized-testing-2/.

Ward, Kelly, and Lisa Wolf-Wendel. 2000. "Community-Centered Service Learning: Moving from Doing for to Doing With." *American Behavioral Scientist* 43, no. 5: 767–80.

Wehling, Susan. 2011. "Service Learning and Foreign Language Acquisition: Working with the Migrant Community." In *Got Languages? Powerful Skills for the 21st Century: Dimension 2011—Selected Proceedings of the 2011 Joint Conference of the Southern Conference on Language Teaching, the Louisiana Foreign Language Teachers' Association, and the Southeastern Association of Language Learning Technology*, edited by Carol Wilkerson and Peter Swanson. Roswell, GA: Southern Conference on Language Teaching. https://eric.ed.gov/?id=ED518124.

Welch, Marshall. 1999. "The ABCs of Reflection: A Template for Students and Instructors to Implement Written Reflection in Service-Learning." *NSEE Quarterly* 25, no. 2: 123–25.

Whitehead, Dawn Michelle. 2015. "Global Service Learning: Addressing the Big Challenges." *Diversity & Democracy* 18, no. 3. www.aacu.org/diversitydemocracy/2015/summer/whitehead.

Wiggins, Grant, and Jay McTighe. 1998. *Understanding by Design*. Alexandria, VA: Association for Supervision and Curriculum Development.

Wu, Chiu-Hui, and Robert Dahlgren. 2011. "Discourse of Advocacy: Student Learners' Critical Reflections of Working with Spanish-Speaking Immigrant Students." In *Problematizing Service-Learning*. Charlotte: Information Age.

Wurr, Adrian J., and Josef Hellebrandt, eds. 2007. *Learning the Language of Global Citizenship: Service Learning in Applied Linguistics*. Boston: Anker. www.aacu.org/diversitydemocracy/2015/summer/whitehead.

Yorks, Lyle, and Elizabeth Kasl. 2002. "Toward a Theory and Practice for Whole-Person Learning: Reconceptualizing Experience and the Role of Affect." *Adult Education Quarterly* 52, no. 3: 176–92.

Zapata, Gabriela. 2011. "The Effects of Community Service Learning Projects on L2 Learners' Cultural Understanding." *Hispania* 94, no. 1: 86–102.

Index

Boxes, figures, and tables are indicated by b, f, and t, following page numbers.

www.ingramcontent.com/pod-product-compliance
Lightning Source LLC
LaVergne TN
LVHW040758070826
844660LV00025B/1187